Beyond **Ridiculous**

STUDIES IN

THEATRE HISTORY

AND CULTURE

Heather S. Nathans,

series editor

Beyond **Ridiculous**

Making Gay Theatre with Charles Busch

in 1980s New York

Kenneth Elliott

UNIVERSITY OF IOWA PRESS, Iowa City

Design by Richard Hendel

Printed on acid-free paper

Library of Congress Cataloging-in-Publication Data
Names: Elliott, Kenneth, author.
Title: Beyond Ridiculous: Making Gay Theatre with Charles Busch in 1980s
New York / Kenneth Elliott.
Description: Iowa City: University of Iowa Press, [2023] | Series: Studies in
Theatre History and Culture | Includes bibliographical references and index.
Identifiers: LCCN 2023002589 (print) | LCCN 2023002590 (ebook) |
ISBN 9781609389192 (paperback; acid-free paper) | ISBN 9781609389208 (ebook)
Subjects: LCSH: Theatre-in-Limbo (Theater company)—History. | Theatrical
companies—New York (State)—New York—History—20th century. |
Elliott, Kenneth.
Classification: LCC PN2297.T48 E45 2023 (print) | LCC PN2297.T48 (ebook) |
DDC 792.097471—dc23/eng/20230213
LC record available at https://lccn.loc.gov/2023002589
LC ebook record available at https://lccn.loc.gov/2023002590

For Ren Gong

Contents

Acknowledgments

I've been working on this project on and off for years while serving as chair of an academic department and directing multiple student productions at Rutgers University–Camden. I have a few friends who thought I would never finish it, and without their encouragement and occasional nudging, I wouldn't have. It was my friends who kept me going.

My college roommate from Northwestern, Roy Cockrum, a wonderful actor who played over 1,000 performances of *Vampire Lesbians of Sodom* at the Provincetown Playhouse and in Tokyo, Japan, read early chapters as I completed them and helped to push the project forward. I will be forever grateful to another old friend from Northwestern, Scott Sublett, for his keen observations and editorial advice, and for suggesting that I submit the manuscript to the University of Iowa Press. The insight that Tom Aulino (yet another old friend from Northwestern) offered as an original member of the Theatre-in-Limbo company was invaluable.

My good friend Jack Sears graciously read the manuscript more than once as I made extensive revisions, and I always appreciated his warm support leavened by dry wit. My late friend, Tom Britt, also read early drafts and provided valued encouragement.

Charles Busch and I got to know Richard Niles in 1991 when he was working on his doctoral dissertation on Theatre-in-Limbo and we were working on a new play called *Red Scare on Sunset*. Richard asked us if he could be a "fly on the wall" during the development and rehearsal process. I'm so glad we said yes; he has become a close friend. His excellent and detailed dissertation has jogged my memory on many occasions, and his thoughtful analysis of the plays and the performance style of Charles Busch has certainly had a big impact on me and on this book. In addition, Richard conducted many hours of interviews with Charles, with me, and with other members of the company while we were in the midst of production. The transcripts of these interviews, now archived at Marymount Manhattan College, where Richard taught for many years, were a great resource because they reveal what we thought at the time, rather than our thoughts on the experience as seen through rose-colored glasses over thirty years later. Richard read multiple drafts of this book, and his feedback always inspired me.

Many thanks to the editors at the University of Iowa Press, Heather S. Nathans, series editor, and Daniel Ciba, associate series editor, for Studies in Theatre History and Culture. I am terribly appreciative that they decided to include this book in their distinguished series. Anonymous readers had a major impact on revisions, and I am very grateful to Sean Edgecomb for his insightful and constructive comments. Meredith Stabel, acquisitions editor, has been enormously helpful throughout the process, as has editorial assistant, Margaret Yapp. Thanks also to Trevor Perri, formerly of Northwestern University Press, for his encouragement.

Librarians are among my favorite people in the world, and I'm particularly grateful to Julie Still at the Paul Robeson Library at Rutgers for her help with my research. Thanks also to Mary Brown, the archivist at the Thomas J. Shanahan Library at Marymount Manhattan College, who provided transcripts of interviews with Charles Busch and other cast members from the Richard Niles/Charles Busch papers housed there.

The idea of writing about my experiences with Theatre-in-Limbo was first suggested to me by the late Leon Katz, who was a visiting professor at UCLA while I was working on my doctorate there, and this book started out as one chapter in my dissertation. The brilliant Sue-Ellen Case was my dissertation advisor, and she provided invaluable editorial guidance. I'm also grateful to Michael Hackett, David Román, James Schultz, and Eng-Beng Lim for their encouragement and thoughtful comments.

It is a pleasure to work with my colleagues in the Department of Visual, Media, and Performing Arts at Rutgers, and their support is greatly appreciated. The Rutgers staff is really terrific. Our department's wonderful administrative assistant, Zulma Rodriguez, has been a great help, and Kate Blair, from the Camden College of Arts and Sciences Dean's Office, solved some thorny formatting issues with the manuscript.

I've relied on Brian Whitehill in many ways since we met in 1984. He designed the sets as well as the posters and advertisements for all of the Theatre-in-Limbo productions with style and wit. He has helped me again with this book by coordinating the photographs, some of which he took himself. I'd like to thank all the photographers who contributed to this project. T. L. Boston stage-managed several of our shows and also occasionally served as a production photographer; two of his photographs are in this book. It is always a pleasure to work with the talented Carol Rosegg, in the studio or on the set. She has long been one of best theatre photographers in the business. One of my favorite backstage photographs, featured in the Introduction, was taken by Andy Halliday. Special thanks to Norbert Sinski for the estate of George Dudley, and Keith Henry for the estate of Marc Raboy, for granting permission to use their wonderful photos.

Whether we've stayed in close touch or not over the years, Theatre-in-Limbo alumni always seem like family, and reunions are a real pleasure. With love and gratitude, I would like to thank the actors, designers, and stage crew who worked on our shows, including Theresa Aceves, Tom Aulino, Michael Belanger, Ralph Buckley, Kathie Carr, Roy Cockrum, John Glaser, Jim Griffith, Andy Halliday, Michael Hunter, Julie Halston, Judith A. Hansen, Arnie Kolodner, Vivien Leone, Becky London, and Sam Rudy. Always in my memory are Robert Carey, Mark Hamilton, Meghan Robinson, Debra Tennenbaum, Bobby Locke, Jennifer Arnold, and Jeff Veazey, who are sorely missed. And of course, I am so grateful to my old friend Charles Busch, playwright, star, and collaborator extraordinaire.

I'd like express deep love and appreciation for my late parents, Donald and Dorothy Elliott, who were unfailingly supportive as I labored through graduate school and early versions of this book. I'm sorry they didn't get to see it in print, but they never doubted it would happen. And finally, I'm especially thankful for my beloved partner of ten years, Dr. Shao Gong, better known to friends as Ren.

Introduction **Beyond Ridiculous**

Kenneth Elliott, Julie Halston, Tom Aulino, Arnie Kolodner, Charles Busch, and Robert Carey in the cramped backstage area at Limbo, preparing for a performance of Vampire Lesbians of Sodom. *Photo by Andy Halliday.*

Ninth Street between Avenues B and C wasn't the most desolate block in Manhattan's East Village on December 1, 1984, but it was dreary enough—mostly shuttered industrial buildings, a rubble-strewn vacant lot, a few dilapidated apartment houses, and plenty of graffiti. But at around 9:30 that evening, an orderly queue of well-heeled young gay men and a few women began forming at the door of a former sanitation garage in the middle of the block. The only indication that there might be something other than garbage trucks inside was a small sign that read "Limbo." Before long, the line snaked down the block and around the corner, past the bodega on Avenue C. It was the last performance of the year for Theatre-in-Limbo in our signature production, a drag extravaganza called *Vampire Lesbians of Sodom*, written by and starring Charles Busch.

Inside the Limbo, a combination art gallery, nightclub, and performance space, I was getting frantic. I was the director and producer of the show, and I was also in the cast. We had been waiting for nearly an hour to begin our setup while a rock band scheduled to perform later that night was completing a sound check. The stage was littered with what looked like hundreds of feet of speaker wire, microphones, amplifiers, and a drum kit. The musicians seemed to have no conception that our show was supposed to start on that very stage in a half hour. As they idly began to clear their equipment, I pointedly glared in their direction while noisily setting up neat rows of white metal folding chairs in front of the stage, sweating, despite the lack of heat in the building, through the heavy stage makeup I always wore when playing the pompous silent screen star King Carlisle. The cast was already getting into costume in the cramped, narrow, alley-like area behind the platform stage. Most of us put on our makeup at home because there were no dressing rooms at the Limbo. There wasn't even a toilet backstage; in case of emergency, the actors had to improvise with cups or soda cans. Our wig designer/stage manager Kathie Carr was giving a last-minute coat of lacquer to one of her outrageous beehive creations. Joe Cote, our production assistant, pulled out a ladder in the midst of the chaos onstage and began hanging our backdrop. The musicians were still sauntering around, unplugging cable and casually chatting amongst themselves, seemingly unaware that they were in the way. Lighting designer Vivien Leone was running a last-minute dimmer check. It was already 9:45, and the show was supposed to start at 10:00. Suddenly, the sound of angry shouting rang out from the back of the room. Vivien had just discovered that the deejay from the previous night's after-hours party had refocused her light plot, and she was giving the house technical director an earful. Kathie dropped her can of hairspray and ran back to the booth to run the board while Vivien scrambled up a ladder to refocus the lights. We would have to hold the curtain, as usual.

Finally, at around 10:15, the stage was set, the lights were refocused, and we were ready to open the house. Marie-Lohr, a beautiful French girl wearing jeans, a T-shirt, and a black leather jacket, was stationed at the door ready to collect $5 from each customer—she was our favorite door person because she was glamorous, with a tough edge, and never let anyone in for free. As the audience filed in, I stood with Marie-Lohr for a few minutes, and then went out on the street to check out the crowd. I was astonished to see the queue still winding around the block. I ran backstage and told Charles that we had never had a bigger audience. The folding chairs were quickly taken and standees soon filled in any vacant space in the room. The bartender was busy dispensing longneck Rolling Rock beers and mixed drinks in plastic cups from the unlicensed bar. The curtain had to be held as more and more people pushed in. They just kept coming. I always made a practice of shuttling back and forth from backstage to the front door to see how sales were going. That night it took me over five minutes just to cross the room because of the mob scene. As I made my way backstage, I noticed some of the crowd filling in the space behind the bar with the bartender, several were sitting on top of the ice machine, and others were perched on rungs of the ladder leading up to the light booth. The Limbo was packed dangerously beyond its capacity, but there wasn't a certificate of occupancy anyway, and nobody cared. Such laws were casually ignored in the East Village of 1984. When our theme music finally blared from the speakers, the audience roared in recognition. Many of them had seen the show several times. The actors waiting in the wings to go on were thrilled but also slightly frightened. I quipped to Charles that this must have been how the Beatles felt before a concert, on a smaller scale, of course—maybe in Hamburg.

It was electrifying to play for Limbo audiences—like riding a wild wave. They got every joke, appreciated every nuance, and the laughs were huge. At the curtain call that night, our unofficial fan club, a group of young men who called themselves "Charlie's Angels," presented flowers to everyone in the cast during the thunderous ovation. The obvious affection that this audience had for the entire company was palpable. Who were they, and why had they come to this converted garage in a marginal neighborhood to see us? Theatre historian Arnold Aronson had attended the previous night's performance and later analyzed the crowd with anthropological precision for the *Drama Review*:

> The audience is primarily gay and conservatively dressed; this is
> not the East Village Punk scene one sees on the street a block or two
> away. It is a cult audience familiar with the work of playwright/actor
> Charles Busch, and with the high-camp style of this company. It is not
> a "theatre audience"—by and large, these spectators are not familiar
> with nor interested in the range of avant-garde theatre available

elsewhere in the city. It is a young audience and many are not familiar with the early work of John Vaccaro, Ron Tavel, Charles Ludlam, and Hot Peaches which is a clear precedent for this performance. This is an audience out for simple entertainment.[1]

The Limbo audiences did not have to be familiar with the historical precedents of Vaccaro, Tavel, and Ludlam to respond to the specifically gay theatrical style those men helped to create back in the 1960s—a style known as Theatre of the Ridiculous.[2] Times may have changed, but the Ridiculous Theatre aesthetic still spoke to a young gay audience with little or no knowledge of its provenance. The critical theorist and scholar David M. Halperin observed that "gay culture is not just a superficial affectation. It is an expression of difference through style—a way of carving out space for an alternate way of life. And that means carving out space in opposition to straight society."[3] The Limbo was that kind of space, and Ridiculous Theatre was that kind of style. Aronson calls it "high camp." Volumes have been written on this subject since the publication of Susan Sontag's 1964 essay "Notes on Camp," and it is a hotly contested term, but it's not something we thought much about at the time, and we weren't concerned with its political ramification.[4] For us, camp mostly meant embracing and exaggerating for effect the highly theatrical performance style of 1930s and '40s film stars, with occasional anachronisms, such as an ancient Roman guard with a New Jersey accent or a Byzantine empress who sends her robes to the local dry cleaner.

Charles Busch, a college friend, introduced me to Ludlam and the Ridiculous Theatrical Company soon after I moved to New York, and we saw nearly every show they produced from 1980 on. We often stopped backstage to chat with Ludlam and members of the cast after performances. Ludlam's brilliant comic turns were hilarious, and I was well aware that Theatre-in-Limbo owed a huge debt to him. But like the young audience described by Aronson, I was unfamiliar with his early work, or that of other artists who had developed the Ridiculous aesthetic decades earlier. It wasn't until my doctoral studies at UCLA, many years later, that I gained a deep understanding of the origins of the type of theatre the Ridiculous Theatrical Company performed and discovered a number of excellent books and articles on the subject.[5] For readers unacquainted with the early Ridiculous Theatre, as I was, I will attempt to sketch a brief history.

The Ridiculous was avant-garde theatre born in the rebellious 1960s.

Although Ludlam later objected to being identified as avant-garde, the earliest Ridiculous Theatre most definitely fit the bill: it was a direct assault on straight, mainstream values. It wasn't necessarily concerned with gay subjects; it was a gay *aesthetic*. Not to be confused with the stark, existentially angst-ridden Theatre of the Absurd, Ridiculous Theatre was outrageous and over the top. It mocked conventional values and pretenses and undermined traditional gender roles and political categories to expose what Stefan Brecht (son of playwright Bertolt Brecht) described as "the utter ridiculousness of institutionalized society."[6] It did so by parodying high and low literary and theatrical forms of the past, especially pop culture. Everything from Christopher Marlowe to Maria Montez movies to *I Love Lucy* could be recycled into the Ridiculous. It was a non-illusionistic, presentational performance style defined by camp, cheap theatrics, the grotesque, sexual ambiguity, and gender-blurring drag performances.

The elements of what would become the aesthetic of Ridiculous Theatre crystalized in the work of Jack Smith (1932–1989), a photographer, filmmaker, and performance artist whom Ludlam would later call "the daddy of us all."[7] Smith developed a philosophy of rebellion against the dominant culture that gave weight to his aesthetic. Rage, based on alienation from postwar mainstream American culture, was what motivated him. He wasn't a playwright in the traditional sense, nor did he regularly produce, direct, or act on the stage. He rejected commercialism so effectively that relatively few people actually saw his work. His most celebrated achievement, the 1963 film *Flaming Creatures*, was banned in New York and twenty-one other states. And yet Smith was influential to such disparate artists as Robert Wilson, Richard Foreman, Federico Fellini, and Andy Warhol. Foreman described his first encounter with *Flaming Creatures* as "the most overwhelming aesthetic experience of my life."[8] Aronson calls him "the lynchpin of the avant-garde."[9] Smith used drag, a staple of gay performance for generations, in a new way: as a critique of gender stereotypes. His flaming creatures intentionally blurred the differences between male and female rather than exaggerating them. He found value in pop culture rejects, such as the B movie goddess Maria Montez, that were regarded as kitsch by highbrow critics. He took what was considered trash and turned it into art. This was his "moldy aesthetic," and it became the basis for Ridiculous Theatre.

The stage history of Ridiculous Theatre began with playwright Ronald Tavel (1936–2009), a screenwriter for Andy Warhol's films, and director John Vaccaro (1929–2016). They founded the Play-House of the Ridiculous in 1965, and their first collaboration was produced way Off Broadway in a gallery called the Coda, which specialized in psychedelic art. Both men were greatly influenced by Smith, but whereas Tavel's inclination was to develop a highly intellectual, text-based theatre (his plays are larded with bad puns and malapropisms, often with sexual connotations), Vaccaro's interest was in manic, over-the-top staging that he called "orgiastic."[10] Their collaboration didn't last long, but it lasted long enough to launch the career of a young Charles Ludlam (1943–1987), who began his career as a scene-stealing actor in a Play-House production, *The Life of Lady Godiva* (1966). He soon broke away to start his own company, where he was playwright, director, and star, and he proceeded to thoroughly transform Ridiculous Theatre during the course of his career.

Smith, Tavel, and Vaccaro had created nonlinear performance events that owed as much to 1960s Happenings as they did to traditional theatre. Ludlam's earliest work was very much a part of that tradition, but beginning with *Bluebeard* (1970), his plays were often in more traditional and accessible forms, such as the well-made play. Many of them earned high praise from the *New York Times*. His adaptation of *Camille* (1973) was a huge hit, and his performance as the consumptive courtesan Marguerite Gautier is legendary. The plunging neckline of his costume revealed his hairy chest, both referencing and making a mockery of the elegant gowns Adrian had designed for Garbo to wear in the 1936 MGM film version; at the same time, Ludlam demonstrated a reverence for his source material by playing key emotional scenes with complete earnestness. It was a delicate balancing act that delighted his gay audiences. He had his biggest success in 1984 with *The Mystery of Irma Vep*, and there was much talk that he was entering the mainstream. But while he sought to "win converts"[11] and expand the audience for the Ridiculous, Ludlam kept his company very much at arm's length from mainstream commercial theater.

Charles Busch and I thought Theatre-in-Limbo was about as far from the mainstream theatre of the time as you could get when we were starting out in 1984. We were a gay company with little experience and no connections to speak of, and our leading lady was a man. Yet over the course of seven years, five Theatre-in-Limbo productions transferred to commercial Off-Broadway runs, and the most successful of them ran for five years and became the longest-running nonmusical Off-Broadway production in history. Since those days, Charles has become a beloved establishment figure of New York theatre. He was nominated for a 2001 Tony Award for his hit

Broadway comedy, *The Tale of the Allergist's Wife*. He was even named an "Off-Broadway Legend" in 2011 by the Off-Broadway Alliance, an industry trade group. The perception of assimilation into the cultural mainstream may explain why Theatre-in-Limbo is often left out of overviews of gay, avant-garde, and Off-Off-Broadway theatre of the period, and why there are so few published accounts of its history. Some East Village performance artists felt we were interlopers from the West Village, and Charles's early plays are often viewed as lightweight commercial comedies, yet our productions were regarded as oddities by the commercial theatre community. We didn't fit comfortably into any category. Theatre-in-Limbo occupied a uniquely liminal space between the avant-garde and the establishment while belonging to neither.

The world was very different in December 1984 when we were performing *Vampire Lesbians* at the Limbo Lounge than it had been nearly twenty years earlier when the first Ridiculous Theatre performances took place. The protest movements of the 1960s, the sexual revolution, the Vietnam War, the Stonewall rebellion, disco, Watergate, and Carter's malaise were all water under the bridge. Although progress had been made on gay rights, major challenges for the LGBTQ community remained. We were in the midst of the Reagan revolution, and the sunny geniality of the president masked the ascendance of his racist, homophobic, anti-feminist supporters such as the Reverend Jerry Falwell and the "Moral Majority." Most important, the relentless tragedy of AIDS was well underway, and it had altered the landscape for gay Americans and how we were perceived by the mainstream.

The decade of the 1980s was a transitional period for New York theatre. Production on Broadway was sharply curtailed from its heyday. Only ten new American plays opened on Broadway in the 1984–85 season, compared to twenty-one in the 1969–70 season just fifteen years earlier—a 50 percent reduction. Times Square was a place to be avoided, not a tourist destination. Some Broadway houses remained dark for the entire season, even after two historic theatres, the Morosco and the Helen Hayes, had been demolished to make way for the ghastly Marriott Marquis Hotel—a harbinger of the Times Square to come. Homeless men and women often slept in the doorways of vacant theatres.

It was a dreary and dispiriting time in New York. Like many young hopefuls, Charles and I had come to the city to start careers in a theatre that seemed to be dying on the vine. We found ourselves thwarted at every turn until Theatre-in-Limbo changed our lives. Charles often refers to himself as an anecdotist, and he likes to frame the Theatre-in-Limbo story as a fairy tale. That evening in 1984, the sudden and improbable success of *Vampire Lesbians of Sodom* certainly felt like one. But of course, it's not that simple. To explore the context and complications of our story, this book draws upon primary and secondary sources, documents, and interviews; however, it is also a memoir of my friendship and collaboration with Charles Busch. While I don't have the critical distance of an objective historian or theorist, I hope to show how central theatre was to at least part of the gay community as the AIDS epidemic took its deadly toll. I'll tell a firsthand history of our company, marked by heady triumphs and devastating tragedy, as a reflection of a pivotal period in New York history, and of a lost theatrical world.

Chapter 1 **Wouldn't It Be Fun?**

Julie Halston, Theresa Aceves, Charles Busch, and Tom Aulino backstage at 8BC. Photo by Kenneth Elliott.

In March 1984, while Charles Ludlam was readying his masterpiece, *The Mystery of Irma Vep*, Charles Busch was becoming desperate and depressed. His solo show, *Charles Busch Alone with a Cast of Thousands* had recently opened and closed in New York at the Shandol Theatre without much notice. It had been the culmination of years of effort as a solo performer, in which he had played short gigs at such venues as the cabaret theatre upstairs at the Duplex in Greenwich Village and the Ballroom in SoHo. He had worked hard to secure bookings at small theatres and cabarets around the country, such as the Valencia Rose in San Francisco and the Source Theatre in Washington, D.C. Although these engagements were often well received by the local press, they did not lead to more prestigious bookings.

I had met Charles (then known as Chuck) Busch over ten years earlier, when I was a freshman theatre major at Northwestern University in the fall of 1973 and we were both cast in a university production of *Romeo and Juliet*. He was jealous of me because, as Paris's Page, I had two or three lines, and he was in the chorus. I would hang out in the green room of Cahn Auditorium with him and his best friend, Ed Taussig, during the long stretches when we weren't onstage. They were witty and worldly sophomores from New York, and they were both openly gay; I was still in the closet, and they enjoyed teasing me about it. We remained friends throughout our college careers, although we weren't in any more shows together. The Northwestern theatre department was like a microcosm of show business, and Charles was frustrated by his inability to land a role in university productions. Slender, effeminate, self-conscious, and somewhat awkward, he was difficult to cast—but he was determined to succeed. When he returned from a semester abroad in Amsterdam in the fall of his junior year, he had a whole new look: dyed red hair, a pierced ear (*very* unusual at the time), and a huge fur coat. As an uptight midwesterner, I was a little unnerved by this cultivated outrageousness but it proved to be a good strategy for him. In his senior year, he made big waves on campus by starring in a student-produced vehicle he wrote for himself and Ed. The play, presented as part of the "Midnight Madness" film series, was called *Sister Act*, and he and Ed appeared in drag as Siamese twin sisters, joined at the hip, who performed in a carnival act. It was clear that Northwestern University had never witnessed anything like this. On the morning of opening night, the front page of the student newspaper, the *Daily Northwestern*, featured a big picture of Charles and Ed in full drag sporting red afro wigs and boas under a banner headline that screamed, "Degeneracy to Reign at Midnight Madness."[1] Naturally, the theatre was packed that night, and when the lights came up on the two of them, the audience roared; Charles felt vindicated after years of being ignored by the university theatre.

The inspiration for *Sister Act* came years earlier when he saw Charles Ludlam and the Ridiculous Theatrical Company performing *Eunuchs of the Forbidden City* back in 1972. He met Ludlam in the spring of 1976 at a symposium sponsored by the University of Chicago while the company was there performing *Camille* and *Stage Blood*. After graduation, he decided to stay in Chicago for a few years to pursue his own version of

Ridiculous Theatre. He wrote another drag comedy for Ed and himself, *Old Coozies* (a spoof based on John Van Druten's *Old Acquaintance*), which they performed at a gay club called La Mere Vipere. He soon formed his own Ludlam-esque troupe called the Imitation of Life Company, and they had some success performing a vehicle he had written for himself, *Myrtle Pope: The Story of a Woman Possessed*, at various Chicago clubs. It was a parody mash-up of women's pictures from *Madame X* to *Mildred Pierce*. I saw it at La Mere Vipere, and it was hilarious. But jealousy and infighting among members of his company soon led to the breakup of the Imitation of Life, and Charles moved back to New York in the spring of 1978. When I moved to the city in the fall of 1979, he was living with his aunt, Lillian Blum, in her elegant apartment at 50 Park Avenue, and she was ready for him to move out. When I visited him there she hopefully pressed the idea that the two of us might get an apartment together. "You're like the man who came to dinner," she said, half teasing, turning to Charles. "You came and never left; you just took over." We pored over the apartment rental ads in the *Village Voice*, but it was hard to find anything we could afford. I was back in Indiana for Christmas when Charles called to tell me he had found our apartment, just slightly over our budget at $450 per month. My heart sank when I saw it for the first time, however: a dreary, cramped railroad flat in a run-down tenement building. He convinced me that the location was the important thing—and it was a great location, right in the heart of the West Village, on Twelfth Street between Greenwich Avenue and West Fourth Street. We moved in together in February 1980.

Charles had changed career strategies when he returned to New York. After the acrimonious breakup of his Chicago company, he preferred to work solo. The act he developed with various directors was a mix of monologues in the style of Ruth Draper and multicharacter sketches in which he played all the roles, male and female. He abandoned drag performance, however, at least partly because, like Ludlam, he did not want to be marginalized as merely a gay act. His ambitions were greater than that, and he wanted to be taken seriously. His costume was simple, almost severe, and androgynous enough to allow him to play both men and women: black trousers, a long-sleeved black shirt, and a white cravat. The emphasis was on his ability as an actor to play a variety of roles and to switch rapidly between them. He accomplished the transitions by changing his focus, a technique he had learned from professors such as Frank Galati in what was then quaintly called the Department of Interpretation at Northwestern (it is now the Department of Performance Studies). *Alone with a Cast of Thousands*, presented by the Meridian Gay Theatre at the Shandol (a shabby showcase house in Chelsea) in January 1984, consisted of several such solo pieces he had written in a variety of styles from naturalism to genre parody. While it was a polished performance, there was very little press, and ticket sales were dismal. Charles had had high hopes for this production, and his sense of disappointment at its failure was profound. He was almost thirty, and it seemed to him that his career was going nowhere.

I was equally desperate. I had moved to New York to pursue a career as a stage director, and my biggest directing credit to date had been my roommate's recently closed solo show. Before coming to New York, I had worked as an assistant stage manager at the Seattle Repertory Theatre and the Academy Festival Theatre in Lake Forest, Illinois (where the Broadway-bound revival of *Morning's at Seven* was developed). Several actors working at these theatres told me I *had* to move to New York, and so I did. However, once I got to the city, I quickly learned the hard lesson that it was not so easy to get Equity stage management positions, let alone directing gigs. Although I had worked part-time at various jobs, my primary employment had been as personal assistant to Michael Stewart, the librettist of such Broadway musicals as *Bye Bye Birdie*, *Hello Dolly*, and *42nd Street*. I got the job through Bob Vandergriff, a stage-manager friend who thought it would provide some good connections, but the connections never panned out. Each day when I arrived at Mike's office in his sprawling apartment in the Wyoming on Seventh Avenue across the street from the Carnegie Deli, he would look up from his typewriter, hand me a small assignment book, and ask "What's on our great list today?" Something about the way he asked that question was a kindly, if ironic, acknowledgment that there was nothing "great" about it. My duties included menial tasks such as answering the telephone, running errands, picking up his linens at the Chinese laundry, and occasionally trimming his ear hair—none of which required a master's degree from Northwestern. Working for Mike had its memorable moments, such as delivering scripts to Jule Styne in his office at the Mark Hellinger Theatre, which looked like a time capsule from 1948 (they were collaborating on a musical based on *Treasure Island*), fielding calls from David Merrick, and handing out engraved Christmas gifts from Tiffany's to the chorus kids backstage at the Majestic Theatre. But after a couple of years, I came to the obvious conclusion that my career in the theatre was going nowhere, and I began applying to law schools as my father had long suggested.

Beyond the desperation Charles and I felt about our own careers, 1984 was a grim and anxious year in New York City. Less than six months after Ronald Reagan's inauguration in 1981, the *New York Times* ran its first story about an epidemic of a disease that soon came to be known as AIDS. I remember reading the article but not worrying about it much at the time; a relatively small number of people were affected. It wasn't long, however, before I started noticing emaciated young men with haunted looks, some with purple lesions on their faces, on the streets of our neighborhood in the West Village. One day a year or so later when I was getting my hair cut at Manuel H. Garza, a posh salon in the East Fifties (an indulgence I justified, despite the fact that I could barely pay my rent, because of my fear of going bald), I noticed that the stylist working in the next chair had lost lots of weight. Manuel whispered in my ear, "Del's got GRID," the acronym used at the time, which stood for gay-related immune deficiency. I never saw Del again. When David Garrett, a good friend from college and a gifted actor/singer, died in early 1983 after a brief bout of pneumocystis pneumonia, the horror of the epidemic really hit home. David was the first person I knew well to die of AIDS, but there were many more to come.

By 1984, New York was a major epicenter of the disease: of 6,402 reported cases of AIDS nationwide by October 1984, 2,651 of them were in New York, according to the Centers for Disease Control.[2] The response of the federal government to AIDS was notoriously slow; Reagan famously failed to even publicly mention the disease during his first term. As the death toll mounted and the administration's indifference to the epidemic became increasingly evident, fear, despair, and anger were everyday emotions in the city's gay communities, where memorial services became frequent, but dreaded, social events.

AIDS was not the only polarizing factor in New York City in 1984. Despite the gradual recovery from a major recession, the Reagan era brought massive budget cuts, reduced services, and increased homelessness to the city. At least 40,000 homeless people were living on the streets that year, turning many neighborhoods into what Mayor Edward I. Koch bluntly called "outdoor psychiatric wards."[3] At the same time, rents were skyrocketing as gentrification forced many longtime residents out of their previously marginal neighborhoods. Although the U.S. economy was pulling out of recession and Wall Street was booming, the disparity between the rich and poor in the city had become more painfully evident than ever. Affluent enclaves such as the Upper East Side contrasted starkly with the poverty of areas such as the East Village, which had developed a reputation as a center of violent crime, drug dealing, and urban decay. For most New Yorkers, the East Village was a neighborhood to be avoided. For some young artists and performers, however, it represented an opportunity because it offered low rents in a city that was otherwise all but unaffordable.

Limbo

On Friday, March 9, 1984, Charles and I attended a performance that our friend Bina Sharif was giving at the Limbo Lounge on Tompkins Square Park in the East Village. Neither of us had spent much time east of First Avenue. When we ventured there one afternoon to watch location shooting for the film *Ragtime*, we felt like tourists visiting a foreign country. (The film's art director had restored a block of East Eleventh Street to its turn-of-the-century glory, obscuring the blight of the surrounding area.) We had received the flyer for Bina's show, but we were nervous about traveling to the neighborhood after dark so we decided to splurge on a taxi. It was an adventure. The streets were lined with buildings that had been torched by landlords hoping to collect insurance money. Alphabet City by night was as ominous as we had imagined. The numerous vacant lots were strewn with rubble. And despite a recent police crackdown on drug dealing ("Operation Pressure Point"),[4] many homeless junkies and alcoholics seemed to be wandering the streets. It was a grim, menacing environment. The Limbo Lounge was appropriately named; the entire neighborhood appeared to be in a state of limbo just short of complete obliteration. If you knew where to look amid the ruins, however, you saw dozens of new art galleries, restaurants, and clubs, mostly run by young people in their twenties and thirties who would have been unable to afford retail rents in more established neighborhoods. Many of the clubs featured various types of performance that theatre historian Uzi Parnes categorized in a 1985 issue of the *Drama Review* devoted to the East Village scene as "Pop Performance, Dada Cabaret, New Vaudeville, entertaining Performance Art, or just plain Burlesque."[5]

This downtown club and art scene, created by Baby Boomers reared on mass culture, had developed a remarkably coherent aesthetic. The Mudd Club, which opened in TriBeCa in 1978, was a harbinger of the emerging East Village performance culture. That same year, Ann Magnuson started

Club 57 in the basement of a Polish church at 57 St. Mark's Place. This club glorified trashy TV shows and films from the 1950s through the 1970s, and featured a wide variety of performances and theme parties that parodied pop culture. John Epperson (a.k.a. Lypsinka) described his first visit to the club, shortly after he moved to the city in 1978, to see a screening of *Valley of the Dolls*: "So I got there, and the audience was screaming just for the credits. When Edie Williams' name came up the crowd went wild. And I thought these kids already know who these people are! They are light years ahead of me! But I'd found my place." Epperson explained that the reaction of the crowd to the film was "both loving and mocking at the same time."[6] Magnuson summed up the general East Village sensibility:

> Most of the people here are trying to make sense of what they grew up with in the '60s and '70s. We take all those elements and put them back together in different configurations and try to make people laugh. And we make them think.[7]

Critic Margo Jefferson identified the source of this aesthetic as "a collective memory crammed with sitcoms, fashion photos, gossip rags, TV news, radio talk shows, Top Forty Lists, comics and cartoons, sci-fi and horror movies, Disneyland, pornography, chorus lines, and trade shows."[8] Gone was the minimalism of 1970s performance artists; the shows at Club 57 were outrageous fun. Although it closed by 1983, its program was typical of the downtown aesthetic in its irony-laden love/hate relationship with mass culture. Numerous other clubs and cafés featuring performance soon sprang up in the neighborhood, including the Pyramid, the Wow Café, 8BC, Darinka, and the Limbo Lounge. Madonna briefly tended bar at Lucky Strike, which boasted a bar in the shape of a penis and testicles. The styles of the performers varied wildly, but the parody of pop culture was a constant.

The Limbo Lounge, located at 339 East Tenth Street, was a narrow, railroad storefront, the floors, walls, and ceilings of which were painted black. When Charles and I arrived there for the first time, a lively crowd of very pale young men and women wearing black were milling around drinking longneck Rolling Rocks while music blared from the speakers. The Limbo Lounge served as an art gallery by day, and an installation of colorful abstract art was for sale. By night Limbo was a performance space and an illegal after-hours club for the crowd at the Pyramid and other neighborhood clubs. We had no idea who these utterly cool, utterly hip, androgynous people were, but the place had the atmosphere of a secret, forbidden party where everyone was in-the-know—a kind of 1980s version of a beatnik hangout. Charles and I were East Village tourists who had stumbled into this fabulous, magical scene that night.

There was no actual stage, only a small area of floor space allotted to the performers at the rear of the front room. The lighting consisted of hardware store clip lights, and there was no seating other than a few booths on one side of the room. There was also a small back room with an unlicensed bar, which opened onto a backyard sculpture garden affiliated with an art gallery next door, which was owned by a woman who had renamed herself after the mayor's official residence, Gracie Mansion. Most of the audience sat on the floor when Bina was introduced by one of the club owners, who called himself Michael Limbo, a handsome young man in his late twenties with an enigmatic smile and a curiously relaxed, low-key demeanor. Bina's act consisted primarily of a lengthy recitation of the names of designer perfumes, delivered with fierce attitude. It was a witty, blistering critique of American consumerism. She got some substantial laughs, and after the performance Charles turned to me and said, without irony, "Wouldn't it be fun to do a show here?" I agreed that it would, and so we approached Michael Limbo, who was mingling with the crowd. He was very friendly, but he had no idea who we were, and he didn't seem to care. We told him we wanted to do a show in his club. Without missing a beat, he checked his date book and gave us a Friday and Saturday slot a little over a month later. It was that easy to break into the East Village performance scene.

We had a booking, but we needed a show. The Limbo Lounge was certainly not an appropriate venue for an evening of severe Ruth Draper–style monologues. But for two nights in a tiny East Village dive, Charles felt he could just let loose and do full drag again without worrying about the ramifications for his career—who would ever hear of it? He had a play in his trunk called *Vampire Lesbians of Sodom* that was the perfect vehicle. (Yes, he had a real trunk in our living room where he stored old scripts, among other things.) He had written it the previous summer, based in part on a vampire script called *Teethmarks* that he had written as an undergraduate at Northwestern. We had held a reading of *Vampires* in our West Twelfth Street living room in September 1983, but nothing happened with it until Charles suggested we resuscitate it for our booking at the Limbo Lounge. Over the course of the next two weeks, he quickly cut and revised the script while working temp jobs at Warner Communications. The finished product was not really a play so much as two tenuously related sketches in the Ridiculous style. Unlike many of the early Ridiculous plays of Ronald Tavel and Charles Ludlam, however, *Vampires* had the semblance of a plot.

Vampire Lesbians of Sodom is the story of two feuding showbiz diva lesbian vampires battling it out over the centuries. The first scene, set in ancient Sodom and Gomorrah ("the twin cities") was in the style of a burlesque sketch. Scantily clad guards bring a young virgin to the mouth of "a forbidding cave." She is to be a virgin sacrifice to the dreaded Succubus monster, so she begs the guards to rape her so she no longer qualifies as a virgin. Rape is certainly not a subject for comedy, but in this context, an outrageous comic reversal leads the potential victim to demand to be raped, while the potential rapists run away in terror, leaving her to the mercy of the Succubus. The Succubus, a "hard-boiled dame" with a touch of grandeur, emerges from the cave and sinks her teeth into the young virgin's neck as the lights black out.

The second scene, set in Hollywood in 1920, parodied the drawing-room comedy genre, with elements of melodrama and French romantic drama. In the intervening millennia, the Succubus has become a silent screen vamp of the Theda Bara school, known as Magda Legerdemain or La Condesa. The young virgin of scene 1, now a vampire herself, has transformed herself into Madeleine Astarté, "the dazzling grande dame of the New York stage," who is La Condesa's greatest rival. Astarté arrives at La Condesa's mansion and casually announces that she has stolen La Condesa's most prestigious future roles at the studio. She then proceeds to steal her girlfriend as well, the young starlet Renee Vain. After Astarté drinks Renee's blood, the two stars confront each other with lengthy *tirades* in which they catalogue the injustices they have inflicted on each other, but by the end of the scene they join forces to destroy a male vampire hunter disguised as female gossip columnist, a Hedda Hopper type with a wild hat, called Oatsie Carewe. Madeleine and La Condesa escape, but their conflict in this early version of the script remains unresolved. Charles was not sure how to end the play, so he left open the possibility of a return engagement by ending the scene abruptly with an announcement: "Did they escape or did they perish with the rising sun? Find out the answer in 'Return of the Vampire Lesbians of Sodom,' coming soon to a theatre near you."[9]

Like his earlier plays *Sister Act* and *Myrtle Pope*, *Vampire Lesbians* was very much indebted to Ludlam's work. Charles was not only a fan; he had gotten to know Ludlam over the years. When he first performed his solo show at the Duplex in New York, Charles invited Ludlam to see it. Ludlam was enthusiastic and encouraging, and he invited Charles to perform his act as a late show at his theatre at One Sheridan Square. Charles had even acted briefly with the Ridiculous Theatrical Company as a replacement in the role of Hecate during a 1979 revival of *Bluebeard*. It wasn't a happy experience. Charles volunteered to bring in his own costume, featuring a black bustier, so he could make a more glamorous impression than had the previous Hecate. He was given only fifteen minutes of rehearsal (which Ludlam did not attend) before finding himself onstage with Ludlam at the climax of the play. The star wasn't happy with his understated performance and demanded that he "ham it up" at the next show. But Charles did not make enough of an adjustment to please Ludlam, who angrily berated him backstage, shouting "Who the fuck do you think you are?" Shaken, at the next show Charles reluctantly tried to deliver the hammy performance that Ludlam wanted. It still wasn't enough, and in the middle of the scene Ludlam humiliated Charles by ripping down his glamorous bustier. After the show, Charles asked Ludlam why he had done that, and he never forgot Ludlam's reply: "I'll stick my finger up your ass if I feel like it!" This ended Charles's desire to work with the Ridiculous Theatrical Company, but he still had a fantasy that he might one day have his own company and, like Ludlam, write fabulous star parts for himself.[10]

Putting It Together

We were too poor to make multiple copies of the script at the local copy shop, so Charles sneaked into the copy room of Warner Communications, where he was working a temp job, to make the needed copies, leaving us ready for our first rehearsal, held March 25, 1984. We still needed a cast, but fortunately we knew plenty of out-of-work actors. Some cross-gender casting was essential to the conception of the play, but the cast was a mix of men and women. Charles had written the plum role of the Virgin Sacrifice/Madeleine Astarté for himself. The two other female roles would be played by women. Charles had Bina Sharif in mind for the other leading role, the Succubus/La Condesa, but she was otherwise engaged. He then somehow convinced Ridiculous Theatrical Company veteran Lola Pashalinski, whom he had met during his brief stint in *Bluebeard*, to take the role. Engaging Lola was quite a coup. She had won two Obie awards for her work with Ludlam (in *Corn* and *Der Ring Gott Farblonjet*), and was an Off-Off-Broadway legend. We billed her on the flyer as "special guest star."

The cast was rounded out with other friends and acquaintances, and the process of assembling them was casual. Charles wanted to include his oldest friend, Andy Halliday, whom he had met when he was fifteen at a theatre summer camp called Beginner's Showcase. Andy was diminutive and slender, with thinning, curly black hair, and he exuded a jittery energy. He agreed to play La Condesa's neurotic butler, Etienne. Theresa Aceves, a petite and beautiful young actress with a touch of madness in her eyes, was an acquaintance of Charles's from Washington, D.C. She was to play the ingenue, Renee Vain. I called a classmate from Northwestern, Tom Aulino, to play the role of the Salazar the Vampire Hunter who was disguised in drag as Oatsie Carewe. We needed two hot young men for the guards. Charles had met Arnie Kolodner the previous summer when they both worked at the Renaissance Fair in Tuxedo, New York. A magician who had recently graduated from the acting program at NYU, he was a good-looking guy with a touch of arrogance who was initially resistant to presenting himself as beefcake. Charles twisted his arm, and he joined the company to play the role of Hujar. I had met Robert Carey at a gay bar on Christopher Street a few weeks earlier, and I used the show as an excuse to call him about playing the other guard, Ali. Bobby was darkly handsome and possessed a spectacular body, but he had never appeared on stage and was terrified at the prospect. At the time, he was working for the reservations office of the Helmsley Palace Hotel. It took some coaxing over cocktails, but he finally agreed to do the part. I was to direct and play King Carlisle, a pompous, airheaded silent screen matinee idol betrothed to La Condesa's girlfriend, Renee Vain, but exposed as a homosexual by Madeleine (using a variation on Harold's words to Michael from *The Boys in the Band*: "You may one day marry, and even have children. But you will always be a homosexual. Always!").[11]

The entire budget for the production was under $50. We rehearsed in the living room of actor James Ray's apartment on Seventh Avenue at Thirteenth Street. I was house-sitting for him while he was in Los Angeles, and it was the largest space I could find for free. The play had no scenery. For lighting, we relied on clip lights provided by the Limbo Lounge. Charles coordinated the costumes, which for the most part were completely makeshift. Some of them were pulled from his closet (he always kept a few wigs and miscellaneous bits of fabric stowed away). His Aunt Lillian worked as a volunteer at a thrift shop near her apartment in Murray Hill, and she was an excellent source of wardrobe items. Bobby Carey cut up an old black leather jacket and sewed the pieces together to make loin cloths for the guards. Theresa Aceves wore a slip with a sash added to give the impression of a flapper. Kathie Carr, who had stage managed Charles's show at the Shandol, styled the cheap Dynel wigs, which had been bought on Fourteenth Street. She teased La Condesa's wig into a truly impressive beehive. Our biggest expense was postage. Charles created a hand-lettered flyer, which he photocopied at Warner Communications. We mailed it to everyone we knew, as well as to the mailing list Charles had developed over the years from his solo show. It was our only advertising.

The night of our first performance (April 9, 1984) we discovered that the East Village audience was not necessarily as monolithic as it had seemed on our first visit. The Limbo Lounge was packed with around sixty customers who paid $3 apiece to see the show, but there was very little evidence of the "local" crowd we had observed at Bina Sharif's performance a few weeks earlier. Our audience that night was predominantly gay men, most of whom were not from the immediate neighborhood—they would have seemed more at home in a West Village bar like Uncle Charlie's. Instead of basic black, pastel polo shirts paired with khaki pants was the favored look. Our performance had attracted its own very specific audience to the Limbo Lounge: our friends.

Although I had seen quite a few of Ludlam's productions at One Sheridan Square, I had never directed a production in the Ridiculous style. In fact, this was the first play with more than one cast member that I had directed in New York, and I wanted to show off what I had learned from Professor James Coakley in his advanced directing class at Northwestern. Advanced directing meant "style," so I approached the heightened theatricality of the script by staging it as a modern Restoration comedy, featuring over-the-top characterizations and exaggerated line readings and playing out to the audience (while maintaining a sense of the reality of the world of the play, of course). But, in effect, my academic approach was remarkably similar to Ludlam's directorial style. Given the limited experience of much of the cast (as well as the director), the result was pretty amateurish—which was also in keeping with the Ridiculous aesthetic. This heightened style was an odd choice for such a small space, where the audience was literally sitting on the floor in the playing area only a few feet from the performers. The stage had approximately six feet of depth and eight feet of width; the single entrance was the hallway connecting the front and back rooms, upstage right.

The opening scene in Sodom was notable for Bobby Carey's awkward line readings and thick New Jersey accent as the guard, Ali, bantering with Arnie Kolodner's Hujar, the second guard:

HUJAR: So what brings you here to Sodom?

ALI: Don't scoff but I've come to seek my fortune.

HUJAR: My friend, you've made a wise move. This city has everything. Have you been to the bars?

ALI: Last night I was taken to a place called "The Galley Slave." The whole place was supposed to look like a slave ship. There was this fellow who they tied up in a sling and . . . and . . . and they shoved a golden pestle up his you know what.

HUJAR: (lewdly) You don't say. Last night, my lover and I went to the baths in Gomorrah. Talk about trolls. It was like open house at the leper colony.

ALI: Hujar, I don't want to offend you but I'm really not into bars and baths. I'm looking for a relationship.[12]

The anachronistic parallels between ancient Sodom and the contemporary gay scene in New York City got some decent laughs, but the audience was truly mesmerized by Bobby's scantily clad body. The main function of this sequence, however, was to set up the entrance of the unconscious Virgin Sacrifice. Charles nestled his face into Arnie's chest as he was carried in, and when they reached center stage, he turned his face to the audience to reveal a virgin who was a cross between a Pre-Raphaelite angel and a burlesque queen.

Lola Pashalinski received an ovation from the audience on her entrance as the Succubus, but it was in the second scene as La Condesa that she demonstrated to the entire company her superb mastery of the Ridiculous style. The tiny stage was so crowded with other actors that she could barely move, so she planted herself dead center when she entered to discover that Madeleine had not only stolen her upcoming film roles but had seduced Renee Vain as well. She delivered her long, angry denunciation speech in the grand theatrical manner of a neoclassical *tirade*. Lola exploited the hauteur of the character with her erect posture and condescending glare. She poured her energy into her vocal delivery, which was stentorian in style, punctuated by touches of Bert Lahr. Her diction was exaggerated, like that of an old-school tragedian. With the exception of a few bold gestures and pointed turns of her head to Madeleine, she remained immovable throughout the monologue, which is essentially a list speech, a catalogue of the numerous lovers Madeleine had stolen from La Condesa over the centuries: a nun in the dark ages, "the most beautiful of Caligula's courtesans," a lady in waiting to Elizabeth I, etc. She began the speech in a contained rage, and as she progressed through the litany of stolen lovers, she increased her energy and intensity, building to a thrilling climax as she explained why she had never previously sought revenge:

> Because I am a great lady, I conduct myself with dignity and grandeur whilst you roll in the gutter, parading your twat onstage and calling it acting. You've got about as much glamour as common street whore. But now, madame, you have gone too far. I am the queen of vampires and I shall never, never relinquish my hold on Hollywood![13]

Lola extended her delivery of the second syllable of the second "never" in the last sentence to such an absurd length that I thought she wouldn't have the breath to make it to the end of the speech. This was a performance we had not seen in rehearsal. I was onstage at the time, and I was startled by the magic that occurs when a truly gifted actor suddenly turns it on. Charles stared at her with awe and respect. She had thrown down the gauntlet, and now he had to follow with his own *tirade*.

He delivered the first line of his speech like a middle-class New York matron, and with a tone of utter boredom that completely undercut and deflated Pashalinski's grandiloquent vocal pyrotechnics: "Are you through?" He got a huge laugh, and he was off and running. He immediately switched to a refined, mid-Atlantic accent that signaled the beginning of the speech as a set piece. The practice of switching of accents in mid-speech can be traced back to some of the earliest Ridiculous productions. Ronald Tavel's stage directions for *The Life of Lady Godiva* (1966) calls for Godiva to speak "*with an exaggerated British accent*" on her entrance, and then in mid-speech inexplicably switch to "*a very thick Brooklyn accent.*"[14] A few pages later she is instructed to "*speak in her natural voice form this point on.*"[15] The character might seem to suffer from multiple personality disorder, but in the world of the Ridiculous such shifts are an accepted element of the style. Charles's vocal switching wasn't written into the script, and it was subtler than that indicated in the *Godiva* script, but it conveyed the same idea of the character's unstable identity.

Like Lola, Charles remained almost motionless throughout much of his speech, employing only a few deliberate grand gestures. Rather than attacking the speech from the top at a fever pitch, he began quietly, emphasizing the lyricism:

> As you desire to relive the past, shall we travel even further back in
> time? Many centuries ago, back in the days of the Bible, there was a
> young girl, a mere child of fourteen, a lovely girl, full of high spirits.
> A lottery was held to choose a sacrificial victim for the dreaded
> Succubus. As fate would have it, she chose the black stone of death.[16]

Charles had obsessively studied accounts of great actresses of the past such as Nazimova, Mrs. Patrick Campbell, and especially Sarah Bernhardt. Although he had seen silent film footage of Bernhardt, he was most familiar with her style through the written accounts he had devoured. The pitch of his voice ran up and down the scale in a manner that recalled Cornelia Otis Skinner's description of Bernhardt playing the title role in *Adrienne Lecouvreur* for an American audience that

> heard nothing but that voice which had in it "the cooing of doves,
> the running of streams, the falling of spring rains." They shivered
> as though with ice on their spines when that voice clarioned in rage
> or anguish and her acting became the flash of forked lightning.[17]

While Charles's delivery of "a lovely girl, full of high spirits" reflected "the cooing of doves," his tone coarsened considerably as he described what happened after the girl "chose the black stone of death," and it occasionally veered into a Glenda Jackson–like nasality as Madeleine vividly describes the ordeal of her assault by the bloodsucking vampire lesbian. She explains how the young victim turned the tables by lodging "her teeth into a vein of the monster" and drinking its blood. He saved the clarion of rage for the finale of the speech:

> And there, on that bleached rocky point, left to rot like a piece of old
> meat, she did not die but was transformed, transformed into one of
> the undead, never to find eternal rest but to stalk the earth forever in
> search of a victim, forever alone, forever damned.

He turned to Lola and posed with his arms extended like a cross as he commanded, "Look at me. I am that girl! And I demand the death of the Succubus!"[18] This was the cue for the audience to burst into applause, and they cooperated. It was also a deliberate evocation of Blanche Yurka as Madame Defarge in a climactic moment from the 1936 film version of *A Tale* of *Two Cities* ("I demand the death of the Evrémonde!").[19] These two *tirades* were the centerpiece of the production. The different styles employed by Busch and Pashalinski recalled Skinner's description of the contrast between Bernhardt ("an incandescent, shimmering aura")[20] and the earlier tragédienne, Rachel ("an Old-School player-queen of heroic build and thundering voice").[21] By the end of the performance, the audience was cheering and shouting "brava!" I was delighted but perplexed. None of us were expecting such a response, even from an audience that consisted mostly of our friends. When we got the same kind of ovation the second night, we thought we might be on to something.

East Village Vaudeville

The original impulse behind our new company was expressed by Charles's question to me after Bina Sharif's performance: "Wouldn't it be fun to do a show here?" Homelessness, crime, crack dealing, skyrocketing rents, and especially AIDS made New York City an extremely hostile environment in 1984. By completely ignoring the realities of the moment and instead embracing utter fantasy, *Vampire Lesbians* provided us and our audience with a much-needed dose of escapist entertainment. The giddy enthusiasm of the response to our first two performances was substantial enough to encourage Charles and me to seek additional bookings for *Vampire Lesbians*. We had the exhilarating sense that we had a hit. Michael Limbo was pleased to see his club filled, and he invited us to play a return engagement in early June. We didn't want to wait that long, so in the meantime we booked the show into another East Village club, 8BC, for a single performance in May.

Unfortunately, Lola Pashalinski wasn't interested in continuing with the show. She offered no reasons for withdrawing, but Charles speculated that she had long since paid her dues performing under such circumstances. After all, she had played Ludlam's *Bluebeard* in a gay dive bar fourteen years earlier. Her departure complicated things. I knew Lola would be very hard to replace, and we had to find somebody fast. Charles had met Julie Halston when he was doing his one-man show in San Francisco. She was a full-time corporate librarian at a Wall Street firm, but she had a comedy act that she brought to the Valencia Rose, an eccentric former mortuary turned cabaret in the Mission District where Charles was performing. Julie had a big personality, knew lots of people, and had proved it when she organized groups to fill the seats at the Shandol Theatre when we were playing to empty houses there a few months earlier. With Julie as La Condesa we were guaranteed an audience, but I thought we should hear her read before offering her the part. She came to our apartment to audition, and she later recalled that she could "see the blood draining" from my face as she read. I asked Charles to meet me in the kitchen, a few yards away, and Julie remembers hearing me whispering through the closed door: "Charles, she's terrible. She can't act." Charles could only lamely reply that she had once played Nina in *The Seagull* at Hofstra University.[22] In the end, we couldn't find anyone else who was willing to learn the part and play one performance for no money in a dangerous neighborhood, so Julie made her debut with our company at 8BC on Friday May 18, 1984.

8BC, as its name suggests, was on Eighth Street between Avenues B and C. It was an 1840 farmhouse that had been converted into a performance space. The audience entered a room, once the basement, with a long, unlicensed bar on the right. The stage was at the opposite end of the room at a terrifying height. It was all that remained of what was once the first floor, the rest of which had been removed. Owners Cornelius Conboy and Dennis Gattra conceived of their club as an East Village "Vaudeville House." They booked three acts a night, the first beginning at nine or ten, the last at around two in the morning. It was usually a mixed bill of theatre, cabaret, music, and dance. In between the featured acts, deejays would play recorded music, often unreleased records from up-and-coming bands.[23]

Vampire Lesbians was the first act that Friday. 8BC was an even quirkier venue than the Limbo Lounge. Someone's pet rabbit hopped around backstage while we got ready to go on. There was a dirty white curtain that looked like it had once been a sheet masking the elevated proscenium stage. When it opened, we experienced the disorienting effect of playing down to the audience, which was standing a full story below us. Julie's performance that night was certainly not as nuanced as Lola's, but she took a very different approach to the role and showed that she had genuine comic instincts—something that had not been apparent during rehearsal. She had been confused by my academic approach to directing, as she said in an interview a few years later:

Boulevard theatre and Restoration comedy, those were the two terms that Kenneth used in talking about *Vampires*, and I remember thinking this guy is out of his mind. I thought we were doing a campy drag show with Charles a cut above, because I had seen his work. I was very confused because Ken was treating this like *Hedda Gabler*.[24]

Julie sensed that we were all nervous about her performance, and at the final dress rehearsal she turned to the company and said, "Look guys, I know I stink, but you put a wig on me in front of sixty gay men and I glow!"[25] Rather than playing a grand tragedian trapped in a tawdry farce, Julie's La Condesa was more of a middlebrow matron with pretensions. She spoke with a Long Island accent, her posture was slouched, and her gestures recalled Joan Rivers more than Rachel. She got big laughs. That night's performance had more than a few fits and starts, but the air of under-rehearsed amateurism was part of the fun. Since most of the audience was drinking and many of them were high on drugs, they were pretty easy to please.

After the show, we descended to the main floor and mixed with the crowd. Performing in East Village clubs was more like hosting a party than acting in a play, and hanging out afterward was part of the scene. Writing in the *Drama Review*, Charles Tarzian described the atmosphere of 8BC as "particularly reminiscent of Germany during the Weimar era,"[26] and there certainly was an aura of Kit-Kat-Klub "divine decadence," which was all the more haunting when we spilled onto Eighth Street at two in the morning. The atmosphere outside the club was more reminiscent of Germany after the Allied bombing. Many of the buildings on the block had been reduced to rubble. Nothing was left but empty shells and vacant lots, illuminated only by the moon because the streetlights didn't work. This particular block of East Eighth Street, known to some as "Little Dresden,"[27] was completely dark and desolate. The only sign of life (and electricity) on this eerie East Village block was 8BC. Looking at the ruins, it was hard to imagine that this neighborhood ever was or ever could be a vibrant part of the city.

Speculators Keep Out!

"East Village" was a sales term invented by real estate agents in the 1960s to lend bohemian cachet to a part of town that had long been known as the Lower East Side.[28] This area had been home to diverse groups of Polish, Slavic, Ukrainian, Jewish, Chinese, Puerto Rican, and other immigrants, and it had been in a state of slow decline since the 1940s. Throughout the 1970s, buildings in the neighborhood were abandoned at an alarming rate, and arson was commonplace. Despite the proliferation of art galleries and clubs, the unrelenting grimness of the East Village in May 1984 made its future prospects as a center of real estate development seem unlikely to the casual observer. But real estate speculators had already seen value in the area. In 1982, the average rent for a Lower East Side apartment was $150, which is what made it attractive to young artists. By 1984, comparable apartments were renting for $600 to $1,300.[29] The average sales price for a walk-up apartment building in Alphabet City rose from $25,000 in 1980 to $223,625 in 1985.[30] Deborah Humphreys, of the community housing organization Pueblo Nuevo, blamed the artists and performers: "Indirectly, the artists are gentrifiers. They supply the housing demand that causes rents to be out of reach for low-income residents. It really hits the poor people who have always considered the Lower East Side home. Where can you go if you can't live there?"[31] There weren't many options, other than to leave town.

The gentrification of the East Village was given a major boost the very week after our 8BC performance, when the widely read and trendy *New York Magazine* ran as a cover story Craig Unger's "The Lower East Side: There Goes the Neighborhood." With its weekly columns on chic restaurants and entertainment tips such as "Ruth Recommends," "Sales and Bargains," and "Best Bets," *New York* delivered to city consumers the up-to-the-minute inside story on what was chic and what they should buy or desire. Unger's article chronicled the explosion of art galleries, boutiques, restaurants, and clubs opening in what had once been an urban wasteland, but its main focus was real estate and gentrification.

Unger illustrated the trend by focusing on one building: Christodora House, a sixteen-story Art Deco shell on Avenue B on the east side of Tompkins Square Park and around the corner from the Limbo Lounge. At that time, Christodora House was in a state of complete disrepair; its doors were welded shut, its windows were broken, and graffiti covered every reachable surface. It was built in 1928 as a settlement house, community recreation center, and residential hotel, but as the neighborhood demographic shifted over the years, the building deteriorated and was bought by the city. No bidders appeared in 1975 when the city put the Christodora up for auction, but when the minimum bid finally dropped to $62,500, it sold to real-estate developer George Jaffee, the sole bidder. A mere eight years later, Jaffee sold it for $1.3 million. One year after that, in 1984, it was sold again—this time for $3 million. Christodora House was emblematic of what was happening throughout the neighborhood. It was therefore not surprising that local residents hung out banners warning "Speculators Keep Out."[32]

Unger's article, accompanied by a handy cartoon map identifying the neighborhood hot spots, had a major impact on the East Village. Now even the most bourgeois Upper West Siders could navigate the area. Most of the

East Village entrepreneurs, including the owners of the Limbo Lounge, were initially delighted by the attention because it was an opportunity to make money. The "scary" Lower East Side was suddenly the hippest part of town. It was not unusual to see limousines parked in front of storefront clubs and galleries on otherwise burned-out blocks. Tourists in search of the latest thing descended in droves, especially on weekends. But the frisson of excitement that accompanied the sudden spotlight on the East Village didn't last long. Just a few years later, a Gap clothing store opened on St. Marks Place, to the dismay of the locals.

The brief period after the "discovery" of the East Village but before its total commodification had an impact on mainstream culture, however. East Village fashion quickly became chic. In the film *Desperately Seeking Susan* (1985), Madonna (the former bartender from Lucky Strike) modeled a dizzying array of black bustiers, spike heels, and Antique Boutique fashions that looked positively glamorous. *Vogue* magazine, the bible of the fashion industry, ran an article on the downtown aesthetic in July 1985. East Village artists such as Keith Haring and Jean-Michel Basquiat were embraced by mainstream galleries. Some East Village performers also moved into the mainstream. Ann Magnuson, the founder of the seminal Club 57 (and who played the cigarette girl in *Desperately Seeking Susan*), had by the end of the decade become a regular on the ABC sitcom *Anything but Love*. The ironically detached view of mass culture that was such a key element of East Village performance in the early 1980s has since become commonplace. The general perception of drag performance as fashionable and cutting edge rather than a stigmatized subcultural practice was also reinforced by the East Village boom. *Vampire Lesbians of Sodom* benefited from all these trends.

As a throwaway tagline in one of his closing paragraphs, Unger mentioned *Vampire Lesbians* (misstating the title): "And, whatever else, the area is rarely boring. Last week's performance at 8BC was called 'Lesbian Vampires From Sodom [*sic*].'"[33] Immediately after Unger's story hit the newsstands, Michael Limbo reported that the reservation line at the Limbo Lounge was ringing off the hook for our next performance on June 2. In those pre-Twitter days, a single, brief reference in *New York Magazine* (even if the title of the play was misstated) seemed to us to be a major media breakthrough. It became the catalyst for our theatrical ambitions. We were convinced that the old cliché about being in the right place at the right time was proving to be true.

Chapter 2 **Fantasy Theatre**

Kenneth Elliott and Charles Busch in costume for Theodora,
She-Bitch of Byzantium, *wearing crowns fashioned by John Glaser.*
Photo by George Dudley.

• •

Fantasy played a huge role in our developing plans, and we started to
get big ideas. The ad hoc company we had so casually thrown together
shifted from a one-shot lark to the focus of our lives. Charles and I had
long after-dinner conversations in our Twelfth Street apartment planning,
plotting, and fantasizing. We needed a name for our company. Since the
Limbo Lounge was our home base, I suggested we call ourselves Theatre

of Limbo as a riff on Theatre of the Absurd or Theatre of Cruelty, a parody of avant-garde theatre movements. Charles liked the idea, but over dinner one night, our friend Michael Feingold, theatre critic for the *Village Voice*, pondered the matter and drily announced that Theatre-in-Limbo (hyphenated like Stratford-upon-Avon) was a wittier alternative. Michael had an authoritative air that was irresistible, so we went with it.

Charles quickly dashed off another play for Theatre-in-Limbo to take advantage of what we assumed would be a groundswell of word of mouth thanks to the mention in *New York* magazine. Again, reflecting the influence of Ludlam, Charles chose as his source material a nineteenth-century well-made play: Victorien Sardou's *Théodora* (1884), which had been a vehicle for Sarah Bernhardt. Unlike Ludlam's complex, full-length adaptation of *Camille*, however, Charles distilled *Théodora* to a broad one-act sketch composed of three short scenes that could easily be played in a noisy club. We needed another vulgar/catchy title to sell tickets, so he came up with *Theodora, She-Bitch of Byzantium*. This time, he tailored the roles specifically for our actors. Naturally, Charles played the title role of the Empress Theodora, who was "trapped in a loveless marriage" to the cruel and perverse Emperor Justinian (my role). Justinian was a prototypical evil queen who was obsessed with his slave boy, Toso (Andy Halliday). Toso was secretly married to his sister, Rita (Theresa Aceves), who was Theodora's hand-maiden. Tom Aulino played the other drag role, Fata Morgana, queen of the Gypsies. Our handsome young men, Arnie Kolodner and Bobby Carey, played revolutionaries plotting to murder the emperor. Initially, *Theodora* had no part for Julie Halston, but we enjoyed having her around so much that Charles just wrote one in (Justinian's Aunt Vulva, a disapproving prude). At this point, the company was still as much a social event as a theatrical one. After the performances, most of us went out for late supper and drinks together at McBell's, an eccentric Irish pub on Sixth Avenue at Washington Place that had great hamburgers, and where theatre people as diverse as Uta Hagen, Charles Ludlam, and Carrie Nye were regulars.

Like *Vampire Lesbians*, *Theodora* was put together quickly and on the cheap, with only six brief rehearsals, including the final dress. But now that we were taking ourselves more seriously, I wanted to bring a bit of polish to our second show, so we persuaded a few pros we knew to help us upgrade the production values. Our loyal stage manager and wig designer Kathie Carr was doubling as the costumer for this production (to be billed in the program as the mysterious "Caracciolo," her real surname), but she needed help. I called my friend (and former roommate) John Glaser, a wonderfully imaginative designer who had access to a first-rate costume shop, to help make the costumes look a little more like Byzantine tunics and a little less like old bed sheets. He used the facilities at Izquierdo Studio, a specialty costume house, to dye and decorate them, adding borders and sequins. John also constructed whimsical crowns for Justinian and Theodora, decorated with plastic forks and spoons sprayed gold. These crowns and the makeshift costumes were descendants of the "moldy aesthetic," that staple of the Ridiculous since the early days of Jack Smith, but John finished them with the panache he would have lavished on a Broadway show. They were simultaneously moldy and slick.

Charles decided Andy Halliday should have a sexy dance in the show, partly because he knew Andy had fantasized about being a Hollywood chorus boy in a Jack Cole production number and partly to mollify him after making him play the creepy butler in *Vampire Lesbians*. In the script, Justinian asks Toso to "provide us with a dance to soothe our ragged nerves." The minimal stage direction that follows simply reads "TOSO GOES INTO HIS DANCE, HIGHLY EROTIC AND PURELY FOR JUSTINIAN'S BENEFIT."[1] What to do with that in six rehearsals? Andy wanted professional help for the number, and his friend Jeff Veazey volunteered to select the music and choreograph. Jeff was an experienced dancer who had appeared on Broadway in shows such as *Sugar Babies* and *Sophisticated Ladies*, and he had also directed and choreographed hotel and cruise ship revues. At the time, he was Susan Stroman's dancing partner in a revue called *Trading Places*, in which they meticulously recreated dance routines of Fred and Ginger and other famous couples from classic films. I am not a choreographer, and I was thrilled to have his help. But I was really amazed by how completely Jeff picked up on the tone and style of the production, bringing a well-structured polish along with genuine wit to the brief dance he created. The music he selected was a brassy, wonderfully anachronistic striptease version of the old Sophie Tucker number, "Some of These Days." After establishing Byzantine exoticism with three poses that might have come from an ancient mosaic, Jeff moved the number into a bump and grind routine that resembled a stripper's Las Vegas lounge act from the 1950s.

Friday, June 8, 1984, was a stultifying day in New York. When we arrived at the Limbo Lounge that evening for the debut of *Theodora*, we were met with the first of many Limbo disasters: no air-conditioning. The place was like an oven, and it was obvious that performing there would be a miserable experience for actors and audience alike. This realization led to a quick change of plans. The imperturbable and Zen-like Michael Limbo arranged with his next-door neighbor, art dealer Gracie Mansion, to allow us to perform in her "sculpture garden," a small backyard behind the tenement storefronts. The sculptures, some of which were six to seven feet tall, looked like grotesque, misshapen totem poles painted with broad, agitated brush strokes, and a collection of oversized scowling masks hung on the fence surrounding the space. The clip lights were simply moved outside with cheap extension cords. A few chairs and benches were set up, and the audience walked through the Limbo Lounge and out the back door. The heat was almost as oppressive outside as it was in, but no one seemed to mind. Playing the show amid a sculpture installation reinforced the idea that our company was a part of the East Village art scene, although just a few months earlier most of us had rarely set foot east of First Avenue. The al fresco opening night, enhanced by car alarms, traffic noise, and sirens in the background, went smoothly enough. But we were thrilled beyond words when on the second night a photographer from *People* magazine showed up to take pictures during the performance for an upcoming story on the East Village scene.

Stock Players

Theodora was remarkably easy to rehearse because the actors were perfectly suited to their roles. Whereas *Vampire Lesbians* had been written long before we assembled our group, Charles wrote *Theodora* with the individual talents of each company member in mind, emphasizing the quirks of their personalities. We fantasized that our actors were like stock players under contract to Louis B. Mayer. This kind of fantasy tracks back to the beginning of the Ridiculous aesthetic. Decades earlier, Jack Smith had created his own imaginary movie studio, Cinemaroc, which in turn inspired Andy Warhol's concept of "superstars." Tavel asserted that the aesthetic of Ridiculous Theatre "was that we were presenting the real actor, not some character. The true mentality of the actor."[2] The disconnect between actor and character typical of earlier Ridiculous Theatre and underground film could produce inspired results on some occasions, pure tedium on others. It was loose and uncontrolled, Brechtian alienation without the didacticism.

Charles and I were not interested in presenting the "real actor." Instead, we worked to create an artificial persona for each member of our company, a kind of typecasting that pushed them into a mold based on certain elements of their personalities that would only vary slightly from play to play. Nothing was left to chance—our rehearsal process involved little or no improvisation. For *Theodora*, Charles sketched a character type for each actor, and he later built upon these personas with each successive script. Knowing that he was writing for specific actors and their quirks made it possible for him to churn out scripts quickly (*Theodora* was written in the course of a few days). Each actor had a certain trademark quality that Charles liked to call his or her "trip," just as eighteenth-century actors had lines of business.

Andreas, the swashbuckling revolutionary who becomes the secret love interest of the Empress Theodora, became the prototype for most of the roles Arnie Kolodner would play. Arnie's characters would always fall hopelessly in love with the female characters played by Charles. He was our handsome leading man, whom Charles thought of as a sort of second-string Robert Taylor. Bobby Carey's lack of stage experience and thick New Jersey accent were endearingly amateurish but limited him to smaller roles. His perfectly sculpted body was a major asset that we exploited as much as possible, however—beefcake sells. In the last scene of Theodora, Bobby was captured by the emperor's guards, stripped, and threatened by Justinian with the kind of torture found in the s/m porn magazine *Drummer*:

> After you have been sodomized by every soldier in my barracks,
> you will be placed upon a rack and the royal surgeon shall remove
> your balls and your joystick, without an anesthetic. Then I shall have
> a three-foot dildo permanently embedded up your butthole. At the
> end of the dildo shall be a horse's tail, and I shall have you trained
> as a gelded pony in my private stable. Am I painting a vivid enough
> picture for you?[3]

This degradation became a running motif in future productions.

Theresa Aceves was a seemingly vulnerable ingénue who would unexpectedly reveal that she was actually tough as nails. She had a trick voice that could switch instantly from a sweetly lyrical timbre to a demented, gravelly rage. She was also expert at bloodcurdling screams. Audiences that had first experienced her scream in *Vampire Lesbians* gave her an ovation when she screamed in *Theodora*. After that response, we worked her scream into every production we did. As if to emphasize the notion of a studio-created starlet, Charles even convinced her to change her stage name from the ethnic-sounding Theresa Aceves to the bland, vaguely Anglo-Saxon Theresa Marlowe. Charles could be somewhat mischievous now and then, and he delighted in writing parts that brought out a manic insanity in Andy Halliday, like Etienne in *Vampire Lesbians*, whose character was perfectly summarized by a line Charles recycled from an old Phyllis Diller routine: "This isn't hair on my head, these are nerve endings!"[4] Charles saw me as an effete villain or an ineffectual lover, a Henry Danielle type. Julie could play grand, but was best when she revealed her inner Long Island hausfrau. Tom Aulino usually played slightly grotesque character parts. In effect, we were all playing double roles: actors in a stock company playing roles in a play. Charles later reflected, "It was easy to write plays for this group because they all were characters already. I knew exactly who they were. I think that had to be part of our success."[5]

While most of the company was playing double roles, Charles was playing a triple role: he played himself as a man playing an actress playing a role. In those days he used no padding to create the illusion that he was a real woman; his silhouette was always clearly male. But he was extremely concerned about creating a glamorous image, and he would never emphasize his maleness as Ludlam had done by exposing his hairy chest in *Camille*. The actress he portrayed was a slightly older leading lady who specialized in theatrical claptrap. Charles found plenty of opportunities within his performances to comically exploit and deconstruct these layers of gender illusion. In scene 2 of *Theodora*, when the empress disguises herself as a boy, the "disguise" consisted of a pageboy wig and an oversized, belted Gap T-shirt, a look that could not have been more androgynous. The wig suggested a New York salon blunt cut more than Prince Valiant, and the T-shirt resembled both a male tunic and contemporary female East Village fashion. Charles's body language was more feminine than masculine, and yet he was obviously a man. When Charles-as-Theodora entered the Gypsy camp in this get-up and struck a mannequin-like pose, Tom Aulino as the Gypsy queen eyed him dubiously and asked, "What can I do for you . . . young man?"[6] Here Charles had found an extra layer of illusion: a man playing an actress playing a woman disguised as a boy. The absurdity of the moment never failed to get a laugh.

In his early Limbo performances Charles's characterizations consisted of a series of fragmented citations of a variety of female stars. In *Theodora* he evoked Sarah Bernhardt in Sardou's *Théodora* by replicating poses from historical photographs and attempting to recreate her more famous moments as they had been described in theatre histories. One famous photograph of Bernhardt in *Théodora* shows her barring the door so that her lover could escape. Charles recreated the pose in our production, despite there being no door (or set) on the stage. In addition to evoking Bernhardt, Charles referenced film stars of the 1930s and '40s. Sometimes these references would consist of nothing more than a fleeting facial expression. In Theodora's soliloquy at the end of scene 1, she complains, "To think that I, Empress Theodora, the unparalleled object of desire to every man over twelve in the Byzantium, should be so trapped in a loveless marriage."[7] Charles punctuated this line by rolling his eyes like Bette Davis. In scene 2, after accidentally swallowing a magic potion, the lovesick Theodora suddenly sounded uncannily like Fanny Brice. A few moments later at the end of the scene, while in the throes of passion with her new lover, Andreas, Charles's Theodora switched to Greta Garbo's voice and accent to deliver the line "Yes, my love, you are the one to change my life. Tonight, I am yours."[8]

At first, the transitions in and out of these citations could be somewhat awkward and choppy, like a collection of impersonations with no through line. But as he gained experience, the performance became almost seamless to the point that this fragmented character actually had a coherent persona: "the star." This star had elements of many stars: A hint of Joan Crawford, Mae West, or Norma Shearer might bubble to the surface, but these citations were a part of, not separate from, the persona of "the star." This beleaguered leading lady of a ragtag troupe was consistent from play to play. Of course, Charles made adjustments for each role depending on the specifics of the plots and situations. But whatever the role, it was played by the same female "star."

The characters as played by the "star" were inherently sympathetic, partly because Charles wanted the audience to like him and partly because of the class connotations in both the writing and his portrayal. The characters had pretensions of grandeur that were constantly undermined by the circumstances of the plots as well as by the limitations of the productions. Although Charles spoke primarily with a refined and polished, vaguely upper-class accent like the Hollywood stars of early talkies who had been forced to take voice lessons, he would inevitably switch his accent to reveal the "common" roots of the character, as in this scene from *Theodora*:

THEODORA: You've known me since I was a child, begging in the streets of Babylon. You know all that I've been, carny dancer, aerial artiste, geek, whore.

FATA: You mustn't . . .

THEODORA: No, let me. I have no illusions about myself. If I've become a Goddess, it is because I fought for it. No one ever handed me anything on a plate. I climbed the ladder of success wrong by wrong and I'd do it again if I had to.[9]

"Wrong by wrong" was a phrase lifted from Mae West, but Charles delivered it with the grim toughness of Barbara Stanwyck. Like most of the characters he wrote for himself, Theodora was a woman of great achievement but humble origins. By being tough, scrappy, and canny she overcame enormous obstacles to achieve her goal. This was a parody of the Reagan-era entrepreneurial capitalist spirit: Theodora was no welfare queen. She proved that, with gumption and hard work, the lowliest beggar in the streets can rise through the ranks to become a goddess.

Charles firmly established a warm and direct relationship between the "star" and her audience by making a curtain speech after each performance. At the end of the curtain call, he would hold up his hands after the applause had crested to greet the audience and to promote our future appearances. He usually began his pitch in the grand manner by thanking the audience with campy pretentiousness. "Bless you, darlings!" was his signature opening phrase. Initially these speeches were brief and to the point; he would ask the audience to sign our mailing list so that we could inform them of future shows because the only advertising we could afford was "a geek with a sandwich board on Avenue C." (The word "geek" was not a synonym for nerd at the time; it meant grotesque, carnival sideshow performers.) But gradually, the speech became a performance in itself, often getting bigger laughs than the show as he would explain how we had "worked so hard ironing in the kinks for you." Offstage, Charles was shy and a bit self-conscious, but as "the star" he had total confidence and proved to be a bold, quick-witted, and skilled improviser. The curtain speeches, which members of the company referred to as "the third act," became a Theatre-in-Limbo trademark and one of our most effective advertisements.

After the first weekend of *Theodora*, Michael Limbo (who sometimes used his real name, Michael Gormley) invited Charles and me to dinner at the apartment above the club he shared with his partner, Victor Mendolia (then known as Victor Anonymous?—and yes, the question mark was part of his name) to discuss the future of our company. He explained that due to neighborhood complaints about noise as well as the sudden wave of interest in the East Village, he had decided to close the Tenth Street Limbo Lounge at the end of June 1984. He had taken a lease on a much larger space, a former sanitation garage on Ninth Street between Avenues B and C, just steps from the decaying Christodora House, and he planned to renovate the new club over the summer and to open in the fall: a new, bigger, better Limbo! The four of us decided that Theatre-in-Limbo would be the resident theatre company of the new Limbo (no longer the Limbo *Lounge*). We planned to open in October with a revival of *Vampire Lesbians* and then change the bill every three weeks, producing new plays as quickly as Charles could write them. Since *Theodora* had gone from blank page to full production in a matter of days, we figured that three weeks to write and rehearse each new play would be luxurious. We devised this ambitious production schedule because we were determined to exploit our association with the suddenly fashionable East Village as it was being gentrified. We had no organizing aesthetic goal at the outset. We simply felt that the explosion of interest in the East Village was an opportunity for us to make our mark in the theatre. I decided to postpone law school to run Theatre-in-Limbo, and I was elated about it. My father, who *really* wanted me to be a lawyer, was supportive, but less than elated. Understandably, he wanted me to start a "real" career, which is exactly what I thought I was doing.

Charles planned to announce our ambitious fall season during the curtain speech after our final performance of *Theodora* on June 30, but first we had to deal with another Limbo disaster. An early evening deluge turned Gracie Mansion's sculpture garden into an unplayable field of mud. When we arrived at the Limbo Lounge, Michael Limbo was once again smiling benignly, utterly unworried, as Victor swept dirty, brown water into a recalcitrant drain. We moved the stage to a small cement area directly behind the club and laid a tarp down over the mud for the audience. Charles threw himself into the cleanup effort with Joan Crawford intensity, getting on his hands and knees to scrub the stage in full wig and makeup, even as the audience started to filter in. The show went on, and we ended our inaugural season filled with optimism for the future of our company.

Nonprofit Theatre

Up to this point, Theatre-in-Limbo performances were like festive parties for the audience and actors alike. But since Charles and I were committed to making this fledgling theatre company a career, and not just a party, for the foreseeable future we wanted to approach it in a professional and businesslike manner. Charles had no interest in business, and everyone else in the company held full-time jobs, so I became the producer while still working part-time for Michael Stewart. Despite his disappointment about my decision not to attend law school, my father helped me with the legal work to organize the company as a nonprofit corporation so that we could accept tax-deductible contributions. We elected a slate of officers for our board of directors: I was president; Kathie Carr was secretary (because she was known to be a superb typist and had worked as a secretary in a medical office); Julie Halston was treasurer (because she worked for a Wall Street firm and therefore must know something about finance); Charles was vice president (a job with no duties other than to weigh in from time to time)—he tended to drift off during our board meetings like the Dormouse in *Alice in Wonderland*. I came up with a fundraising goal of $2,000 to cover the start-up expenses for the fall season. George Dudley, an acquaintance who had a greeting-card business, took studio production shots for publicity purposes soon after the final performances at the old Limbo Lounge. I brought the contact sheets and a few enlargements to Sam Rudy, a friend of a friend and a press agent with Shirley Herz Associates, who at the time was representing the Broadway musical *La Cage aux Folles*. I wanted to capitalize on the attention we had received in *New York* magazine. Sam was dubious at first, but he was amused by the photos and ultimately agreed to represent us for the fall season at the new Limbo. We weren't interested in reveling in our obscurity, and now we had a Broadway press agent to make sure that wouldn't happen.

Charles unexpectedly picked up a prestige gig for his one-man show at the Indiana Repertory Theatre in my hometown of Indianapolis in August, followed by another booking back at the Valencia Rose in San Francisco. It was essentially the same show we had done at the Shandol Theatre a few months earlier, so it didn't require much rehearsal, but I went along to set the lighting and sound in Indianapolis. This gave us the opportunity to organize a board of directors retreat at my grandmother's summer cottage in northern Indiana. Julie, Kathie, and Andy joined Charles and me for a long weekend at Lake Maxinkuckee, where we continued to plan our season and fantasize. Charles and Julie were really into the mod London fashion scene, so we developed a parody of 1960s British films: *Sleeping Beauty or Coma*. We decided that this would be perfect as a curtain raiser for our gala opening night at the new Limbo. Charles wrote no part for himself in it because he was going to be out of town for much of our rehearsal period. It didn't matter—we only intended to give one performance of this play anyway. It was a throwaway.

Meanwhile, we were waiting, waiting, waiting for the big East Village article in *People*. As a spin-off of *Time*, a "serious" news magazine, *People* legitimized celebrity gossip and within a few months of its initial publication in 1974 it became one of the highest circulation weeklies in the United States, reaching a broad mainstream readership. If anything could have topped a mention in *New York* magazine, it was a picture in *People*. The story finally appeared in the August 20, 1984 issue, which featured a small photo of Charles, Julie, and me in our *Theodora* costumes, framed by totem poles in Gracie Mansion's garden. It appeared with an article titled "Art after Midnight," which simultaneously romanticized the downtown club scene and distanced the reader from it:

> Long after midtown office towers have been deserted for the day, as many New Yorkers snuggle into bed in their high-rise apartments, another world comes to life in the seedier districts of Lower Manhattan. From 11 p.m. to 5 a.m., Monday through Sunday, the young and the active pack into musty East Village basement bars, cavernous lofts in warehouse districts, or short-lived speakeasies that, because they lack liquor licenses, tend to fall prey to police raids. Disdaining the laser lights and droning beat of '70s discos, these clubs offer an '80s alternative: riotous after-hours vaudeville complete with drag shows, art auctions, raunchy comedy revues and theme parties celebrating such diverse topics as sexual obsession and Tupperware. The purpose, believe it or not, is art.[10]

The point of view of the article affirmed mainstream, middle-class values by characterizing the downtown scene as "outlandish." At the same time, the description of the "riotous" entertainments available to those who were in the know made it all seem smart, trendy, fun, and tantalizingly out of reach to the humdrum office workers who go to bed after the eleven o'clock news. The article included a photo of Michael Limbo and his partners standing outside their club, along with the announcement that Limbo would "soon be moving to a better location in Manhattan's East Village."[11]

This "better location" was further east and even scarier, on a typically desolate East Village block. When I returned to New York from the lake, I encountered another Limbo disaster: construction delays. The new Limbo was a big, empty, unfinished space that Michael, Victor, and their partners were renovating over the summer of 1984 with the $22,500 they had received for the sale of the lease on their old space. Transforming a garage for garbage trucks into a cutting-edge art gallery/club/theatre was more complicated than anyone imagined, especially since the owners were doing much of the construction work themselves. It was very slow going, and it dawned on me that all our planning and board meetings would be for naught because the Limbo would never be finished in time for the opening.

The new space, at 623 East Ninth Street, was enormous compared to the old Limbo, and its size reflected the optimism that was felt about the future of the East Village. Whereas the old Limbo Lounge was a combination art gallery and club, the new Limbo separated those functions. A large gallery space, painted white, occupied the front of the building. The cavernous, high-ceilinged club room was in the rear, down a long narrow corridor, accessed by a separate entrance. It had a bar on the right and at the back of the room, a simple platform stage, approximately eight feet by twenty feet. But not everything had been thought through. Fire codes were apparently not a major consideration, because there was no rear exit. The "backstage" area was a claustrophobic alleyway three feet wide between the stage and the cement block back wall of the building, hardly enough room for a company of eight actors with wigs and costumes. There were no wings; the performers could only access the stage by climbing steps left and right— not the most graceful way to make an entrance. There were no drapes or masking of any kind on the stage. There was no lighting equipment. And there were no chairs for the audience. I asked Michael where the audience was going to sit, but he hadn't really thought about it—maybe on the cement floor. This conflicted with my fantasy of running a theater company, so I ordered fifty cheap white, metal folding chairs from Conran's and had them delivered to the Limbo. Our $2,000 budget was already stretched before we started rehearsal, and there was more to come.

The larger scale of the space obviously required some minimal scenic elements and real stage lighting, not just hardware-store clip lights. In a panic, I called a lighting designer friend, Vivien Leone (we had met doing a show at Lucille Lortel's White Barn Theatre in Connecticut), and begged her to help. She agreed to light the shows for the fall season, and I carved out some money from our budget to rent lighting equipment. After consulting with her, I purchased what would be the basic scenic elements of all the Theatre-in-Limbo productions staged in the new space: two sets of legs, a border, and a muslin drop. All of these soft goods were equipped with tie-lines so that they could be quickly hung before the shows and removed immediately afterward. Our shows needed to be as portable as possible because usually another group, often with very different scenic needs, was scheduled before or after our performances. The Limbo offered very little storage space, and anything left there was likely to be missing the next day, so Charles and I made certain that the productions never required any furniture. They were what we called "stand-up" plays: the time and place were established with brief exposition rather than scenery. The necessity of keeping it simple affected the visual aesthetic of the shows as well as the scripts. Both *Vampire Lesbians* and *Theodora* exploited antique theatre conventions, and I had staged them in a presentational style. Our new wing and drop configuration, which suggested a nineteenth-century touring company, created a visual concept for Theatre-in-Limbo. Vivien came up with a simple but effective design that played on this idea by including footlights in the plot for every show. The scenery and lighting thus complemented Charles's performance as an old-school "star" with her stock players.

Not long before the opening, Vivien introduced me to a friend of hers who would have a huge impact on our company: Brian Whitehill, a graphic designer for Channel 13. We met mainly to talk about flyers and newspaper ads, but by the end of the meeting I asked him to be our resident set designer as well. We discussed ways to visually amplify the idea that we were a touring stock company performing an eccentric repertory of plays. The old-fashioned legs, borders, and footlights that Vivien had suggested emphasized the idea that the company had just trouped into town, but otherwise there wasn't much going on scenically. The muslin backdrop brought our outrageous thrift shop costumes into sharp relief for *Vampire Lesbians*, but it was very plain. Brian suggested that he paint the drop for our second production, the *Theodora* revival. Charles loved the idea of a painted backdrop, and he hoped for a romantic depiction of a castle for the court scenes and a leafy forest for the gypsy camp, but Brian's idea was more abstract and wittier. The drop he created had the look of ancient mosaics, but it took the form of a New York City subway station for a stop called BYZANTIUM. In the center of the drop was a subway map with lines that resembled the profiles of the emperor and empress. Charles was disappointed when I showed him Brian's sketch because it didn't exactly reinforce his Sarah Bernhardt fantasy, but it proved to be the perfect way to alert the audience to the off-center quality of what they were about to see. Brian designed both the scenery and the advertising for every show we did from that point.

Brian strongly believed that the experience of seeing a show actually begins when a potential audience member sees an ad in the newspaper or receives a flyer, and he felt that the design of the ads should coordinate with what was on the stage. His ads and fliers did just that. He designed a Theatre-in-Limbo logo that consisted of an oval-shaped medallion with the company name, flanked by two reclining nude cartoon figures, a male on the left and a female on the right, supporting cartoonish comedy and tragedy masks. Stretched across the top of all our flyers, these elements suggested the decorative entablature of a proscenium arch. Performance information at the bottom of the flyer was enclosed in a box that represented a stage. A row of abstract, triangular footlights rested on top of this box, seemingly shining on the photos and logo for the show being advertised. Brian used the same elements for the few newspaper ads we could afford in the *Village Voice* and the *New York Native*. He gave Theatre-in-Limbo a distinctive, instantly recognizable trademark look that was consistent from the ads to the fliers to the stage.

A Vegas Finale

As we prepared for our grand opening at the new Limbo, we worried that the two scenes of *Vampire Lesbians* would seem truncated and too brief (at a half-hour) in our grander new surroundings. While he was working at the Indiana Repertory Theatre, Charles wrote a third scene for *Vampire Lesbians* to provide a resolution of sorts for the production at the new Limbo. It is set in a contemporary Las Vegas rehearsal room. Madeleine Astarté, the silent screen vamp of scene 2, has transformed herself into Madeleine Andrews, a tough-as-nails showbiz broad on the order of late-career Lucille Ball. The scene opens with Madeleine's gay chorus boys discussing recent vampire attacks on the Vegas strip, but it soon escalates into a queeny fight between two of the veteran dancers:

Brian Whitehill's flyer for Theodora, She-Bitch of Byzantium.
Design by B. T. Whitehill; photo by George Dudley.

ZACK: First we have vampires on the strip, now I've got an hysterical faggot to deal with.

DANNY: I wouldn't be worried about vampires, Whorina. Your ass is hardly virgin territory.[12]

These exaggerated, stereotyped portrayals of bitchy gay chorus boys could easily be considered toxic and homophobic in another context, but as written by a gay man and played by gay men for an audience largely composed of gay men, this scene is an example of the strategy the late scholar José Muñoz called "disidentification," in which such stereotypes can be recycled "as powerful and seductive sites of self-creation."[13] We did not avoid the unflattering, limp-wristed clichés of these characters; we exploited them for laughs—but we were laughing at ourselves.

Madeleine, the "star," enters (in a wig by Kathie Carr that resembled fluorescent red cotton candy swirled into a bouffant) and explains to Danny that she was forced to fire his lover, David, from the act because "where this show is concerned, I am ruthless." She immediately softens her image and imparts some philosophical thoughts to Danny:

MADELEINE: I detest being a boss lady. It's so unattractive. Danny, I'm very fond of you, I'd like to give you some good advice. You're better off without him.

DANNY: Madeleine, I don't want to sound rude but . . .

MADELEINE: Listen to Mama. You want to be a star?

DANNY: (*Sullenly.*) Yeah.

MADELEINE: Take this advice. You can't have it all. A long time ago, I made up my mind that there were certain things I had to give up on the road to fame. One of those things was personal happiness. Well, let's get to work.[14]

Charles satirizes the gay fetishism of diva worship in this inverted world where nothing is more important than the sheer fakery of show business—including "personal happiness." The phoniness is further demonstrated as Madeleine and the boys then proceed to rehearse the new number for her act: "Maniac" from the movie *Flashdance*. Jeff Veazey staged a dead-on parody of a Vegas act, partly inspired by Lauren Bacall's recent performance in the Broadway musical *Woman of the Year*, in which the chorus boys do all the dancing and the aging star barely moves as she croaks to a recorded track: the "star" is nothing but image, propped up by her cadre of boys.

The number is interrupted when a disheveled charwoman enters with a mop and bucket. Madeleine recognizes her as La Condesa, down on her luck. The old resentments bubble up, the two old vampires bicker, and Madeleine threatens to destroy her longtime enemy with a curse she learned from a "tribal witch doctor named Pooji Dung." In one of the silliest routines of the show, Madeleine chants and grunts nonsense syllables to cast a spell to eliminate La Condesa once and for all. Charles experimented with various endings to the scene. In one version, Madeleine realized that she and La Condesa have identical rings, which meant that they were bound together forever. The ring business, a device as old as the Greek comedy of Menander, was eventually cut, and in the final version Madeleine simply realizes, in the midst of executing the Pooji Dung hex, that she can't live without her old nemesis, and she breaks down:

MADELEINE: . . . I can't! I can't kill you! Then I shall be truly alone. I've shed a tear. I feel something. Is it impossible that in this whole world, there is only you with whom I can travel through time?

LA CONDESA: (*Tough.*) Save it for Valentine's Day.

MADELEINE: (*Simply.*) I need you.

LA CONDESA: (*Touched.*) You need me. Someone needs me?

MADELEINE: In an odd way, your presence has always been a comfort.

LA CONDESA: (*In reverie.*) You need me. I am needed.

MADELEINE: Isn't that what life's all about? Funny.[15]

Here the dialogue parodies the cheap sentiment found in tacky television dramas, while at the same time embracing the sentimentality for an uplifting ending. Ludlam had employed a similar technique when he mocked the nineteenth-century conventions of *Camille* while genuinely playing the pathos of Marguerite's death to wring tears from the audience as well as laughs. In a moment of largesse, Madeleine proposes to La Condesa that the two of them do an act together. As the lights fade out, an orchestral tag of "Everything's Coming Up Roses" swells as the two of them contemplate their future as partners on the stage.

This utterly contrived ending provided both irony and warmth, which was in keeping with the tone of the show as a whole. Each scene was a separate genre parody: scene 1 was a burlesque sketch, scene 2 a drawing room comedy/melodrama, and scene 3 a contemporary Vegas act. But in each case, the parody was tempered, in both the writing and the acting, by the fact that we loved the styles that we were mocking. My goal as director was to get the actors to believe what they were saying, no matter how silly or outrageous the dialogue. And so, despite the intentionally provocative title and the occasional vulgarity, *Vampire Lesbians of Sodom* was as sweet as it was edgy. The ultimate message of the show arrives in Madeleine's discovery that she and La Condesa need each other. The mutual contempt that had fueled their feud for centuries is replaced by the redemptive power of love.

East Village Repertory Theatre

Despite the construction setbacks at the new Limbo, we miraculously opened our new season on schedule on October 4, 1984, with a "gala" performance of *Vampire Lesbians* paired, for one performance only, with *Sleeping Beauty or Coma* and a solo piece performed by Theresa Aceves (*Angel Dust,* by Robert Perring). We had barely recovered from the opening when we started rehearsing our next show, a revival of *Theodora.* Things didn't always go smoothly during the course of the season because Limbo operated in a very loose way, with lots of musicians and performance artists coming in and out with little regard to scheduling. Victor did keep a schedule—but nobody paid much attention to it. I had been trained as a stage manager and prized organization above all else, and Vivien was used to working in the relatively controlled environment of professional theatres. Throughout the fall season, we grew to anticipate regularly occurring calamities that would stop us dead in our tracks and that we called the "eight o'clock surprise." More than once we arrived for sold-out performances to find a rock band, with equipment spread out on the stage, just beginning a sound check. One time, in preparation for an upcoming installation, wet paint was slopped over the entire club as we arrived. I often had to call Vivien at the last minute to rush over and refocus lighting equipment that had been repurposed. It was the East Village way.

Sam Rudy sent out press releases, arranged for some interviews, and did a great job of getting the word out, but the mainstream press we received for the fall season was somewhat limited (*People* did not do a follow-up piece). Our audiences nonetheless steadily grew. An item appeared in *Variety*'s "Legit Bits" column,[16] there were a handful of reviews in such publications as *The Villager* and *Backstage,* and the gay press was highly supportive. Michael Sommers's review of *Vampire Lesbians* in the gay newspaper *New York Native* was instrumental in helping to reach our target audience:

It's a riot; tracing the exploits of a deadly duo from their first meeting in biblical times through the fleshpots of 1920s Hollywood to present day Las Vegas. The plot is a delicious mishmash of Maria Montez epics, full of overripe lines and overblown theatrics done strictly for laughs. Luckily, this giddy show runs a mere 45 minutes, or the audience would hyperventilate in its hysterical glee.[17]

Brandon Judell, writing in the *Advocate*, also raved: "Far within the bombed-out realm of Alphabet City (between Avenues B and C), comic genius is running amuck."[18] We did have the misfortune to open at almost the same time that the Ridiculous Theatrical Company was opening Ludlam's brilliant vampire play, *Irma Vep*, which our friend Michael Feingold pointed out in his *Village Voice* review:

> Charles Busch's *Vampire Lesbians of Sodom* suffers in my mind from the inevitable comparison with *Irma Vep*, next to which it looks as bloodless as Helen Chandler after a bout with Lugosi. It has enough humor and cheerfully spunky inanity to pass its brief time well enough as a late show in a liquor-serving establishment, but it hasn't much dramatic drive or substance, and the stage arrangements at the new Limbo Lounge are so lofty they demand something bigger and richer.[19]

Lofty? It was actually a pretty rudimentary setup. This was one of the first of many critical comparisons between Ludlam and Busch, but we always thought it a little unfair to juxtapose our first fledgling effort with Ludlam's masterpiece.

Three weeks later we changed the bill, and *Theodora, She-Bitch of Byzantium* reopened on schedule. That night, Charles got huge laughs during the curtain speech when he plugged our third scheduled show of the season, *Gidget Goes Psychotic*—but we weren't laughing during rehearsals. Theresa Aceves, who often had an appropriate hint of madness in her eyes, was cast in the role of Gidget, but Charles hadn't quite gotten a handle on how to make her psychotic episodes funny. Up to this point, it wasn't a given that Charles would play the lead in every production (he hadn't even appeared in *Coma*). We had the egalitarian notion that it would be generous to give other members of the company the lead from time to time, as Ludlam had done with his company. But if he wasn't writing a central role for himself, Charles wasn't as adept at focusing the script. You could just feel in the rehearsal hall that this show was not going to get laughs, and we had no time to make adequate script changes. It was pretty obvious that we were overwhelmed and couldn't open a new play every three weeks after all, so I decided instead to extend *Theodora*, and play it in rep with *Vampire Lesbians* to give us more time to plan our next production.

As it turned out, the only new show we ended up doing in the fall of 1984 was our holiday play, *Times Square Angel: A Hard-Boiled Christmas Fantasy*. Charles had written to me from San Francisco in late August with the seed of an idea:

> Just got back from doing my laundry and I had a great idea for a Christmas show—
>
> We all play the inhabitants of a seedy boarding house circa 1930—Julie is the hard-boiled landlady who always thinks she sees the face of Jesus in everything. You and I are married pair of old actors, à la the Lunts, who are broke. You are going senile + reliving past triumphs. I am very Dame Beatrice [an aging actress character in his one-man show]. Theresa's an embittered blind girl. Tom is a Scrooge-like old man, Arnie, a charming gigolo, Andy, an urchin or street performer, and Bobby, a prostitute (female variety). All of our fortunes are dwindling. You and I are destitute + about to be living in the street. And then we all see the face of Jesus in the landlady's pie crust—but a fight breaks out + someone throws the cream pie + it hits Theresa (the blind girl) in the face + she's cured. Then Bobby, the whore, takes a little piece + sticks it up his dress + he's cured of the clap. A telegram arrives and we learn we have roles in a movie— and everyone lives happily ever after + maybe we have Mr. Ray on tape as the voice of God à la Orson Welles—with lots of inspirational music. And at the end, we all sing "Auld Lang Syne" + then lead the audience in a round of Christmas carols. What do you think of that general idea?[20]

I loved the general idea, but I worried that there wasn't enough of a story to fill a forty-five-minute slot at the Limbo. What was the action before we were served this miraculous pie?

The plot we ended up with was completely different, but the inspirational holiday theme of redemption was retained. Charles had a 1940s red dress with shoulder pads in his closet that he wanted to wear in a play, and one night over dinner in a Grove Street restaurant Andy Halliday suggested a reworking of the Henry Fonda/Lucille Ball film *The Big Street* (1942). Elements of *It's a Wonderful Life* (1946) and Dickens's *Christmas Carol* also figure into the plot of *Times Square Angel. Angel* is the story of Irish O'Flanagan, a gangster's moll working as a nightclub chanteuse who is on "a quick road to disaster" because of her greed and selfishness. The Lord (heard only on tape, and played by James Cahill rather than James Ray) sends an angel down to Earth to "show her the path that will lead her to heaven." He takes her on a "trip into the future" to show her that her self-centeredness will lead to ruin and a lonely death if she doesn't change her ways. Like Scrooge, Irish undergoes a sudden but complete transformation to become almost insanely thoughtful and loving. Like Madeleine in *Vampire Lesbians*, Irish realizes that she can't go it alone: she needs her friends. The play concludes with Irish leading a group of carolers on the streets of New York as snow gently falls (white confetti sprinkled by our diminutive production assistant, Joe Cote, who looked for all the world like a street urchin from a 1930s Hollywood film leaning over the top of the backdrop), and the angel returns to heaven knowing that he has done his duty.

There was plenty of knowing irony in the treatment of the familiar source material for *Times Square Angel*, but Irish's conversion and the inspirational ending were played for real. A G-rated sentimental Christmas pageant about the importance of love, generosity, and human kindness might seem a strange choice for an East Village club like the Limbo, but these were strange times. Many of the young men in our audience had AIDS; we all had friends who were sick; and all of us, actors and audience alike, were weighed down by the unimaginable devastation of the epidemic. As a producer, I was thrilled to see the line for tickets snake down the block to Avenue C, but it is difficult to describe how heartbreaking and scary it was to see so many people with AIDS enter the club, to look at a gaunt face and think, "He's got it." In the back of everyone's mind was the question: "Who's next?" At the time, AIDS had no effective treatment, and a positive diagnosis was pretty much considered a death sentence. We had to rely on the love and care of friends to get through the horror of that reality, and so it was very easy for our audiences to relate to Irish O'Flanagan's conversion. It was an ugly world that cried out for kindness and empathy, even from the most hard-boiled New Yorkers.

Unlike Larry Kramer's *Normal Heart* and William Hoffman's *As Is*, Charles's plays did not address the subject of AIDS directly, but it was very much present in the subtext. And there was a sense in which

Theatre-in-Limbo was providing welcome relief from the miserable reality of AIDS. Although the official government closing of the baths and sex clubs was still a year away, gay nightlife was already sharply curtailed by fear. The audience that traveled to this inconvenient location on a desolate street to gather in a converted garage had a real sense of community, as confirmed by theatre historian Arnold Aronson's account for the *Drama Review* of a typical Limbo presentation:

> The audience seemed to be a participant in the performance—not through any physical involvement, but through enthusiastic, spontaneous responses to the performers, characters and lines. Lavish costumes, favorite actors (several performers were clearly known to the audience from other shows), in-jokes and clever parodies brought cheers, raucous laughter, and applause.[21]

All of us, actors and audience alike, wanted to escape from AIDS, and that desire was a major force shaping our company. We may have been in a converted garage on East Ninth Street, but the atmosphere at the Limbo in the fall of 1984 had the feel of a USO show on a battlefront during wartime. And all too soon, AIDS would insinuate itself into the lives of members of our company, with tragic results.

Chapter 3 **Off Broadway**

La Condesa (Meghan Robinson) and Madeleine Astarté (Charles Busch) both have their eyes on the young starlet, Renee Vain (Theresa Aceves), in this publicity shot for Vampire Lesbians of Sodom. *Photo by Marc Raboy.*

The cavernous bar/performance space of the Limbo was unheated and could get pretty cold in December, but that didn't matter to the enormous and boisterous crowd that packed into the space for the closing-night performance of *Vampire Lesbians* on December 1, 1984. It was our biggest crowd yet, and it was intoxicating to play for an audience that seemed to know all the lines but still laughed at the jokes as if they were hearing them for the first time. The adrenaline rush of that performance convinced me that our show might have a future beyond the East Village.

Throughout the fall, I wrote letters and made phone calls to numerous producers about the possibility of transferring *Vampire Lesbians* to a commercial Off-Broadway theatre, but I got nowhere. The title alone was enough to frighten most of them. The general response was that the show belonged at the Limbo Lounge and would never attract audiences at a more "legit" venue. And there was the implicitly homophobic notion that a cult gay show should stay in the closet. One mainstream producer did express interest. Broadway veteran Arthur Cantor was the general manager of the Provincetown Playhouse on MacDougal Street, which had been dark for some time, and he was looking for a tenant. Arthur came from another time and place. He had started his career as a press agent in the 1950s representing shows like *Inherit the Wind* and *Auntie Mame*. He moved into producing in 1959 by partnering with Saint Subber to present Paddy Chayefsky's *Tenth Man*, directed by Tyrone Guthrie, which went on to win the Pulitzer Prize. He was a protégé of the legendary producer Billy Rose and became a mainstay of Broadway in the 1960s and '70s, producing many shows of the "prestige" variety. He had a magnificent suite of offices at Seventy-Third and Broadway lined with framed window cards; he lived at the Dakota. He was Harvard educated, clever, charming, urbane, streetwise, and paternal—and I didn't trust him at all. I couldn't put my finger on exactly why that was, but it probably had something to do with the fact that although he was terribly enthusiastic about transferring *Vampire Lesbians* to the Provincetown Playhouse, he wasn't willing to put a dime in the show. Instead, he encouraged me to produce it myself, something I initially thought of as a laughable idea. The typical capitalization of an Off-Broadway show in 1984 was over $250,000, with some shows pushing $400,000 or higher, far more money than I could dream of getting my hands on. Arthur, who was legendarily cheap, insisted there was nothing to it, that there was no need for a show to cost that much, and that I should call him back when I had enough front money—money that can be spent before the show is capitalized—to put down a deposit on the theatre. I didn't know what front money was, but with a good deal of trepidation, I decided to take his advice.

My friend Michael O'Rand, who had introduced me to Sam Rudy, was a company manager who worked with the producer Richard Barr and had been the managing director at the Academy Festival Theatre when I was a stage manager there. He helped me to cobble together as low a budget

as we could possibly devise by paring everything to the bone: a capitalization of $55,000. This budget had no fat and almost no reserve fund, which
meant it depended on everything going right and assumed the show would
be an instant hit. I made an appointment with Paul Woerner, a handsome
young theatrical attorney with the firm Linden and Deutsch, whom I knew
through Michael Stewart.[1] This was a "white-shoe" law firm with elegantly
appointed offices. The reception room was decorated with tasteful sofas
and fine oriental carpets, and the secretaries served coffee in bone china
cups and saucers. When I went in to talk to Paul at his immaculate desk,
he studied the budget for a few minutes and then sat in silence. He looked
troubled when he finally spoke. He explained that the capitalization was
so low that he couldn't possibly do the legal work—his fee would be unaffordable. I asked him how anybody could produce low-budget shows if legal
work was so prohibitive. He said he didn't know. He was very nice about it
all, but I was pretty discouraged.

Michael O'Rand just giggled when I told him what happened and suggested I call another entertainment lawyer he knew, Leonard Kolleeny. In
contrast to the refined environment at Linden and Deutsch, Leonard's office furniture appeared to have been purchased at a thrift shop, including
a garish, bright orange Naugahyde sofa in the waiting room. When I was
called into his office, we sat at a round table that was far from immaculate—it was covered with stacks several feet high of manila files stuffed
with legal papers. Leonard didn't serve coffee; he kept a bottle of scotch
in an old, gray metal file cabinet, which he poured into Styrofoam cups.
But he loved the theatre, and he told me not to worry about the fee, that
he would do the legal work for "whatever you can afford to pay." I hired
him. My father was appalled by the partnership agreement he produced, a
literal cut and paste job, with the previous general partner's name simply
whited out by Leonard's secretary. It was sloppy, but it was legal, and I am
forever grateful to Leonard.

It was hard to raise money to move a show that wasn't running. Potential investors invariably asked "Can I come and see it?" So, we returned to
Limbo for an encore engagement in March 1985. But in the meantime, Julie
Halston had decided that she needed to concentrate on her Wall Street day
job and couldn't continue with the company. Once again, we had to recast
the role of La Condesa, and once again Charles and I held auditions in our
West Twelfth Street living room. We ultimately chose a friend of Julie's,

Meghan Robinson, as her replacement. Meghan (pronounced Meh-GANN) was an experienced stage actress who had also done a stint on the soap opera *Search for Tomorrow*. She possessed a smoker's husky voice, a throaty laugh, a grand manner, and she understood the style of the play without a lot of coaching. She was passionate about everything, and we were immediately entranced by her. She came from a family of artists (she called her father by his first name, Victor), lived in the East Village, and dressed glamorously with high style in clothes purchased from her neighborhood thrift shops. She always accessorized with whimsical jewelry and had a collection of hundreds of cheap earrings (her favorites included dangling red plastic lobsters). She was a handsome, if somewhat androgynous woman, who was on at least one occasion mistaken for a drag queen. Charles described her face as resembling "the prow of a ship." She was married to a gay man, the Canadian actor Maxim Mazumdar.[2] She loved him ("Max is *so* wonderful!"), but she explained that it was not a physical relationship; they were married so that she could work in Canadian theatres and he could work in the U.S. Charles and I thought that arrangement sounded very sophisticated, but not all of the other actors were so taken with Meghan; she could be condescending toward anyone she considered to be amateurish—a category that included almost everyone else in the company. Meghan reframed the role of La Condesa to her own powerful personality. She had not even a hint of the Long Island matron about her—she was from Connecticut!

Thanks to our return to Limbo, I found a co-producer who was willing to come in with $10,000 or so (Gerald A. Davis), but we were still short. The money-raising continued in dribs and drabs—some investments were as small as $275—from friends, family, and a few of the cast members. I cooked a spaghetti dinner in our kitchen for Charles's two aunts and his sisters so that we could put the squeeze on them. While I was stirring the sauce, Charles pitched the show. You could almost hear the violins playing as he described how we were on the brink of success after years of struggle, stymied only by the lack of a few thousand dollars. I talked up what a great, moneymaking opportunity this was, and presented the partnership papers Leonard had drawn up. I thought we were sunk when Aunt Lillian repeated that her late husband had a golden rule: "Don't drink, don't smoke, and don't put money into show business." His sister Margaret quipped, "Be careful, you get dessert, they'll wipe out your retirement fund." But before they left the table, Aunt Lillian and Margaret had signed on as investors, and Aunt Belle agreed to put up front money. For years afterward, they never tired of teasing me about the most expensive spaghetti dinner they ever ate. Margaret figured it was about $75 per strand. Although my parents would have preferred that I finally go to law school, they made a generous investment as well. Even Michael Stewart, my former employer, and his sister, Francine Pascal, kicked in. We weren't there yet, but with Aunt Belle's front money, I was able to give Arthur a deposit for the Provincetown Playhouse.

The move from the Limbo to the Provincetown Playhouse was physically only a few blocks across town, but we were entering the entirely different world of Off Broadway. One night in April, Bobby Carey and I were having dinner at a Village restaurant, and I had the keys to the Playhouse in my pocket. After dinner, we walked over to 133 MacDougal Street. I opened the doors, turned on the lights, and we sat in the back of the empty theatre staring at the tiny stage, imagining what it would be like to play there. I was trying to impress him, but I ended up being in awe myself. The Playhouse had been dark for some time, it was rat-infested, more than a little shabby, and in need of a coat of paint; but it was legendary. The Provincetown Players, searching for a winter home for the company they had established on Cape Cod, had transformed the pre-Victorian building, just off the southwest corner of Washington Square, into their theatre in 1918. Like most Off-Broadway theatres at the time, it was a converted space. According to Helen Deutsch and Stella Hanau, the building had previously been "a storehouse, a bottling-works and a stable."[3] It opened with one-act plays by Edna St. Vincent Millay, Eugene O'Neill, and Florence Kiper Frank. The Provincetown Players were a vital part the avant-garde of the late teens and early twenties, but in the intervening years the Provincetown Playhouse had become a commercial Off-Broadway rental house. Many famous actors had performed there; Bette Davis made her New York theatre debut on this stage. The famed plaster cyclorama dome, which George Cram Cook commissioned for the premiere of O'Neill's *Emperor Jones* (1920), starring Charles Gilpin, was still intact.

But Off Broadway in 1985 was a very different place than it had been in O'Neill's time. The Provincetown Playhouse had become too expensive to house noncommercial experimental theatre, yet at 175 seats it was considered too small to be profitable. And Off Broadway was no longer the incubator of avant-garde theatre that it once was; it was largely a lower-priced version of Broadway. Having challenged mainstream sensibilities by introducing playwrights such as Edward Albee and directors such as Jose Quintero and Alan Schneider, Off Broadway became part of the mainstream. At the same time, audiences for adventurous, new drama on Broadway were diminishing—a trend that has continued to accelerate. A new play without a star that might fill a four-hundred-seat theatre Off Broadway would have been a flop in a larger Broadway house. So shows from the 1984–85 season, like *Orphans* by Lyle Kessler and *The Foreigner* by Larry Shue, and holdovers from previous seasons, like Wendy Wasserstein's *Isn't It Romantic?* and the Howard Ashman/Alan Menken smash musical *Little Shop of Horrors*, which might have been produced on Broadway a few decades earlier, instead enjoyed profitable runs Off Broadway.

So moving across town from the East Village to the established Off-Broadway Provincetown Playhouse was a physical move from the fringe to the mainstream. As Bobby and I sat in that empty theatre, it was intoxicating to imagine that our fantasy theatre company would perform there, complete with a marquee, a box office, a lobby, and real theatre seats. The audience would buy actual tickets, and they would be given *Showbills* (then the Off-Broadway version of *Playbill*). There would be ads in the *New York Times*, and we would be reviewed by all the major newspapers. The cast would be working under Actors' Equity Association contracts. These were the corporeal signs that it was no longer a fantasy. *Vampire Lesbians* would be the first-ever play with a Ridiculous aesthetic to transfer to a commercial Off-Broadway run. Charles Ludlam's *Irma Vep* was a huge hit that season, but the Ridiculous Theatrical Company remained non-Equity to the end and operated on a nonprofit basis.

Moving West

The running time of *Vampire Lesbians* was only forty-five minutes: perfect for a club, but not long enough for a full evening in an Off-Broadway theatre. We considered various ways of lengthening the show by adding scenes showing the feuding vampires in various historical periods, but it all felt like padding. Charles was also nervous that the show was too lightweight and insubstantial to survive the scrutiny of the New York theatre critics. One bizarre scenario he proposed was that the show should end with La Condesa and Madeleine fleeing vampire hunters via helicopter to a bunker in South America. I was horrified as I listened to him pitch this depressing evocation of Nazi war criminals. That night I had a nightmare that we did the show at the Provincetown with all these revisions, and the audience hated it. The theatre erupted into loud, angry booing, and then they started screaming, "This isn't what we paid for! This isn't what we came to see! We want *Vampire Lesbians of Sodom*!!" I woke up in a sweat. The next day over breakfast, I told Charles that we had to do the show exactly the way we did it at the Limbo Lounge because it worked. No changes! He finally agreed to leave well enough alone, and we decided to add a curtain raiser to fill out the evening. Charles wanted to add *Theodora* to the bill, but I argued that it was too similar in tone and style to *Vampire Lesbians*. I also felt that some of Justinian's pornographic speeches were too over-the-top vulgar for an Off-Broadway production. I had a hunch that matinee ladies were not ready for *Drummer* magazine fantasies.

Sleeping Beauty or Coma, the one-act Charles had written for the "gala" opening of the new Limbo in October 1984, was finally chosen as the curtain raiser. It is a sweetly nostalgic play that provided a context for a parade of dozens of outrageous costumes. The story is the Sleeping Beauty legend set in the milieu of the fashion industry of swinging mod London in the 1960s. The evil witch is a queeny establishment fashion designer (Sebastian Loré, played by me) who transforms an incompetent office temp (Enid Wetwhistle, originally Julie Halston's role, now played by Meghan) into a supermodel whom he renames Rose, the sleeping beauty figure. Rose falls into a coma as a result of a bad acid trip after Loré's prune-faced secretary (Miss Thick, played by Andy Halliday) pours toxic LSD into her drink at a party. Charles, who wasn't in the original version, expanded one of the roles for himself: up-and-coming designer Fauna Alexander, who challenges the establishment fashion world with her revolutionary new aesthetic. The play parodied multiple British films of the 1960s, from Richard Lester's Beatles movies to Michelangelo Antonioni's *Blow-Up*. We called upon Jeff Veazey again to choreograph a dance number set in a London club that was a catalogue of 1960s dances such as the Frug, the Twist, the Swim, and the Jerk. To try out the newly polished script and put together the last bits of financing, we went back to the Limbo with *Coma* for eight performances in May.

Despite the relatively straightforward storyline, Charles managed to include a classic gender-blurring moment between Fauna and Enid that always got an enormous laugh:

FAUNA: *(extremely vulnerable)* I suddenly have this urge to kiss you.
I've never felt this way about another woman.

ENID: Then kiss me. *(They tentatively move closer and gently kiss)*

FAUNA: Oh dear, does that make me a lesbian?[4]

The scene did not reference a specific film, but it was redolent of 1960s-era British kitchen sink dramas, such as *A Taste of Honey* and *Darling*, where two girls might be doing something relatively innocent but act as if it were shocking and forbidden. In the text of *Coma*, the forbidden kiss is between two women; Fauna is uptight, but Enid is free of inhibitions and ready to experiment. Enid dismisses Fauna's question about her potential lesbianism ("You're just lonely and want to be loved!"). But of course the audience was aware that one of the women was a (gay) man in drag, rendering the concern about lesbianism absurd. Charles played the moment trembling with gravity, as if he had just violated the ultimate taboo, a witty critique of the absurdity of homophobic social conventions.

While we were in the midst of our run of *Coma* at the Limbo and simultaneously gearing up for our Off-Broadway opening the following month, the money finally came together at what seemed like the last possible moment. It was an intense period of multitasking, so I hired David Lawlor, a grouchy, unpleasant, bitter general manager, who nonetheless came highly recommended, to handle the unions, contracts, payroll, and all the other business details while I focused on directing, acting, and crafting a publicity campaign. Lawlor was in his sixties at the time, and I felt lucky to have an experienced old pro to guide us through the byzantine complexities of opening an Off-Broadway show. Sam Rudy was taking some time off, so Pete Sanders from the Shirley Herz office handled the press. With our low budget we couldn't afford big ads in the *Times*, so instead we put our money into posters. Brian designed three "one-sheets" with campy studio glamour shots by Marc Raboy (one for each scene of *Vampire Lesbians*), and I had them posted on construction sites all over town. The fact that it was technically illegal to do so ("Post No Bills!") gave the campaign a fugitive allure.

Thanks to the tryouts at Limbo (our equivalent to Philadelphia and New Haven), the shows were rehearsed and ready to go by the time we moved into the theatre, which was lucky, since there was no money in the budget for rehearsal pay; we went right into techs and dresses. Julie Halston missed being a part of the company, so she rejoined us as the female understudy while keeping her day job on Wall Street. I splurged by hiring

Michael Belanger as the male understudy weeks earlier than required by Equity so that he could go on for me while I divided my time between acting on stage and directing from out front. In a quiet moment during one of the dress rehearsals, I took a break and walked down to the lower lobby. As I was sipping water from the fountain at the foot of the stairs, I was startled by a loud thumping noise. I looked up to discover an enormous rat staring at me from the landing. We both froze for a moment, then the rat proceeded to thump down the remaining stairs, walk right past me, and head into the lounge. I was in my pink Sebastian Loré costume with a white bouffant wig, so it must have known I was harmless. Another rat made a dramatic appearance on a ledge just above the actors' heads one night when I was giving notes in the green room. The rats weren't used to so much activity in their theatre. I made a mental note to call Arthur about getting an exterminator.

The move from Limbo to the Provincetown Playhouse required a substantial upgrade of the physical production. We tried to find the balance between tweaking the production values for an Off-Broadway venue and maintaining the East Village sensibility. Brian Whitehill designed a proscenium arch with the Theatre-in-Limbo logo (including the reclining cartoon nudes across the top) that reinforced our branding. He created the illusion of gilded filigree by attaching found objects such as aluminum TV dinner trays, crutches, Styrofoam cups, and plastic cutlery and highlighting the arrangement with gold spray paint. If you squinted from the back of the house, it gave the impression of a rather elegant proscenium arch. On closer inspection, it was obviously created from junk. To emphasize our concept of a traveling stock company, he designed a roll drop as a front curtain emblazoned with the logos for the two shows to be performed along with three other shows that we didn't perform: *Theodora, Times Square Angel*, and *Pardon My Inquisition*. *Pardon My Inquisition* hadn't even been written at the time, although Charles had frequently mentioned the title in his curtain speech. This drop was seen by the audience as they entered the theatre, and it created the impression that Theatre-in-Limbo was a company with a repertoire and that any one of these plays might be performed on a given night. As the houselights dimmed, Vivien lit the title of the play that was about to begin.

Vampire Lesbians had been performed in front of a plain muslin drop at the Limbo. Brian retained the muslin backdrop as a cyclorama for the transfer, but decorated it with black triangles that suggested stylized stars.

Brian Whitehill's design of the roll drop and proscenium arch for Vampire Lesbians of Sodom *at the Provincetown Playhouse, shown here in his rendering, suggested that we were traveling company with a repertory of five plays. Photo by B. T. Whitehill.*

He also added a crescent-shaped black groundrow, which was seen in silhouette. A rectangular frame in the shape of a large picture postcard was mounted on top of the ground row, and he created a different postcard for each scene. The scenery provided a graphic comment on each scene's setting while remaining in the background. The acting area downstage was empty, as it had been at the Limbo; there was no furniture. Vivien attached small "inky" lamps as footlights to the edge of the stage, which Brian concealed with decorative reflectors made of oblong aluminum pans spray-painted gold and black. For *Coma*, a roll drop was lowered in front of the groundrow that depicted a page casually torn from a fashion designer's sketchbook. Playing on the sleeping beauty's name, Rose, the doodling on the page included a thumbnail of a 1960s frock that resembled a stem for the skirt and a bloom for the collar, as well as a pair of Twiggy-type eyes with rose makeup. Brian, who always likes to work a visual joke into the scenery, created flat, cardboard eyelids that closed through slits in the drop when Rose went into her coma. When she woke up, the eyes opened, always getting a nice laugh.

Since the show was performed on an empty stage in front of a drop, the costumes were an especially important visual element. John Glaser created some forty costumes for the two plays on the bill. The basic designs were mostly the same as they had been at the Limbo, but they were substantially enhanced for the transfer, and generous amounts of glitter and sequins were added. *Coma* became a genuine fashion show, which gave John the opportunity to create an eye-popping array of garish, 1960s-inspired frocks, including a minidress made entirely of sparkling red and black plastic squares hooked together. He really outdid himself with the flamboyantly elegant Erté-inspired gowns for the two divas in the Hollywood scene of *Vampire Lesbians*, which beautifully evoked silent screen vamps. The parade of outrageous costumes downstage of Brian's witty backdrops, framed by the proscenium arch and footlights, created a highly stylized and theatrical look. It was redolent of Jack Smith's moldy aesthetic, but made over with uncustomary slickness and polish.

The show sold well during the two weeks of previews at the Provincetown Playhouse (thanks, in part, to low-priced $15 previews), and the audience response was generally consistent with what the show had received at the Limbo. Audiences were vocal, and there were lots of laughs. But at a critics' matinee preview the Sunday before the opening, we experienced a very unexpected response: almost total silence. Lines that usually received big laughs didn't seem to register at all. To make matters worse, we were all aware that the famously venomous John Simon, critic for *New York Magazine*, was in the audience that afternoon. The deathly stillness was shocking to the cast, and we responded by pushing desperately. The performance concluded with tepid applause that fizzled out before we had completely left the stage. Yet just a few hours later, at the Sunday evening performance, the audience response was once again deliriously vocal. That matinee performance was the first instance of what was to become a disconcerting phenomenon that persisted throughout the Off-Broadway run of *Vampire Lesbians*. Some audiences seemed attuned to every reference and were convulsed with laughter from beginning to end. Others simply didn't get it, and they sat in baffled silence. The cast immediately began to theorize about the cause of this radical shift in audience response from one performance to the next, and there was soon general agreement that predominantly gay audiences laughed at the show, and predominantly straight audiences didn't. While mainstream audiences were curious and attentive, they were not fully attuned to the Ridiculous camp aesthetic that gay audiences were so familiar with. They weren't in on the joke, and the coded, camp humor of the play either baffled or bored them.

The suddenly inconsistent audience response made the cast more than usually nervous as opening night (June 19, 1985) approached. The opening night audience was warm, but far from ecstatic. After the performance, friends and well-wishers invaded the green room downstairs. As the backstage crowd swelled, production assistant Joe Cote, wearing a cap that made him look like an old-time newsboy, rushed in with an early edition copy of the next morning's *New York Times*. He whispered to me, "I think you'll want to read this." A hush fell over the room at the sight of the newspaper. Everyone knew that the *Times* review was the only one that mattered. Neither Charles nor I was up to reading it aloud, so Ed Taussig grabbed the paper and began reading D. J. R. Bruckner's review. It is impossible to recreate the feeling of ecstasy that erupted in the room as we realized it was a rave. The first paragraph set the tone for the entire review:

> In Charles Busch's "Vampire Lesbians of Sodom" and the accompanying "Sleeping Beauty or Coma" the legitimate stage, if that's what it can be called in this case, may have found the answer to "The Rocky Horror Picture Show." One can imagine a cult forming. Costumes flashier than pinball machines, outrageous lines, awful puns, sinister innocence, harmless depravity—it's all here. And it is contagious; this kind of campy show that transforms everything it touches attracts audiences that could take over and finish the performance if the cast walked out in the middle.[5]

Bruckner praised the writing, the direction, the choreography, the performances, the production design, and the costume design. He concluded by observing "the audience laughs at the first line and goes right on laughing at every line to the end, and even at some of the silences. That's no mean achievement."[6] Charles retired to his dressing room to cry. The scene in the green room was a joyous cliché right out of a Busby Berkeley backstage musical as everyone headed out for the opening night party at AREA, the chic, downtown club of the moment, hosted by Michael Musto.

The key word in Bruckner's review that helps to explain the commercial success of the show is "harmless." He reassures his readers that the outrageousness of the production is all in good fun and in the spirit of innocence. The strongest word he uses to describe the show's satire is "irreverent." He states that Busch tweaks his satirical targets "without assaulting any of them directly." In other words, the audience need not fear that its values will be seriously challenged. Other critics agreed that *Vampire Lesbians* could not be considered social critique. Mary Campbell of the Associated

Press asserted, "the play, which doesn't have a bite of redeeming social value, might disappoint some theatergoers because there's no nudity and it isn't even very offensive."[7] The lack of offensiveness was affirmed by Robert Feldberg of the *Bergen Record*, who praised the show for its "good natured combination of outrageousness and let's-dress-up-and-have-a-good-time innocence."[8] *Variety* pronounced it "silly,"[9] while Marilyn Stasio of the *New York Post* patronizingly labeled it "a giddy little drag show."[10] The dreaded John Simon was not amused, calling the production "a twin bill of lower-than-low camp that I made single by departing after the first item, *Sleeping Beauty or Coma*, which left me just sufficiently uncomatose to stagger out. I was told that the title play is funnier (how could it not be?), but I had forgotten to bring my calipers."[11]

Busch versus Ludlam

At the heart of much of this criticism was the comparison of Charles Busch and Theatre-in-Limbo to Charles Ludlam and the Ridiculous Theatrical Company (the *Times* review was one of the few that did not mention Ludlam). The critics generally found us to be lightweights by comparison. Michael Feingold had led the charge months earlier with his review of the Limbo production in the *Village Voice*. Stasio complained that "one waits in vain for the literary conceits and clever phrase-mongering that makes Charles Ludlam and his Ridiculous Theatrical Company so amusing."[12] Don Nelson of the *Daily News* noted that "like the RTC, Busch and cohorts play multiple roles both male and female, but their material does not project the innovative comic brilliance that Ludlam is capable of."[13] Allan Wallach of *Newsday* felt that "theatergoers familiar with the similar work of the Ridiculous Theatrical Company may miss the often clever wordplay and ingenuity of Charles Ludlam's best efforts,"[14] while William A. Raidy, writing in the Newark *Star-Ledger*, noted that Busch "does not as yet have Ludlam's finely honed sense of double dimension comedy or his incredible ability for facial expression."[15] John Simon noted with disdainful contempt that "compared to Busch, Charles Ludlam is Elenora Duse and Sarah Bernhardt rolled into one."[16]

It was almost as if the critics created a high culture/low culture divide between Ludlam and Busch, an ironic stance considering that so much of Ludlam's work was concerned with demolishing that very divide. Theatre scholar Richard Niles argues that this condescending critical attitude reveals "a basic uneasiness about the presence of drag in performance, and a need to justify its use by discerning an underlying seriousness of intent."[17] And yet *Vampire Lesbians*, seemingly devoid of underlying seriousness, attained commercial success beyond that of any of Ludlam's plays. It played to sellout crowds throughout the summer of 1985, and although attendance dipped after Labor Day, the running expenses of the show were low enough to enable it to run for almost five years. The gay cult audiences that launched the show were eventually supplanted by audiences largely composed of tourists, and its extended run in an established Off-Broadway theatre created a greater awareness and acceptance of Ridiculous Theatre among mainstream theatergoers.

The commercial viability of *Vampire Lesbians* was due more to the differences between Busch and Ludlam than to their similarities. The original impulses of the two artists were entirely different. Ludlam founded his company before Stonewall, and his aesthetic was marked by oppression. He wrote that "camp is motivated by rage,"[18] and in his manifesto he urged testing out "a dangerous idea, a theme that threatens one's whole value system."[19] Busch was a generation younger, and he was fueled more by ambition than anger. He wrote no manifestos, but he stated that *Vampire Lesbians* "was created merely to entertain a late-night crowd on a hot summer night in the East Village."[20] While Ludlam was a provocateur, Busch was innocently "irreverent," with an overriding desire to please the audience. Ludlam reveled in the grotesque, like the artificial genital Black-Eyed Susan wore in the final scene of *Bluebeard*, or the appearance of a five-hundred-pound nude woman in *Salammbo*. Busch preferred beauty and glamour, which was reflected in his approach to drag and in the composition of our company. "There was a sweetness about us," Busch later noted, "a childlike quality about the actors. Ludlam's original group was decadent, grotesque. I adored it, but they were not a loveable group and he was not a loveable actor. He was a genius performer, dangerous."[21] Ludlam's scripts were self-consciously erudite, often containing references to a vast array of novels, plays, and philosophical tracts as well as to Hollywood films and pop culture. Busch's references were almost entirely pop-oriented, usually centered on his obsession with Hollywood films of the 1930s and '40s. Moreover, Ludlam was ambivalent about mainstream success, whereas Busch desperately desired it.

Nevertheless, it isn't exactly true that *Vampire Lesbians of Sodom* was intended "merely to entertain." The very title of the play was deliberately offensive to the conventional values of the dominant culture. While it may

The marquee at the Provincetown Playhouse attracted a lot of commentary from passersby and often helped generate significant walk-up business at the box office. Photo by B. T. Whitehill.

seem only mildly titillating in retrospect, it was genuinely shocking to the mainstream sensibility of 1985. Passersby on MacDougal Street would often stop in surprise upon seeing the title treatment up on the marquee. Some laughed, but not everyone did; some were indignant. The *New York Times* advertising department even initially declined to run ads for the show. It was implied (the *Times* doesn't explain such things) that the title violated its sense of decorum. This could have been a disaster, since *New York Times* ads are essential for Off-Broadway shows. Could the word "Lesbians" have been considered toxic, or was it the implication of what those lesbians might have done in Sodom? The *Times* didn't say. After some negotiations with our advertising agency and press agent (powerhouse veteran Shirley Herz herself had to intercede), the *Times* finally agreed to run our ads if we eliminated a tagline we had been using on posters and flyers: "You just can't keep some gals down!" Apparently, they read this line (in combination with the title) as distastefully prurient, something that had never occurred to me. When we dropped the tagline, they agreed to run our ads. But the very idea that we were almost banned from advertising in the *New York Times* gives some sense of the power of the title.

There is no question that the cultural critique expressed in *Vampire Lesbians* was mild compared to Ludlam's radical agenda, and that made it more acceptable to a broad audience. But the central metaphor of ambitious movie stars as bloodsucking vampires was more than a silly excuse to dress up. It was a pointed commentary on the cult of celebrity in superficial contemporary culture. *Vampire Lesbians* also marked an important step in the assimilation of drag into the mainstream. In 1985, the very act of appearing in drag could still be considered "a dangerous idea." While drag performance was not unheard of on commercial stages, it was still considered freakish. The hit musical *La Cage aux Folles*, which had opened in 1983 and was still running when *Vampire Lesbians* opened, depicted the drag queen Albin as a pathetic outsider who had to summon all the inner strength he could muster to sing "I Am What I Am." There were no moral qualms about drag in Busch's performance, and he was clearly enjoying himself. He played his female characters with the aplomb and self-assurance of the 1930s Broadway star Ina Claire in a boulevard comedy.

Ludlam and his partner, Everett Quinton, attended a performance of *Vampire Lesbians* not long after the Off-Broadway opening. They stayed to congratulate us, and both of them were very kind; however, there were reports that Ludlam was less than pleased with what he saw. Ludlam biographer David Kaufman claims that he was "enraged" that "superficial elements of his work had indeed been stolen, but without any of their substance."[22] Years later, Everett made a point of telling me that Ludlam had no animosity toward Busch, and he wanted to dispel any notion of a "feud" between them. But Busch was an upstart rival, and a successful one at that.

The commercial prospects of the Off-Broadway transfer of *Vampire Lesbians* were enhanced by a theatrical trend of the mid-1980s: it opened during a period of growing mainstream acceptance of plays with gay subjects and themes. Soon after the Provincetown opening, the show was featured in a *Variety* article by Richard Hummler that trumpeted this "visibility for gay legit."[23] He pointed to the Broadway production of Harvey Fierstein's *Torch Song Trilogy* (1982) as the beginning of the trend, and cited *La Cage aux Folles*, *As Is*, *The Normal Heart*, Emily Mann's *Execution of Justice*, and Terrence McNally's *Lisbon Traviata* as evidence that gay plays were "demonstrating new mainstream box office vigor":

All of which points up the theater's perennial function of mirroring society. Although many gays feel social repression continues to exist, there's little doubt that homosexuals have made vast strides in the past decade or so in overcoming prejudice and obliterating stereotypes.[24]

That three of the seven plays discussed in the article dealt with the subject of AIDS demonstrates the major impact the disease was having on the broader cultural awareness of homosexuality. Yet it was unclear at the time exactly what that impact would be. Some feared, as Frank Rich argued in a 1987 essay in *Esquire*, that AIDS would set off "a new and more virulent round of Anita Bryant–style witch hunts."[25] This predicted backlash did not gain much traction, however, and the growing mainstream acceptance of gay men and lesbians continued unabated.

A Sure-Fire Idea

The sell-out crowds during the summer of 1985 gave me the giddy, but mistaken, notion that I knew what I was doing as a producer. Charles and I decided it would be fun to bring back *Times Square Angel* for the holiday season and play it in rep with *Vampire Lesbians* at the Provincetown. I convinced myself that this was a sure-fire idea. We had successfully played in rep at the Limbo, so why shouldn't we do the same Off Broadway? I thought it would be a great way to get our Limbo fans to come back, and it would be terrific publicity. But there are good reasons why repertory is very rarely done in commercial theatre. It's hard to effectively advertise two shows in one theatre without confusing the audience. New scenery would have to be designed and installed on an already crowded stage. Since *Vampire Lesbians* was a commercial enterprise with a fiduciary responsibility to the investors, the funds had to be kept completely separate, which meant I had to form a new partnership for *Times Square Angel*. And that meant I had to start raising money all over again and work out another deal with Arthur Cantor, since my license agreement for the Playhouse did not allow me to present other shows. Casting two shows with one set of actors can be a nightmare. The cast of *Times Square Angel* did not precisely correspond to the cast of *Vampire Lesbians*, so two additional actors would have to be put on the payroll.

I was undeterred, but I needed to go to Actors' Equity to get permission to increase the actors' workload. I assumed the salaries would have to go up, but Ken Greenwood, the Off-Broadway representative, explained to me that we were already paying the actors *twice* the required minimum.

I couldn't believe what I was hearing. I had hired David Lawlor and endured his snide put-downs to avoid making mistakes like this. He had been in the business for decades, and I had gotten assurances from colleagues that he could easily handle the job. Shirley Herz told me, "He's a bitchy old queen who's difficult and moody, but he knows what he's doing." I had approached him after the first paychecks came out because they seemed much higher than I thought they should be. He peremptorily informed me that I was wrong, to leave the business affairs to him, and that I didn't know how to read the sliding scale of the Actors' Equity contract. As it turned out, I had read it correctly, and David had mistakenly overpaid the actors, costing the company a substantial amount of money. I was furious, but I couldn't help feeling sorry for him for making such a foolish mistake. He was a proudly obstinate curmudgeon, and it was very difficult for him to admit an error, but he ultimately made a settlement to partially repay the company. As part of the settlement, he also worked for free for another six months, remaining bitter to the end. If I hadn't decided to produce *Times Square Angel*, I might never have discovered his error, and the high (for Off Broadway) salaries we were paying the actors would have forced me to precipitously close the show. However, that proved to be the only financial benefit of reviving *Times Square Angel*.

Like *Vampire Lesbians of Sodom*, the Limbo version of *Times Square Angel* was too short to sustain a full evening at Off-Broadway prices, so we extended it by creating a prologue made up of a cavalcade of ten scenes spelling out just how and why Irish O'Flanagan became such a selfish, hard-boiled dame. The scenes are short blackout sketches, some of which are hilarious, and all of which play on the conventions and clichés of 1930s and '40s film melodramas. Young Irish is a smart, hopeful, idealistic, and generous tomboy, forced by her abusive, alcoholic father to quit school and work in a zipper factory. She escapes the life of a factory drudge by breaking into burlesque, where she discovers her good looks and how to use them. She falls in love with a young aristocrat, Dexter Paine III, who proposes marriage. But Dexter's snobbish dowager mother has other ideas, and they don't include her son marrying a burlesque artist. In a life-changing reversal, Irish takes a payoff from the condescending Mrs. Paine to call off the wedding. She learns then and there that the only important thing in life is money. Everyone in the cast, including our two understudies, doubled (and in some cases tripled) to play the twenty-three roles in this new version.

The prologue was pasted onto the existing Limbo script, making for an entertaining, if occasionally patchy and distended, holiday pageant that would have gone over like gangbusters in a downtown club. But expectations are quite different on Off-Broadway stages.

Walter Goodman, the third-string critic sent by the *New York Times*, likened it in an otherwise bland review to "a movie reel that has run out of control."[26] While *Times Square Angel* was warmly received by most of the critics, it didn't generate much interest at the box office, and the cobbled together prologue actually diluted the power and effectiveness of the forty-five-minute original Limbo version. I tried to keep it open past the holidays, hoping it would pick up steam, but it soon closed, losing its entire investment. I returned our company to playing *Vampire Lesbians* eight times per week, now on much-reduced salaries at the correct Off-Broadway rate (around $225 per week, at the time). It was the last time I would produce an Off-Broadway show without first trying out the material in another venue.

Moving to an Off-Broadway theatre had been our dream, but we discovered that playing a regular Off-Broadway schedule to audiences that grew less and less sophisticated as the months wore on could be a grind. Meghan received magnificent reviews as La Condesa, but her run in the show was marred by health problems. She had a persistent cough, exacerbated (we thought) by her heavy smoking. She missed many performances, forcing Julie Halston to go on far more often than she had planned, a conflict with her day job on Wall Street. Not everyone in the company was sympathetic with Meghan, but Charles and I found the situation very worrying. She assured me that she was fine, that it was nothing but a case of "walking pneumonia." I didn't know what that was, but it didn't sound good. She finally gave her notice in May 1986. I left the show (as an actor) at the same time to take over the management of the production from our disgraced G.M., who was stepping down as part of his settlement agreement. I moved a file cabinet into the kitchen of our Twelfth Street railroad flat, and it became my office. Charles would often wander in to have his morning bowl of cereal while I was going over payroll with the company manager.

The general manager is responsible for overseeing all the business aspects of the show. When I took over the position, *Vampire Lesbians* was well past its status as a hot ticket. The box office receipts lurched inconsistently from week to week, depending on such factors as holidays, the time of year, and the weather. There were nights when we sold as few as eleven seats at full price, which threw me into a state of complete panic. A few nights later we might sell out, and I would heave a sigh of relief. It was hard to read the tea leaves, but a few colleagues sensibly suggested that it was time to close the show, that it had run its course. I wasn't sensible, and I couldn't bear the thought of closing before we had repaid our investors. Instead, I focused on cutting costs. Charles and I took no royalties, and the designers agreed to defer theirs. I tried to slash any expense that wasn't fixed, from advertising to dry cleaning, and I managed to pare the running costs of the show to around $12,000 per week—a good thing, since some weeks we didn't even gross that much. But we kept going.

Back in the East Village

Everyone in the company missed the thrill of performing new shows for our Limbo audiences. Charles and I both wanted to do a new show just for fun, without the pressure of opening Off Broadway, so I called Michael and Victor to see if they would be open to letting us do some late shows at the Limbo. But things had changed since our last gig there. Picking up on all the publicity the area had received, the police were cracking down on illegal clubs. Victor and a bartender had been busted for selling liquor without a license, and so they had converted the Limbo from a club to a nonprofit arts center in order to stay alive. Randy Rollison and Denise Lanctot were brought in to run the performances in the space, and they did not seem particularly interested in having us come back. Understandably, they wanted to curate their own type of theatre (a more intellectually respectable avant-garde, I supposed), and we didn't fit the bill. There was a sense that we were too commercial, too polished, that we didn't fit in with the East Village aesthetic. But Michael and Victor wanted us to come back, so Charles and I met with them to pitch the show we wanted to do: a Spanish period piece called *Pardon My Inquisition or Kiss the Blood off My Castanets*. This title had never failed to get a laugh when Charles plugged it as an upcoming production in his curtain speeches, but when we ran it past Randy and Denise they sat stone-faced. There was plenty of tension because Charles and I rather arrogantly thought we *were* Limbo Theatre and viewed Randy and Denise as interlopers, but we finally agreed to some dates in May 1986.

Once again, we had the intense pleasure of throwing together a costume epic with about one week of rehearsal. Charles had seen an old photograph of Bernhardt playing a Moorish Gypsy in Sardou's *La Sorcière* (1903), and that was the catalyst for *Pardon My Inquisition*. He never read Sardou's play, however, and the story he devised bears greater resemblance to *A Tale of Two Cities*, with elements of the Bette Davis potboiler *Marked Woman* thrown in. He dashed off the script, and I made a few suggestions to tighten the structure and clarify motivations. This time Charles played two roles that highlighted his usual common-versus-grand duality: a great lady, the Marquesa Del Drago, and "the tackiest slut in old Toledo," Maria Garbonza, two women who happened to look alike except for their hair color. Since we weren't paying the actors, we packed a cast of eleven onto the tiny Limbo stage. "It had the feeling of a tired melodrama being performed by a tacky company on tour. It was so hokey, hackneyed," Charles remembered. "I think Ken directed it with great brio. We did it very quickly; I think we rehearsed the whole thing in a week. Like a quick sketch, Ken would say 'go over here, go over there,' bam, bam, bam and on we went."[27] Michael Belanger recalled that during a note session with the cast after rehearsing the big tavern scene, I complained "that scene looked like it was from the world's worst summer stock production of *Man of La Mancha*." They all looked downcast until I added, "It was absolutely perfect. Do it exactly the same way every night!" That gives a pretty accurate picture of the production style.

I arranged to have a van pick up the cast on MacDougal Street to drive across town to the East Village. The audience, already crowded into the Limbo when the van finally made it to East Ninth Street, burst into applause as the actors rushed backstage. The faux Spanish costumes, which must have come from old productions of *Carmen* or *La Mancha*, were pulled by our *Vampire Lesbians* wardrobe supervisor, Bobby Locke, who had a day job at Eaves-Brooks Costume Company. Best of all, we got to indulge in the kind of outrageous vulgarity that would have been out of place at the Provincetown Playhouse, such as this exchange between Maria and Pepe (Bobby Carey) at the end of scene 1, as she tries to make her lover, Don Arturo (Arnie Kolodner), jealous in front of a crowd of onlookers in a tavern:

MARIA: (*to Pepe*) I want you. I want you.
PEPE: Let's go to my place.
MARIA: I want you here, Pepe. Now. (*She pulls down his pants, his back is to the audience*) Oh Pepe, you are magnificent.

ZULIMA: Maria, do not degrade yourself.

(*Maria proceeds to go down on Pepe, as the men cheer her on. Pepe moans and groans with pleasure. Don Arturo is disgusted and leaves. Just as Pepe is about to burst with pleasure, Maria lets him go, laughs raucously and exits.*)[28]

This moment provided what Michael Sommers, writing in the *Native*, called "the traditional Theater-in-Limbo sight of Robert Carey's expressive buttocks flushing with shame."[29] Bobby was embarrassed about being exploited in this way, and years later was still explaining that Charles didn't really give him a blow job.

Pardon My Inquisition, which premiered at a time when hopelessness about AIDS was increasing, is all about forbidden sex, lust, and love. It even included a condom joke to parody the new safe sex guidelines:

DON ARTURO: Educate yourself, Bruno. Intercourse is no threat if one covers one's member with a goatskin sheath.

TOPO: Don Arturo is that most modern of men.[30]

We didn't invite the critics, but a few came anyway. *Pardon My Inquisition* wasn't for everyone, although the *Advocate* touted it as "one of the best evenings in town."[31] It certainly was for us. We achieved our goal of having fun, and the experience left us ready to embark on another new Limbo adventure.

Chapter 4 MacDougal Street Empire

Becky London as Berdine, Charles Busch as Chicklet, and Michael Belanger as Marvel Ann go on a "manhunt" in a publicity shot for Psycho Beach Party. *Photo by Carol Rosegg.*

Charles sometimes dreamed up outrageous titles as jokes and announced them as coming attractions during his post-show curtain speeches. If a title got a reaction from our fans, it was then regularly incorporated into his monologue and an expectation developed that a production was actually in the works. The title *Gidget Goes Psychotic* got laughs (and sometimes cheers) long before a line of the play was written. Today, the notion of a comedy about a girl who suffers from mental illness would probably not be so enthusiastically received; practices in the theatre have changed considerably, becoming more sensitive, empathetic, and inclusive on this topic. We had every intention of producing a play with that title at the Limbo in the fall of 1984, but the first version of the script was a misfire that we abandoned after a few rehearsals. It had featured Charles in a supporting role as Alana Anders, a mysterious transgender woman who moves in next door to Gidget's house in Malibu. In a climactic scene, Alana exposes Gidget's father (played by me) as a homosexual, exactly as Madeliene Astarté had done to King Carlisle in *Vampire Lesbians*. Charles thought this ritual unmasking would be an amusing convention to repeat from play to play. The title character was to have been played by Theresa Aceves, which was, in theory, good casting. But Theresa was actually quite vulnerable and convincing as a mentally unbalanced young girl, so a plotline in which she was sexually abused by her psychiatrist while under hypnosis proved to be more disturbing than funny (and, of course, today such a plotline would be met with absolute horror). Another problem was that neither Charles nor I were particular fans of the Gidget films, so we just weren't inspired by the project. We dropped it and moved on. Almost two years later, however, when we were looking for a follow-up to *Pardon My Inquisition*, we started discussing a rewrite of *Gidget*. I persuaded Charles that there were two obligatory expectations that he could not ignore: Gidget had to go psychotic, and *he* had to play her.

We wanted to get the milieu right, so we turned to our well-stocked local video store, The World of Video—our research library—and rented VHS tapes of every 1960s beach party film we could get our hands on. Although we weren't looking forward to sitting through this collection of kitsch, we were surprised to discover that the original *Gidget* was actually a pretty good movie and that Sandra Dee's performance in the title role was much more nuanced than we had expected. But Charles was used to the grande dame roles, and he was nervous about playing a cute and perky teenage girl with pigtails—it wasn't his trip. He was more than comfortable going psychotic, however, which his Gidget did every time she heard the word "red." As in his original script, Gidget was to suffer from multiple personality disorder, giving Charles the opportunity to step outside the peppy surfer girl and transform into several other characters, most notably Ann Bowman, a louche dominatrix with a throaty Tallulah Bankhead voice who had a penchant for giving unsuspecting victims complete head and body shaves. Charles got the idea of head-to-toe shaving as the ultimate in erotic madness from *Drummer* magazine, years before full Brazilians became almost commonplace. We also studied films such as *The Three Faces of Eve*, *Suddenly, Last Summer*, and the Hitchcock classics *Spellbound*, *Psycho*, and *Marnie*, the plots of which were based on notions of mental illness and its causes that had already become quite dated, even ridiculous, by 1986.

The finished rewrite had multiple plotlines and parts for everyone in the company who wanted them. The discovery of Gidget's psychosis and the absurd Freudian analysis of its root causes was the main plot, which was intertwined with the love story of Gidget and Moondoggie, a handsome surfer boy who hoped to become a psychiatrist, played by Arnie Kolodner. Ralph Buckley, an old friend from Northwestern who had already created roles in *Times Square Angel* and *Pardon My Inquisition* was the macho Kahoona, king of the surfers, who was secretly a submissive masochist obsessed with serving Gidget's alter ego, Ann Bowman. Charles explained, "Ralph Buckley is always playing the macho straight male who is always humiliated. My revenge on straight men is through Ralph Buckley. I wanted him to be in bra and panties and he said no way, forget it. He wouldn't do it."[1]

Charles wanted to mollify Bobby Carey and Andy Halliday, both of whom had been dissatisfied with their recent roles, so this time Bobby would not have to show his ass, and Andy would not have to play a grotesque. They played a couple of surf bums, Yo-Yo and Stinky, who fall in love with each other, come out, and become pre-Stonewall gay activists. Theresa graciously gave up the title role and got a part tailored much more effectively to her talent: Bettina Barnes, a sweetly dizzy Hollywood starlet with a ruthlessly hot temper when dealing with studios and agents ("I'll have his balls on a plate"),[2] who was on the lam from the set of her latest B picture. Charles created the drag role of Marvel Ann, a slutty, vapid high school beauty queen, the ultimate mean girl, for *Vampire Lesbians* understudy Michael Belanger. Julie Halston was still maintaining her Wall Street career, so Becky London, who had replaced Meghan in *Vampire Lesbians*, got the plum role of Gidget's brainy sidekick and best friend, Larue. I told Charles that I would rather not act in this one so that I could concentrate on directing and producing, but this left Gidget parentless. Fortunately, Meghan Robinson was rested up after having a few months off from *Vampire Lesbians*, and she readily agreed to play Gidget's mother, the perfect homemaker with a deep, dark secret.

All the strands of the plot are resolved in a climactic luau scene on the beach. The kids are enjoying a limbo contest when a disheveled Marvel Ann enters screaming, her head all but completely shaved. She tearfully explains that someone knocked her out, and she woke up just as the assailant was shaving her head, adding with a sob, "They'd already shaved my beaver."[3] Everyone is shaken, but the big talent show must go on. Charles included a reference to his own earlier play, *Sister Act*, by having Gidget and Larue enter costumed as Siamese twins. They dive into their number, "The Lady in Red," and every time the lyric insistently returns to the word "red," Gidget's face grows more distant and then contorted as she transforms into the monstrous Ann Bowman, terrifying Larue who is still tightly strapped to Gidget in the Siamese twin costume. With a lascivious, triumphant laugh, Gidget/Ann pulls out an enormous straight-edged razor and threatens to give everyone on the beach a full head and body shave. Moondoggie and Kahoona finally subdue her and free Larue from the costume just as Gidget's mother enters, desperate to stop the proceedings. Gidget experiences rapid-fire personality changes: Dr. Rose Mayer (a matronly radio personality), Tylene (an African American grocery store check-out girl), Walter Mullin (a queeny florist), and finally Gidget's younger self. In a flashback scene that recalls Hitchcock's *Marnie*, we see that Gidget's mother was a prostitute called Ann Bowman (in a vivid red dress) who neglected her children while she turned tricks. This long-repressed memory spurs Gidget to launch into a monologue that evokes the climax of another film, *Suddenly, Last Summer*, as she recalls the traumatic death of her younger brother. Moondoggie neatly provides a ridiculously logical, Freudian analysis for Gidget's psychosis, reminiscent of the tidy explanation of Norman Bates's aberrant behavior in the final scene of Hitchcock's *Psycho*:

> It's really very simple. Gidget did her best to suppress this traumatic childhood episode by denying herself all normal human emotion, so she created various alter egos to express emotion for her. She associated the sex drive with her mother, so she in effect became her childhood vision of her mother, Ann Bowman, whenever placed in a potentially erotic situation.[4]

Bettina options Gidget's story for the movies, Stinky and Yo-Yo announce that they are moving to New York as lovers, Larue vows to become a novelist, and, in a romantic coda scene, Moondoggie gives Gidget his pin. Everyone is happy—except Marvel Ann, who is still bald.

The luau scene cried out for a big ensemble musical number, and Jeff Veazey outdid himself. I loved the idea of Theatre-in-Limbo doing an actual limbo number, and I suggested to Jeff that we use the classic Chubby Checker recording. As usual, he and I didn't need to have a long discussion about the number. Our preproduction conversations usually lasted only ten to twenty minutes, but I always knew that he understood perfectly what was required and that whatever he came up with would fit seamlessly into the show. He was the ideal collaborator, and the wittiest, most imaginative choreographer I've ever encountered. The number began as a simple limbo contest, emphasizing a character moment as each actor approached the limbo stick. After the first chorus it graduated to a full-fledged production number that evoked the 1960s beach party movies we were parodying. Jeff was a tough-as-nails Broadway pro who whipped the cast into shape with focused discipline, yet he was always willing to modify his ideas to accommodate the less coordinated members of our company. By the time he was through, they all looked like dancers.

Most of our team had been working together for over two years when we started rehearsing *Gidget*. We had the production of Limbo shows down to a science, and we trusted each other. Brian came up with another witty, abstract backdrop that simultaneously suggested a surfer girl with a 1960s flip hairdo holding a surfboard in each arm, and a Rorschach test with phallic imagery. Vivien varied her light plot with some grotesque colors such as magenta, blue-green, and yellow, both to evoke the vivid color schemes of the original *Gidget* films and to accentuate Gidget's transformations into madness. John Glaser wasn't available to do the costumes, so our *Vampire Lesbians* wardrobe master, Bobby Locke, pulled together some appropriate 1960s beach wear. Kathie Carr had a field day with the wigs, creating some terrific 1960s hair helmets. As usual, the rehearsal period was brief. We started in the last week of September, and we opened at Limbo on October 10, 1986, just as much of the city was captivated by the thrilling World Series contest between the Mets and the Boston Red Sox.

Midnight Theatre

Once again, I hired a van to transport the actors who were still performing in *Vampire Lesbians* across town, but the curtain almost always had to be delayed because I had come up with an impossible schedule. Friday nights at 11:00 p.m. were not a problem, but *Gidget Goes Psychotic* was set to begin at midnight on Saturdays, just ten minutes after the curtain came down on the late show at the Provincetown. We were lucky if the van made it to East Ninth Street by 12:30 on those nights. I mollified the audience by passing out free beer, and Charles (who was taking a few performances off from *Vampire Lesbians*), delighted them with a comic monologue out of drag. Since he had just gotten a very short haircut, he got a big laugh when he joked that he looked like Vanessa Redgrave in the television holocaust drama, *Playing for Time*.

I assumed that *Gidget*, like *Pardon My Inquisition*, would be another show just for our Limbo audiences—an amusing diversion for a few weeks, especially because Charles wasn't particularly interested in playing Gidget. Since I wasn't in the show, I brought a portable black-and-white TV along so I could watch the Mets games in a small coat closet at the back of the house. I had never been a baseball fan, but this World Series was compelling, addictive drama. The audience response to the show drowned out the game. There were substantial laughs from the beginning, but the first huge laugh of the evening came when Charles as Gidget removed her blouse to change into her swimsuit, revealing an utterly flat chest. With genuine teenaged angst, Charles sighed, "I'm hopeless. I'm built just like a boy. I wonder if I'll ever fill out."[5] Since Charles's bare, hairless chest was completely androgynous, this moment didn't have the jarring impact of Ludlam's hairy chest as Marguerite Gautier in his adaptation of *Camille*. But the gender-blurring acknowledgment of the male actor playing a female role was hilarious, in part because Charles played it for real. He was strangely believable as a young girl, even shirtless.

Gidget's line at the top of scene 2, "Mom, I'm home," was the perfect setup for Meghan's entrance as Mrs. Lawrence. With her tight bouffant hairdo, blood red lipstick, and pearls, she was the image of the perfect 1960s mother, as well as an uncanny dead ringer for Joan Crawford as played by Faye Dunaway in *Mommie Dearest*. The audience roared in recognition of this before she said a word, and she threatened to steal the show in the scene that followed. All is sweetness and light until Mrs. Lawrence denies Gidget's request for $25 to buy a surfboard. When Gidget presses the point ("I want a motherfucking, cocksucking surfboard!"), Mrs. Lawrence transforms into a gorgon, accusing Gidget of looking for an excuse to hang out with boys: "You don't know how lucky you are being a virgin, pure and chaste." As the scene escalated, Meghan violently jabbed her finger in Charles's chest to demonstrate "how repugnant it is to have a sweaty man's thing poking at you." When Gidget continued to contradict her, Meghan's voice became a startling baritone growl: "The male body is coarse and ugly."[6] To make her point, she pulls a jockstrap from her bodice, explaining, "For years I've kept this, anticipating this very moment." The scene builds to an hysterical climax as Mrs. Lawrence beats her daughter with the jockstrap to discourage her attraction to male genitalia. By the end of the scene, Meghan was heaving with rage. She hurled the jockstrap at Charles, who was cowering on the floor, and exited to an enormous round of applause. The scene was both hilarious and terrifying because Meghan brought such electric, Medea-like intensity to each moment. I wondered how the rest of the show would play after this tour de force, but each subsequent scene got substantial laughs.

As usual for our Limbo shows, there was no furniture, allowing for swift movement from scene to scene. The staging was simple and clean, punctuated by a few truly cheap theatrical touches to recreate film effects. When Gidget finally goes surfing with the boys for the first time, I wanted to suggest a phony montage shot in the studio. The lights come up on four guys facing the audience, miming a struggle to keep their balance riding a big wave, while Gidget jumps from one board to the next, dancing and joyously clowning, nearly causing a few wipeouts. There were no surfboards, but two downstage groundrow units made of foam core board that Brian painted with blue and white swirls masked the surfers' feet. He mounted circular cutouts with a target pattern on each unit, which were spun around by actors hiding behind them. They simultaneously suggested the movement of the waves and a mind spiraling out of control. I underscored the scene with the relentlessly absurd 1950s' doo-wop tune "Rama Lama Ding Dong" by the Edsels. Another moment of physical business that elicited a huge response from the audience was a fight scene between Moondoggie and Kahoona. As they both throw punches, Gidget steps between them and is knocked out. I staged it all in slow motion and scored it with descending chords of strings lifted from the Bernard Herrmann score to *Psycho*. We were turning it into a living movie. We didn't need a falling chandelier to get a big response from our East Village audiences. They loved these crude, theatrical recreations of classic film devices like montage and slow motion.

The thunderous response to the sold-out late-night performances of *Gidget Goes Psychotic* at the Limbo was even more intense than it had been for *Pardon My Inquisition*. Once again, I started thinking about the possibility of a commercial transfer. The Mets won the World Series, so why couldn't we have another Off-Broadway hit? This time I would not make the mistake of introducing a new show into rep with *Vampire Lesbians*. I would finally replace all the remaining original cast members and open *Gidget* at a separate theatre. After checking out various available Off-Broadway houses, I decided the only affordable option was the Players

Theatre. Not only was it cheap, but it had the additional advantage of a MacDougal Street address just blocks away from the Provincetown Playhouse. Theatre-in-Limbo would own the street!

The Players

The Players Theatre was a rarely booked house almost as dilapidated as the Provincetown. The auditorium was long and very narrow, with a claustrophobically low ceiling. This created a tunnel effect from the back of the house that made the postage-stamp-sized stage appear to be even smaller than it was. Like most Off-Broadway houses, it was a converted space, originally a stable for New York's mounted police and later a garage. It was owned and operated by Donald H. Goldman, who had acquired it in 1958 as a home for Shakespearewrights, the classical acting company he ran. Mr. Goldman was a quiet, dignified, owlish gentleman with very thick glasses and a mildly pained expression. He had an unusually formal manner for an Off-Broadway impresario (he always called me "Mr. Elliott," and I always called him "Mr. Goldman"). He almost always wore a slightly threadbare gray suit with a white shirt and a dark tie. He had an air of resigned weariness, and he seemed quite old to me at the time—but he was positively youthful next to the cadaverous house staff. The usher had a thick head of pure white hair offset by his bright red gin blossoms and the deepest creases I had ever seen on a human face. He wore a black polyester suit that sorely needed dry cleaning, and he always appeared to be mildly, benignly soused. The house manager was a little younger, but he had had his larynx removed and spoke through a hand-held device that he placed on his neck. I worried that they would spoil the cool, East Village cachet of our show (and felt guilty for worrying about it), and wished we could bring back Marie-Lohr in her black leather jacket to greet our patrons.

I can't imagine that Mr. Goldman's dark, dusty office, located backstage at the top of the steps, had changed much since 1958. A black rotary phone sat on his cluttered mahogany desk, and yellowing Shakespearewrights posters lined the walls. I didn't realize that his company had been a real Off-Broadway force in the 1950s, rivaling Joseph Papp's New York Shakespeare Festival. Brooks Atkinson described them as "a young, healthy company with vigorous voices and shattering vitality."[7] They received rave reviews beginning in 1954 for productions of *Twelfth Night*, *Julius Caesar*, and *Macbeth*, among others. Their company included some notable actors, such as the young Pernell Roberts, M'el Dowd, and Lester Rawlins. That was all in the distant past by the time I approached Mr. Goldman about booking his theatre. Nothing about the premises bespoke vitality, but the price was right, and Brian thought he could jazz up the curb appeal by painting his blue and white hypnotic swirls on the dowdy lobby walls.

One nagging question troubled me, and I wanted to get it sorted out before I committed myself to raising money and giving Mr. Goldman a deposit. I was worried that we might be sued by Columbia Pictures, which owned the rights to the *Gidget* movies, for copyright infringement. The original 1959 theatrical release, based on a 1957 novel by Frederick Kohner (*Gidget, the Little Girl with Big Ideas*), had been successful enough to generate two sequels: *Gidget Goes Hawaiian* (1961) and *Gidget Goes to Rome* (1963). The 1965 television series starring Sally Field lasted only one season, but it was fondly remembered by lots of Boomers. Charles took the names of many of the characters directly from either the film or the series (Gidget, Larue, Moondoggie, the Big Kahoona, Stinky), and of course the title *Gidget Goes Psychotic* was a direct parody of the two sequel titles. It's not easy to come up with a title that never fails to get a laugh, and I couldn't bear the idea of changing it, so I hired an attorney with expertise in copyright law to study the issue and provide an opinion letter. He vigorously argued that we had every right to use the *Gidget* characters for satirical purposes, but he added that Columbia Pictures might well sue us anyway. That was all I needed to hear. Despite the fact that our attorney seemed to relish the idea of taking on a major motion picture studio and thought we would have an excellent chance of winning the lawsuit, Charles and I reluctantly decided that we would change the title.

It was relatively easy to switch out the character names. Gidget Lawrence became Chicklet Forest ("I've always been so darn skinny, a stick, a shrimp, so when other girls turned into gorgeous chicks, I became a chicklet.").[8] Moondoggie, Kahoona, Larue, and Stinky became Starcat, Kanaka, Berdine, and Provoloney. Changing the title, however, was agonizing. We wracked our brains trying to come up with a pithy alternative, but inspiration did not strike. Finally, we made indecision a virtue by announcing a "Name That Play" contest. Charles concocted a plaintively cute letter that we sent to our mailing list: "I'm in a tight spot and I need your 'input,'" he wrote. "The powers that be don't like us using the name 'Gidget.' I think they're wrong, but to avoid hassle I'm on the lookout for a new title." The David versus Goliath implications of this contest piqued the interest of the press, and Enid Nemy ran it in her Friday "Broadway" column in the

New York Times. The prize for the best title was $300 and a hamburger with Charles after the show. We got some promising responses such as *Pygtalion*, *Screaming Bikinis*, and *Attack of the Psychotic Surfer*, but none of them was quite right. Charles finally came up with *Psycho Beach Party* on his own, but we had to announce a winner, so we invented the fictitious Betty Stahl of Newburgh, New York. Thankfully, the fact-checkers at the *Times* weren't too concerned with this item, which ran on June 26, 1987.

I capitalized *Psycho Beach Party* at $150,000—almost three times what was spent on *Vampire Lesbians* just two years earlier. This was still low budget by Off-Broadway standards, but it at least included a reserve fund that would allow us to survive for a few weeks if we didn't get brilliant reviews. I hadn't met any rich theatrical angels in the two years since producing *Vampire Lesbians*, so raising the money was a time-consuming slog. Jerry Davis once again partnered with me as co-producer, and Julie Halston raised some money and signed on as an associate producer. By the time the show was capitalized, we had more than seventy investors. In addition to Charles and me, several of the actors invested in the show, as did Brian Whitehill, the company manager (Terry Byrne), the press agents (Pete Sanders and Shirley Herz), and the accountant (Robert Freedman).[9] To have this kind of support from members of the company gave the production a genuine feeling of family. We were all in it together, and we were confident that lightning could strike twice.

A number of upgrades and changes to the production needed to be made for the commercial transfer. The music I had selected for *Gidget Goes Psychotic* was a mix of buoyant early 1960s pop tunes and film underscoring that I lifted from soundtrack LPs, and not all of it was going to work for the new production. In an intimate scene with Gidget, Arnie Kolodner as Moondoggie had lip-synched to a corny love song, taken from the soundtrack of the *Gidget* film, that included the refrain, "Gidget's the girl for me . . . ." In the middle of the number, I had the sound cue mixed to repeat itself like a needle stuck on a record. The needle was carelessly yanked off the record with a scratching sound while Arnie obliviously continued to silently mouth the words until Charles nudged him in the ribs and glared at the stage manager in the booth, forcing Moondoggie to say, "I guess I'll have to *tell* you how I feel." It was a nice metatheatrical moment that pointed up the phoniness of clichéd Hollywood love scenes and called attention to the theatrical device being used, but Gidget's name was in the lyric, so it would have to be changed. I wrote the lyrics for a parody version, with music by Tom Kochan. I had always served as my own sound designer for our shows, but Tom convinced me that I should replace all the incidental music in *Psycho Beach Party*. He wrote a superb original score that included multiple themes. I kept some of the pop tunes, though. I couldn't let go of "Rama Lama Ding Dong."

The physical production got an overhaul as well. The costumes needed to be bumped up a notch, and I really wanted John Glaser to do them. Bobby Locke had been very kind to pull together the costumes for the Limbo production, but they were a little bland and too realistic. I felt terrible about firing Bobby, especially since he was still working for me as the wardrobe master for *Vampire Lesbians*. It was an unbearably painful scene when he came to our apartment to get the news. He desperately wanted the job, and tears started to well up in his eyes as I was hemming and hawing. I tried to ameliorate the situation by promising him I would hire him to design a future show that was more suited to his talents. Not only was he gracious, but he asked to be the wardrobe supervisor for *Psycho Beach Party*. John's costumes did not disappoint; they were eye-popping, colorful, outrageous, highly theatrical, and, thanks to some discreet sequins, they sparkled. Brian's scenic upgrade for the Players Theatre maintained consistency with the look of *Vampire Lesbians* at the Provincetown, but added an early 1960s gloss. Once again, he created a proscenium arch of found objects, this time of items that had associations with teenage girls of the early 1960s, like princess phones, curlers, and 45 rpm records, all vacuformed with a light-gray, pearlized plastic. Like *Vampire Lesbians*, the show curtain was emblazoned with the logos of other Theatre-in-Limbo shows, but Brian added a chiffon overlay redolent of classic television variety shows. The otherwise empty stage was framed by a series of hard portals painted with snappy electric yellow and lavender hypnotic swirls and backed by the hot pink and white Rorschach drop.

Before we could get going with *Psycho Beach Party*, I had to figure out how to replace Charles in *Vampire Lesbians*. I had gradually been replacing the other original cast members, but Charles was a special case. The drag persona he had developed was so idiosyncratic, with its complex blend of film and stage references, that it was more an embodiment of a sensibility than acting in any traditional sense. I wondered if there were another actor in New York who could pull it off without upsetting the balance of the show—and if there were, how could I find him? During the nearly two years that he had played the show, Charles had taken very little time off, although Tom Aulino had filled in for him when Charles took a trip to Florida. (Charles bragged when he returned from his Key West vacation that he was whiter than when he left.) Tom had a very different take on the role, but he understood the style, he knew how to get the laughs, and he had been a part of the company from the beginning, so he was able to fit in seamlessly. But he had another job offer, and he wasn't interested in taking over the role permanently. We considered some East Village club performers, but we worried that they lacked the discipline to play eight shows a week, and they weren't really right for the part anyway. It was turning into the search for Scarlett O'Hara, and we weren't coming up with any real options.

I turned to casting directors Stuart Howard and Amy Schecter, who had some experience with drag performance, having cast *La Cage aux Folles* on Broadway. They assured me that they could find someone for the part—and they did. After days of auditions and many callbacks, we were finally able to cast David Drake, who later became known for his one-man show, *The Night Larry Kramer Kissed Me*. He carefully studied Charles's every gesture and inflection and managed to give a credible performance after a cruelly brief rehearsal period. Eventually he made the part his own and demonstrated genuine charisma.

But replacing actors in a long-running show is an unnerving process. If you get it wrong, the show changes irrevocably, the emphasis shifts, laughs disappear. We had developed an efficient, four-day routine for putting in replacements—but efficiency isn't always a virtue in the theatre. Each new actor watched the show and took notes on Tuesday and was then taught the blocking by the stage manager working with the understudies on Wednesday. On Thursday, I would come in for an afternoon of scene work and notes. Friday afternoon there would be a "put-in" rehearsal with lights, sound, and costumes, and that night they would be on. One night, well into the run, I showed up at the theatre to take notes, and I was distressed by the desultory performance. The words were all there, the blocking looked familiar, but it wasn't remotely the same show we had performed at the Limbo Lounge. The style was all wrong. Some actors were pushing; others seemed to be walking through it. The staging was larded with calcified comic bits and choreographed double takes. And there were times when the cast didn't seem to understand what they were saying, but were just delivering a coarse imitation of their predecessors—and it wasn't their fault. The chore of maintaining *Vampire Lesbians* after nearly two years had become a bore, and I had gotten lazy about it. As I sank lower in my seat in the back of the house, I realized that none of the actors onstage had ever actually rehearsed with each other. I called a full company rehearsal the next day, but it was difficult to create an ensemble from a company of actors who had each been "put-in" separately. It was a hard lesson in the discipline it takes to maintain a long-running show.

We were in the midst of preproduction for *Psycho Beach Party* when Charles and I were both stunned by a front-page headline in the *New York Times*: "Charles Ludlam, 44, Avant-Garde Artist of the Theater, Is Dead."[10] By 1987, AIDS was everywhere, and dozens of our friends and colleagues were among the thousands of New Yorkers who were sick, but Ludlam's death was shockingly abrupt. He was at the peak of his career. I had seen him perform in his brilliant and hilarious play, *The Artificial Jungle*, just a few months earlier, and it seemed only a few weeks earlier that Charles Busch and I had run into him and his partner, Everett Quinton, at McBell's. The lead paragraph of the obituary ironically emphasized that Ludlam "seemed to be on the verge of breaking into the mainstream of American culture," as if that were something to be desired, when part of what made him great was his rejection of the mainstream. Charles, Julie Halston, and I attended the funeral at St. Joseph's Church the next morning. As we walked across Sheridan Square toward Sixth Avenue, we were overwhelmed by the floral tributes and lighted candles on the sidewalk outside the Ridiculous Theatrical Company. A dozen or so people were standing nearby, tears streaming down their faces. The church was packed with friends, fans, and colleagues from the downtown theatre scene. More than a few of the mourners appeared to be deathly ill themselves. The formal Catholic funeral mass was appropriately theatrical from the first strains of the organ as his coffin was carried down the aisle to the traditional hymn, "Our God, Our Help in Ages Past." Leon Katz delivered a moving eulogy, which he concluded by quoting Nanine's final farewell from Ludlam's adaptation of *Camille*: "Toodle-oo, Marguerite."[11] There was a collective sob in the sanctuary.

The Theatre-in-Limbo family was already affected by AIDS as well. Jeff Veazey had been diagnosed when he collapsed after a performance with his dance partner, Susan Stroman, in Las Vegas at the MGM Grand in August 1986. Neither he nor Susan had any idea that he was HIV positive. "We were blaming everything on that Las Vegas air," she later recalled.[12] Fortunately for Jeff, he was diagnosed on the same day that the drug AZT

The façade of the Players Theatre on busy MacDougal Street during the run of Psycho Beach Party. Photo by B. T. Whitehill.

was released. He kept his diagnosis a secret for as long as he could because he wanted to work, and producers were unlikely to hire a dancer with AIDS. He worked hard to keep himself healthy, and initially he responded well to AZT, despite its toxicity. Eventually he even became a motivational speaker for the Gay Men's Health Crisis, discussing what it was like to be a person with AIDS. But by the time we started rehearsals at the end of June he was very thin and gaunt, and I was worried that he wouldn't be able to do the show. He threw himself into the process with his customary tough, chorus boy demeanor undiminished, however; he expanded the number and supervised new dance arrangements. "Try it again, fatso," he snapped at Bobby Carey after a sloppy run-through. Bobby, who had recently picked up a few pounds, was "plucked" by that remark; he was used to having his body admired. He went on a diet immediately after that rehearsal.

Leftovers

Previews went smoothly, and audiences were responding well to the show, but the reviews in the daily papers the day after we opened were what one might call "mixed positive," with an emphasis on mixed. Howard Kissel's tepid notice in the *Daily News* bore the headline "Leftovers Again?" He admitted the show had "virtues," but he was simply bored by the whole idea of another "spoof of Hollywood."[13] Kissel was a rave compared to Clive Barnes in the *New York Post*, who observed under the banner headline "Beach Party Washout," "everyone around me seemed to be having a wild and wonderful time. I was not."[14] Both Kissel and Barnes were straight men who didn't relate to the camp humor, so we took some solace in the all-important *Times* review by a gay critic, Stephen Holden, who called it "a comic trash compactor of a play that takes an already silly genre—early 1960s surf and beach blanket movies—and sends it to camp heaven." Compared to *Vampire Lesbians*, Holden felt that *Psycho Beach Party* was "solidly constructed," with an "amusing plot premise" that "gleefully defies logic as it subverts clean-cut Hollywood stereotypes." While he admired Charles's performance as Chicklet (it had "an aura of cheerful, poker-faced clownishness"), he was ecstatic about Meghan's evocation of Joan Crawford, calling it "the production's coup de théâtre," asserting that she "steals the show."[15] Charles wasn't amused by that.

The meeting at the ad agency the next day was far from euphoric. Holden's review was positive without being enthusiastic, and it was virtually impossible to pull an effective endorsement from it. Quotes like "solidly constructed" and "amusing" don't set the box office on fire. And he qualified it all in his closing paragraph with a familiar comparison to the recently deceased Ludlam: "If Mr. Busch's brand of camp theater has grown in craft, it still lacks the high style and classical aspiration of Charles Ludlam's theatre of the ridiculous." He ended his review with a back-handed compliment, noting that *Psycho Beach Party* "revels in trash for trash's sake." This sentiment was echoed by Barnes's somewhat cruder (and meaner) analysis of what he viewed as the apparent binary opposition of Busch and Ludlam: "Well, it's the difference between processed cheese and Stilton, between diet Pepsi and Dom Perignon, between spoof and satire, between camp and art." There were plenty of other critics who found Busch "less profound" and less intellectual than Ludlam because his work wasn't steeped in classical literature and theatre history. The implication of these snobbish observations is that Busch should learn his lesson from Ludlam and start boning up on the classics, an absurd idea that Ludlam himself would have rejected, considering that cultural "trash" is a primary subject of Pop Art and Ridiculous Theatre.

We got some better news as other reviews started to trickle in, although most of them were at least mildly condescending, emphasizing the play's complete "silliness." Almost all of these critics were middle-aged men, but two prominent female critics were able to look beyond the silliness on the surface. Writing in *The New Yorker*, Mimi Kramer observed that unlike most drag theatre, *Psycho Beach Party* is not misogynist; rather, it "uses cross-dressing to send up the mores and assumptions of heterosexual behavior."[16] Laurie Stone provided a very perceptive feminist analysis of the play in her *Village Voice* review:

> In Busch's art, to go from boy to girl or girl to boy is not an arduous climb or a decadent fall but a pass through a door inside the self. . . . Busch's art has passed through anxiety. He can say anything, imagine anything, and not despise himself for it. This unembittered acceptance is the key to his radicalism, allowing him to venture bravely into his fantasies without minimizing their scariness.[17]

Charles was thrilled that Stone looked past all the clichés about drag, camp, and trash to pinpoint so accurately the underlying essence of what all his performances were about.

Hope Springs Eternal

Despite the smattering of good reviews, business remained so-so at best during the weeks after we opened, and I grimly pursued every avenue I could think of to promote the show. When our press agent, Pete Sanders, called to tell me that Frank Rich, then chief theatre critic of the *New York Times*, would be attending the Sunday evening performance on August 9, the frisson was intense and physical, like being on a roller coaster approaching the highest peak. Rich was far from universally beloved among theatre people (some called him the "butcher of Broadway"), but his prose was so intelligent and vigorous, and he wrote with such genuine passion, that when he loved a show his endorsement was like a ringing command to go see it. This was our chance! I got on the phone to discreetly paper the house, which is always a risky proposition since you can never predict how people who have been given free tickets will respond. Some recipients of this largesse feel it is their duty to be boisterous and spoil the jokes by laughing at the setups, while others, having no stake in proceedings, sit on their hands. But I wanted the house to be full that night, and it was. I was too nervous to watch the show, but I couldn't tear myself away either, so I paced in the lobby listening for laughs. I peeked in from time to time, and to my extreme relief the performance was solid and the audience was laughing in all the right places. Charles and I were elated as we walked over to McBell's for supper after the show. It couldn't have gone better, and we were convinced that Rich would love it.

We checked the paper every morning, but nothing appeared all week. We tried to read the tea leaves. What could it mean? Our answer came on Friday, August 14, when Rich delivered a stinging jeremiad over the airwaves during his theatre roundup on WQXR, the *Times* radio station:

> Mr. Busch has the tight, limited range of a one-note night-club
> stand-up comic. . . . The jokes are pedantic and utilitarian rather
> than inspired. . . . Nor are the other performers particularly funny. . . .
> The direction by Kenneth Elliott is also amateurish, generally
> requiring the performers to line up in a neat row to recite their lines.[18]

We were stunned by this rebuke. Pete Sanders had the comforting air of a funeral director when he urged us to look on the bright side. After all, it was only on the radio. He hadn't panned it in the *Times*.

Not, that is, until the following Thursday's "Critics' Notebook," where Rich expanded on the points he had made on the air. I was stunned to read that he interpreted our lighthearted romp as a polemical attack on "heterosexual oppression." That sounded like box office poison to me. He identified "the didactic gay-liberation dialogue" along with "the perfunctory drag impersonations" as the source of this attack.[19] I puzzled over how "perfunctory drag" could be considered an attack of any kind, but I was even more mystified by the accusation of didacticism. Only one short speech in the entire play had anything to do with liberation politics, and it occurred in the denouement when Yo-Yo and Provoloney come out to their astonished friends at the luau. Charles thought it was funny for a knuckleheaded, early 1960s beach bum to anachronistically spout politically correct gay rights rhetoric. Bobby Carey delivered the lines awkwardly, but with passion and a raised fist:

> I've read all about the persecution of homosexuals, how in big cities,
> bars are raided and innocent people arrested, their lives ruined.
> But someday, someday we're going to fight back and the laws will
> be changed, and our brothers and sisters will march down the main
> streets of America shouting that we are proud to be who we are![20]

At the end of the speech the entire company sighed, as if to say, "Isn't that sweet?" In context, the speech is a comic reversal: an airhead transforms into a prescient political activist. But it was not a bald statement of authorial intent. Theatre-in-Limbo didn't do agitprop. To add insult to injury, Rich included yet another familiar disparaging comparison:

> Charles Ludlam, a true deadpan artist, never made his characters spell out authorial themes, and that's why his inversions of old movie genres, like last season's "Artificial Jungle," got the subversive laughs that elude Mr. Busch.[21]

By this time, Charles and I were growing inured to the mention of Ludlam's exalted status, but the bit about the laughs really hurt. And considering that our carefully handpicked audience had laughed appropriately in all the right places, I thought it would have been more accurate to say that the laughs eluded Mr. Rich.

In high dudgeon (and possibly a state of temporary derangement), I wrote Frank Rich an indignant letter and made a point of copying his boss, Arthur Gelb. I accused Rich of not getting his "facts straight," a tactic I assumed would be more effective than disputing his low opinion of the show. In the "Critic's Notebook," Rich had stated that "In 'Psycho Beach Party,' the beach boys frequently reveal themselves to be gay." Aha! That word "frequently" was not precisely correct. I righteously pointed out that "there are only two gay characters out of a cast of twelve. They fall in love with each other and reveal it ONCE," not frequently. Rich had gone on to claim "the girls who stuff the wild bikinis are often played by boys." Often? Not true, I argued, "only two of the six female roles are played by men." How could he call that "often"? I scolded him for "misstating these facts" and giving "the impression that PSYCHO BEACH PARTY is a gay propaganda play, which it is not." In the next paragraph, I officiously explained that "neither Mr. Busch nor I are concerned with or interested in the subject of 'heterosexual oppression.' The main theme of the play is much simpler: things aren't what they seem to be."[22] That was a respectable theme that *Psycho Beach Party* could share with classic comedies through the centuries, from *Twelfth Night* to *The Importance of Being Earnest*.

Rereading my argument today makes me cringe. While it is true that the main plot has nothing to do with liberation politics, the subtext of the entire play obviously *is* an "attack on heterosexual oppression." Chicklet, Mrs. Forest, Kanaka, Provoloney, and Yo-Yo attempt to project an identity that conforms to the normative ideal of the period but is completely at odds with who they really are. They each conceal a sexual secret, and they either choose to come out or they are publicly outed. These secrets are the source of the play's tension, and once they are revealed, equilibrium is restored. Freed from the shackles of the dominant, heterosexual culture, these characters can live happy lives without the burden of presenting a false, but culturally acceptable identity. This theme may not have been overtly or didactically expressed, but it was embedded in the action of the play.

As soon as I mailed the letter, I was terrified that I had made a huge mistake and that by complaining to Frank Rich I had doomed my theatre career. A couple of weeks later, my heart leapt when I opened our mailbox and discovered a letter to me from the *New York Times*, with Rich's name typed above the familiar *Times* logo in the return address. Not surprisingly, he stood by his account, adding that he thought my reading of his piece was "a bit humorless." I wasn't sure how he expected me to find humor in a devastating pan, and it rankled that he also suggested my explanation of the "main theme" was "a bit disingenuous."[23] I realize now that it rankled because it was true. I was in denial because I did not want *Psycho Beach Party* to be pigeonholed as a gay play—I wanted a mainstream success. Rich ended his letter on a kind note, and I was grateful for that. Perhaps my career wasn't over after all. But my internalized homophobic paranoia was further exacerbated around this time when Pete Sanders convinced *People* magazine to do a feature on the show. I was thrilled about this potential break until I learned that they were only interested in doing the story if they could out Charles and me. The writer wanted to include a relatively innocuous phrase, something like "They're just roommates, not lovers." Amazingly, neither of us would agree to that, a position that seems, in retrospect, at least "a bit disingenuous." Who did we think we were fooling? And yet, ten years before Ellen DeGeneres came out as a lesbian on her sitcom, it was still considered a bad career move to be publicly identified as gay.

By the fall of 1987, the casts of both of our shows needed something to boost their morale. Andy and Meghan came up with a plan to get everyone from both shows together for a celebratory soiree: "The First Annual Theatre-in-Limbo Peoples' Choice Awards, brought to you live from Mc-Bell's." The mock ceremony was co-hosted with campy flair by Jeff Veazey and Julie Halston. *Everyone* got an award from "The Academy of Limbo Arts and Sciences," and Charles composed a poem for the occasion honoring the *Vampire Lesbians* replacement cast that began,

Let's pay tribute to those at 133 MacDougal
In terms rapturous, and not the least bit frugal.
This group is divine from top to bottom,
The cast and crew of *Vampire Lesbians of Sodom*.[24]

There were lots of laughs, the standing ovations were as free-flowing as the drinks, and everyone left in a buoyant mood. It was a perfect metatheatrical celebration of our fantasy theatre. The very next day, October 19, 1987, was later known as "Black Monday," when the stock market unexpectedly crashed.

Public Diversion

With two shows running, I had to move my management office out of our kitchen. Two company managers working on payroll was too intrusive while Charles was eating his shredded wheat, so I rented studio space on Fourth Street, just off MacDougal, around the corner from both shows. It was fun to have two shows running just blocks from each other, but it was also a constant worry. *Psycho Beach Party* kept going, but it never made money. The marginality of the play's success affected the morale backstage, and the result was lots of squabbling among the actors, who were confined to very cramped, poorly ventilated dressing rooms at the Players. Meghan's imperiously condescending attitude, which Charles and I found amusing, was the source of some of the resentment. Less than six months after we opened, I had to start replacing actors, some of whom gave notice primarily because of the toxic backstage atmosphere.

I was sitting in my office one sunny afternoon in April 1988, poring over numbers with company manager Terry Byrne, anxiously trying to figure out how to cut *Psycho Beach Party* expenses to keep the show running, when I received a phone call from Joseph Papp. With much fanfare, he had attended a performance of *Psycho Beach Party* a few weeks earlier, and he had hired me to direct a reading of a new musical that was in development at the Public. But I was surprised to hear from him and even more surprised to hear why. "I have a show called *Zero Positive* by Harry Kondoleon," he said. I told him that I had heard of it and would love to see it. "You can't," was his immediate reply. "I've closed it. We unfortunately had to replace the leading actor and the director. Would you be interested in directing it?" I asked if I could read it first. "I'll send it over now. Call me as soon as you've read it." It arrived by messenger within the hour, and I read it immediately. The subject was AIDS, although that acronym was never mentioned in the play. It was not a documentary examination of its devastation of individual lives, like *As Is*, nor was it a polemical, agenda-driven drama, like *The Normal Heart*. It was more of a highly stylized meditation on confronting death. It had lots of witty, arch, and rather ornate dialogue that bordered on camp, and the final scene was a mock Greek tragedy play-within-the-play in the high Ridiculous style that was campy in the extreme. But the plot took very strange, seemingly arbitrary turns, and the ending was mystifying. I was reticent when I called Mr. Papp back. I told him that I enjoyed reading the script but had to confess that I didn't understand it. I've never forgotten his succinct reply: "You don't have to understand it. You just have to direct it." How could I argue with that? He asked me to come to his office the next day to get started.

"A classic in the theatre horror story genre: Firing an Actor" is how Alex Witchel described the machinations that led to the *Zero Positive* hiatus in her "Inside Theater" column for the magazine *Seven Days*.[25] Most features about theatre productions up to this time were puff pieces with flattering interviews that any press agent would love, but Witchel was pioneering a new, hard-hitting approach to theatre reporting that was not afraid to examine the ugly side of show business by quoting unnamed inside "sources." She tracked the saga from the first rehearsal, where "Kondoleon passed [director Mark Linn-] Baker a note about lead actor Reed Birney that said, 'Reed's perfect,'" to the previews where one of her sources observed that "Harry suddenly couldn't stand a gesture Reed made or a word he said." Another unidentified wag claimed that that Baker "couldn't control the actors." The real problem was that early preview audiences did not like the play, and Harry was panicking. According to Witchel's account, "Kondoleon implored Papp to attend one of the previews. Papp did, and Baker made what others considered a lethal mistake by skipping that show, saying he didn't feel well." Kondoleon persuaded Papp that it was Birney's performance—not the play—that was the problem, but "Baker balked" when he was informed that Birney would be fired. Another source explained that the director's departure was due to "a power struggle with Joe he couldn't possibly win. So he quit before he was fired." It was an ugly situation, and Witchel described it vividly.

Aside from Birney, the rest of the company (an excellent cast that included Frances Conroy and Tony Shalhoub) was still under contract, and they were all in various states of shock. A few of them were visibly angry about what had happened. They had rehearsed for four weeks under Mark Linn-Baker's direction and had played a week of previews before the axe came down. Audiences had started to respond more favorably by the end of the week, and Birney later told me that he had no idea he was going to be fired when he got a call on Monday from Barbara Carroll, Mr. Papp's executive assistant, asking him to come in for a meeting at 5 p.m. At that meeting, Mr. Papp simply explained that "Harry is very unhappy with your work." When Birney asked him why, Papp cryptically replied, "You'll have to ask Harry."[26]

There was to be a hiatus of two weeks for rehearsal and to work in David Pierce (later known as David Hyde Pierce), the replacement who, with great efficiency, had already been hired. (Witchel reported that Papp had gotten him out of jury duty.) Two more full weeks of previews would follow before the press was invited. When I arrived at his office on Tuesday morning, Mr. Papp surprised me by explaining that he thought it best that he direct the play and run rehearsals for a few days. I was to sit in the back of the house observing like a voyeur, which was an unnerving and awkward situation. I watched him try various improvisational techniques to elicit performances from the actors, and they responded gamely for the most part, but there was a sense of treading water. Finally, Mr. Papp seemed to tire of these exercises, and he handed the reins over to me.

The first read-through was so slow, quiet, and mournful that my immediate impulse was to lighten the tone and play against the self-pitying responses of the two main characters, Samantha and Himmer, to the news that they had tested seropositive, or "zero positive" as Himmer pronounces it, "the zero for the infinite nothingness and the plus sign like the cross on a grave."[27] I did not realize at the time that Harry himself had recently been diagnosed as HIV positive. He died of AIDS in 1994 at the age of thirty-nine. I restaged much of the show and encouraged the actors to pick up the pace. I worked in some ironically upbeat incidental music. I convinced the costume designer, Susan Hilferty, to perk up Franny Conroy's look. Her original costume was rather dowdy, but I wanted Samantha to have a chic, self-possessed, East Village sense of style—like Meghan. Susan, Franny, and I went shopping together at various East Village boutiques, and initially we went too far. When Franny made her first entrance in costume she looked like a psychedelic Christmas tree (we toned it down the next day). But I felt I was making some important changes that would highlight the comedy that was undeniably present in the script, despite its grim subject matter.

Harry and I got on famously during the rehearsal period. He took me to his favorite Indian restaurant on East Sixth Street, and we had a fun evening of laughs and gossip. At rehearsal, he seemed to be all in favor of the radical changes I was making, sitting in the house chuckling at the clever lines now being delivered in the manner of a Noël Coward comedy. As soon as previews resumed, however, his attitude changed. Lines that he expected to get laughs didn't get them, at least not consistently. Just as before, the Public Theater subscription audiences did not love the play. I was still rehearsing and making adjustments, but Harry was impatient. In midnight phone calls to some of the actors, he urged them to ignore my direction and go back to the old line readings. Eventually, he called casting director Rosemarie Tichler and others on the staff to complain. Naturally, this intrigue finally made its way to Mr. Papp, who called a company meeting after the matinee on Saturday, May 14. History seemed to be repeating itself, but I made certain that I didn't miss that matinee.

That afternoon I arrived at the lobby of the Public during the intermission, where Mr. Papp was having an animated conversation with several patrons. He was smiling, even laughing. That was encouraging. When he saw me, he walked over, cheerfully patted me on the back, and said, "It's going very well." I wondered if that meant I was about to be fired. I sat through the second act and then waited for the cast to gather in the auditorium. When everyone was present, Mr. Papp entered to address the cast, followed by Harry, who glanced at me with an ambiguous smile. Mr. Papp acknowledged that Harry's telephone whispering campaign was the reason for the meeting. He said that he was sympathetic to the playwright's concerns, and that he knew the play was complex and difficult. He said that he had seen real progress, however, and congratulated the actors on their hard work. Then came the pronouncement: "Therefore, I am putting my full faith in the director, and the playwright is banned from the theatre until opening night." And with that, the cast applauded, and the meeting was over. If Mr. Papp weren't already my hero, he was from that moment forward. Harry approached me after the meeting and casually said, "It really was a very good matinee." Despite my relief, I was still resentful of the tempest in a teapot he had created, so I just curtly said "thank you" through clenched teeth. Mr. Papp was in a great mood, and he and his wife, Gail, graciously took Harry and me out for an early dinner. Harry had a marvelous time telling charming, witty anecdotes over drinks, laughing heartily. I was less ebullient, and I probably even glowered from time to time. As we were walking out of the restaurant, Mr. Papp said to me outside of Harry's earshot, "It really is an extraordinary play, isn't it?" That's what it was all about for him. He loved the play, and he wanted the playwright to be pleased—and he had the power to do anything to achieve that end.

The very next day, half of my MacDougal Street empire collapsed when I had to close *Psycho Beach Party*. It had a respectable run (16 previews, 344 performances), but it lost its entire investment. The day after that, on Monday evening, we held a memorial service in the Provincetown Playhouse for Jeff Veazey, who had died of complications from AIDS a few weeks earlier on Easter morning. He had been thirty-three years old, and *Psycho Beach Party* was his last work as a choreographer. We rented some high-end video equipment for the service, which was organized and led by Susan Stroman. Eulogies and tributes alternated with video clips of Jeff. We saw his choreography and his spectacular dancing, and we saw him discuss his work with GMHC and how he dealt so positively with being a person with AIDS. We even saw him in drag doing a spot-on impersonation of Carol Channing. Jeff's panel for the AIDS Memorial Quilt was displayed in the lobby. The staging of memorial services was becoming an art form during these years, especially among theatre people. Susan did a beautiful job with Jeff's, and it was devastating to sit through it.

I had the luxury of continuing to work on *Zero Positive* without Harry's interference through another week of previews before the press performances began. But Harry wasn't the only one interfering. One night after a preview, while I was downstairs in the dressing room giving some notes to the actors, I was summoned to the empty auditorium of the LuEsther Theater, where Mr. Papp was sitting with Rosemarie Tichler. My heart stopped when he told me that he had identified the remaining problem with the production: the performance of Edward (Teddy) Atienza as Himmer's father. "He's not believable as a father. He's too airy, too light, too sylph-like," he explained with a gesture that made it clear that these were all euphemisms for "too gay." Rosemarie chuckled quietly, but didn't say anything as Mr. Papp announced a proposed solution: fire Teddy, recast the part, and go back into rehearsal again. After a beat of stunned silence, I begged him to let me work with Teddy. I assured him that I could make the appropriate adjustments, and Mr. Papp relented. At rehearsal the next day, Teddy was furious when he pressed me to explain why he had been called in for private coaching, but he agreed to butch it up at some key moments, and the issue blew over. I later suspected that the whole thing was a strategy of Mr. Papp's to get the changes he wanted.

Two Sundays before we opened, a huge story on the production appeared in the *New York Times* "Arts and Leisure" section, covering more than half of the first theater page and continuing for nearly another half-page later in the section. I was amazed that this little play got so much press, but Harry, who had won numerous awards and honors for his playwriting, including an Obie, was very hot at the time. Like Witchel's *Seven Days* piece, this article focused more on the backstage drama than on the play itself. In it, Harry gave a brutally candid interview regarding the firing of Reed Birney: "We'd made an error. I felt we had to correct it. There was a consensus to wait a little longer. My answer was 'N-O.'" He was unremorseful about his role: "I'm not blood-happy. I've never done this before. But playwrights have a lot of rights, you know. I exercised them."[28] The article was accompanied by a staged photo of David Pierce and me rehearsing a scene with Harry in the background, peering at us from behind a pillar, which perfectly captured the tensions. *Zero Positive* was my first professional directing gig outside of my own company, and I couldn't help but reflect on what an unsettling experience it had been, so different from the joy that I always felt working on a Theatre-in-Limbo show.

Meghan was to be my date for opening night, but she didn't show up. I waited for her in the lobby of the Public Theater until the last possible moment. It was very unlike her, and I was disappointed because I wanted her to see how I had attempted to model Franny Conroy's character after her. The next morning the reviews were mixed but respectful for the play, but mostly positive for the actors and the production, including Frank Rich in the *Times*. I was delighted that my epistolary rant seemed to have had no effect on his review. But my relief was tempered by the fact that I still hadn't heard from Meghan after leaving several messages on her answering machine. I soon found out she was in Lenox Hill Hospital with pneumonia. When Charles, Bobby, and I went up to visit her, she was in good spirits, but very cagey about what was wrong. Bobby told us on the way out that he had gotten a look at her chart and had checked out the medicines she was taking. He was sure she had AIDS.

Chapter 5 **The Lady in Question**

Karel (Robert Carey) does not respond well to the advances of the Baron von Elsner's niece, Lotte (Andy Halliday), in The Lady in Question. *Photo by T. L. Boston.*

The pace of gentrification in the East Village picked up rapidly in 1988, and as a result many of the clubs and galleries that had initially attracted the media spotlight disappeared due to skyrocketing rents. Limbo was one of the victims, but Charles and I barely noticed; we were too busy. *Vampire Lesbians* and *Psycho Beach Party* had opened doors. Charles had an agent at the prestigious William Morris Agency, George Lane, who had gotten him work writing a television pilot for CBS (which, like most pilot scripts, was never made), and the Goodspeed Opera Company hired him to rewrite the book for a revival of *Ankles Aweigh*, a dated 1955 musical originally written as a vehicle for the Kean sisters (Jane and Betty). Joseph Papp at the Public Theater had reached out to me again, and I was working on the development of a new musical based on Joe Orton's unproduced screenplay, *Up Against It*, with music and lyrics by Todd Rundgren. But we were still planning to open a new Theatre-in-Limbo production, this time at an established Off-Broadway nonprofit theatre rather than a club, thanks to the networking skills of Jane Allison.

Jane was a charmingly eccentric and vivacious socialite and doyenne of Indiana ex-pats who lived in a penthouse overlooking Washington Square and who wrote a column for *The Indianapolis News* called "Hoosier in Manhattan." She knew lots of interesting people of an earlier era. At one of her cocktail parties, I chatted with an older gentleman who said he was a publicist. "Oh," I said, "What do you publicize?" He replied, "*The Bell Telephone Hour*," a television show that had been off the air for two decades. At the same party, Charles and I were thrilled to meet the great ballerina Tamara Geva, George Balanchine's first wife. Jane devoted a couple of her columns to me and Theatre-in-Limbo. I can only imagine what some of her Indianapolis readers thought of *Vampire Lesbians of Sodom*, but her articles could not have been more enthusiastic. She called me one day to tell me that she wanted to connect me with a fellow Hoosier in Manhattan, Albert Poland, a successful producer and general manager. He and I arranged to meet for dinner at Al Ponte Vecchio, a classic (now defunct) Italian restaurant on Thompson Street not far from Washington Square. Albert was astonished when I told him that I was keeping the running costs of *Vampires* as low as $12,000 per week, and he said that I had to meet his friend, Kyle Renick, another tight-fisted producer who was the artistic director of the WPA Theatre. The WPA was a well-regarded theatre at the time that had generated hits like *Little Shop of Horrors* and *Steel Magnolias*. Charles joined me for dinner with Kyle and Albert on April 3, 1988, and over the course of the meal the two of us pitched an idea we had been discussing: an anti-Nazi World War II melodrama. By the time the check arrived, Kyle had committed to produce the play without seeing the script—which was lucky because it wasn't written yet. This time there wasn't even a title.

Sex Slaves

Before we could get started on our new prestige project, we both got sucked back into the vortex of what was left of the East Village club scene. Andy Halliday, who had long been competitive with Charles, perhaps going back to summer camp, was tired of playing supporting roles. He wrote a star vehicle for himself and convinced Julie Halston (who had gotten a taste of producing by raising money for *Psycho Beach Party*) to produce it. Although the Limbo was gone, Michael Gormley had gotten a job booking acts into a new East Village club called The World, and he gave Julie some midsummer dates. Andy's script was true to the Ridiculous style: a mélange of camp films such as the Maria Montez classic *Cobra Woman*, various Betty Grable musicals, and biblical epics like *The Prodigal* (1955) starring Lana Turner. He wrote it as a tribute to Jeff Veazey, and it was based on the kind of films they had loved to watch together. Susan Stroman agreed to choreograph, and Andy approached me to direct it. I came up with some excuse for refusing, but the real reason was that I was worried about being pigeonholed as a director of campy comedies and tired of the stressful process of producing plays in clubs. I was hoping my work at the Public would lead to more gigs at prestigious theatres. There was a very handsome (and very straight) actor who had been a replacement in *Psycho Beach Party* who was interested in starting a directing career, and Andy gave him the job.

Andy thought the script needed some jokes, and he asked Charles if he would be willing to punch it up, which he agreed to do. He ended up doing a lot more than adding a few gags, however; he completely rewrote almost all of the dialogue, and even came up with a title from the Theatre-in-Limbo playbook: *Sex Slaves of the Lost Kingdom or I Dream of Weenie*. According to Andy, when Charles was through with his rewrite the only things that were left from Andy's draft were the original characters and a semblance of the plotline.[1]

Rehearsals did not go well. The handsome, straight director did not understand the (very gay) sensibility of the play. Andy was in a panic and wanted to replace him. I was still reluctant, but Julie Halston convinced me to take over. Very snobbishly, however, I insisted that I did not want my name on the production, and so I invented the pseudonym Henry Yates, who became the director of record. Unlike the original director, I had no trouble understanding the play, but rehearsals were still not easy. My trepidation about working in clubs was well founded, and the conditions at The World were far worse than they had ever been at the Limbo Lounge. On July 21, 1988, I wrote an entry, dripping with condescension, in a journal that I kept sporadically (the overly grand style and syntax can probably be explained by the fact that I was reading *The Noël Coward Diaries* at the time):

> Yesterday was a "never again" day. I vowed that I would never again have anything to do with a show in an East Village club. . . .

SEX SLAVES had its tech/dress last night at the World on East Second near Avenue C. It was excruciating.

The show is being played on a tiny stage in a lounge-like room beneath the main disco. During the rehearsal the huge *moderne* chandelier which hangs in the middle of the room would shake furiously from the dancing upstairs. Apparently, the load-in was a complete nightmare, one which I fortunately missed. Naturally, the denizens of these clubs work very hard to thwart every legitimate activity undertaken by our crew. The rehearsal itself was OK, the usual stops and goes. The nightmare really began for me after the rehearsal. The entire set, our light board and tape deck as well as all the props, costumes, etc., had to be struck. What is worse, Michael Limbo (the "booker") couldn't guarantee the safety of any of these items, so they all had to be loaded into taxis. In the pouring rain. We had to wade through three inches of water with our cumbersome packages to get to the taxis.

The best (or worst) story from this night of hell involved Andy, the author/star. Twenty minutes after the rehearsal broke as the set was being struck he was still running around the room wearing nothing but a G-string. When I asked him what was wrong (he didn't look happy) he told me that he couldn't find his clothes. I had to laugh, dreadful as it was, at the thought of Andy trying to hail a taxi on Avenue C wearing nothing but a G-string. A few minutes later I saw that he had dressed—"boxer" type shorts and a pink tank top. When I asked him where he had found his clothes, he said that the bartender was using them as rags to wipe down the bar. Charming![2]

My relentlessly negative attitude toward the production changed when I heard the response of the audience on opening night, described in this journal entry from July 22, 1988:

SEX SLAVES opened last night—triumphantly, all things considered. The guards went up on their lines rather glaringly a few times, and Dea missed her big entrance in sc. 4, which left poor Andy onstage alone and panicking. "For Christ sake will someone come out here!" he said. But the amateurish moments contributed to the charm of the enterprise, oddly enough. I was thrilled it came off as well as it did. Packed house of mostly gay men seemed to enjoy themselves thoroughly.[3]

The limited run pretty much sold out, and the show made back all its expenses. Andy was very upset by Charles's tepid reaction to the production, however. He recalls that Charles came backstage after a performance, saw Andy, and said in a deadpan, "Oh, nice costume."[4] They had a very complicated relationship, and it was not improving. The critics were kind without being enthusiastic. Writing in the *Advocate*, Craig Rowland noted that "the show doesn't pretend to be anything more than entertainment; escapist fantasy is what you get. We leave the theater with a chuckle, not a message—and that's a relief during the anxious '80s."[5]

Bad News

The "anxious '80s" just kept getting more anxious. Meghan was released from the hospital, and although we all knew she was recovering from pneumonia she was still cagey about her diagnosis. A few weeks after her release, I took her to a performance of *Much Ado about Nothing* starring Kevin Kline and Blythe Danner in Central Park, but we left in the middle of the first act because it started raining steadily, and I didn't think someone who had just recovered from pneumonia should be sitting outside in the rain. We went back to my place for a drink, where Meghan had a very unnerving coughing fit, which she insisted was nothing more than a summer cold she was having trouble shaking (like Edmund in *Long Day's Journey into Night*). Rumors about her health were flying in our circle. One mutual friend told me she had emphysema, which I almost wanted to believe. Bobby Carey knew better.

The very next night I invited Bobby over to dinner, and he had some news of his own. He said he had something to tell me—then decided he didn't want to tell me. Of course, I had to coax him, and he finally told me that he felt that he was dying. He said he had the classic textbook symptoms of pre-AIDS: night sweats, diarrhea, indigestion, lack of breath, and occasional painful breathing. He was sure he only had at most a year or two to live. It got very maudlin. We both cried. I asked him if he felt ill, and he said no but that he hadn't really felt right for over a year, since before *Psycho Beach Party*. We held each other for a long time, and then he went home. I cried for about ten minutes after he left and prayed to God that Bobby was wrong. Unfortunately, he was not wrong. I didn't get much sleep that night, but one of the strange things about this period was adapting to the horror of AIDS and going about your business while all around you friends and loved ones confronted death. The next day I had an advertising meeting uptown, went running, and distracted myself by watching a VHS recording of *Notorious*—research for our new project and, as I noted in my journal, "a good old-fashioned Nazi picture."[6] I compartmentalized, but I could never fully shake the anxiety and grief.

The next weekend, Charles and I rented a small house right on the beach in Fire Island Pines. Meghan and I rode out together on the train and opened the house on Friday evening. The two of us made dinner and then sat on the deck watching the surf, never mentioning her illness. Charles and Andy joined us the next day. Bobby, Julie, and other friends came later in the week, and the weather was spectacular. Charles had to interrupt his vacation for a couple of days to attend *Ankles Aweigh* rehearsals, and the producers flew him up to Connecticut from the Islip airport in a two-seater, which we all thought was very glamorous. But he returned furious with everyone at Goodspeed, which dampened the mood of the house a bit. And he continued to drop periodic digs at Andy's performance in *Sex Slaves*. Andy, who was very sensitive to the slight, became increasingly resentful. It all boiled over when some friends of Andy's came out for the day and later decided they would spend the night on the deck chairs. Charles and I didn't want the extra guests, but neither of us had the nerve to tell Andy. Julie Halston, who was less shy, volunteered to tell him, and he did not react well to it. Later that day when a few of us returned from a cocktail party, the house was empty. Andy and his friends had gone back to the city, and Andy had left a blistering note for Charles.

One of the many projects I was working on when I got back from the beach was the Off-Broadway transfer of John Epperson's tour de force, *I Could Go on Lip-Synching!* I wanted to present it as a late-night show at the Provincetown Playhouse after *Vampire Lesbians*. Charles and I had seen John's postmodern drag act at the Pyramid Club and were both blown away by it. It was hilarious and sophisticated and, as brilliantly staged by Justin Ross, the antithesis of typical drag acts. John is tall, willowy, and reed-thin, and his exaggerated makeup as Lypsinka with its wildly arched eyebrows and bloodred mouth gave the impression of a woman constantly on the verge of a panic attack. Rather than impersonate a gay icon like Judy Garland or Peggy Lee by simply lip-synching to an old record, without ever speaking a word John created his own unique character through ingenious sound editing by juxtaposing brief clips of various stars in outrageous combinations. The resulting montage provided a running commentary on outdated gender clichés, but what was most dazzling about his performance was how he managed to make these disparate recordings cohere into the persona of Lypsinka, the ultimate troubled star. The fragmented characterization was similar to the star persona Charles had created, but Lypsinka only spoke via audiotape. During the course of John's performance, the multiple voices of the character led to a climactic nervous breakdown, followed by a denouement in which she accepts an Academy Award with excessive humility. Undaunted by the recent failure of *Psycho Beach Party*, I had high hopes that it would be a big hit, and I started negotiations with Arthur Cantor to add late shows for a limited run at the Provincetown Playhouse. Lypsinka certainly generated lots of buzz, attracting celebrities like Elton John, but the stress of running two shows at the same time in one tiny, antiquated theatre was difficult to sustain, and when the announced run ended I did not continue with the project, which transferred for an extended run at another theatre.

The Silly Series

I had another meeting with Kyle Renick, this time in his cluttered, windowless office on the third floor of the (since demolished) WPA Theatre on Twenty-Third Street west of Tenth Avenue. He had to clear a place for me to sit because enormous stacks of manuscripts were piled everywhere. His pained, troubled expression gave me the uneasy sense that he was having second thoughts. He told me he was still very gung ho about producing our play but unclear about how or when to do so, because he felt we would be out of place in his regular subscription season. This was disheartening news. The Theatre-in-Limbo aesthetic, unfortunately, did not fit in with the stated mission of the WPA, which was to produce new and rarely revived American plays from the *realistic* tradition. Partly to accommodate us, Kyle came up with the idea of a low-budget second season of outrageous plays that would harken back to the wild, old days of early Off Broadway. He called it the "Silly Series," a designation I wasn't crazy about—it seemed unintentionally demeaning, and I had never considered our work to be merely "silly." The words "low-budget" also made me nervous, since even the regular season WPA shows were not particularly lavish. Nevertheless, I was pleased that plans for our show seemed to be moving forward. A few weeks later, Kyle called to tell me that he was giving us the slot right after the regular subscription run of Larry Kramer's new play, *Just Say No*. We were set to open for a sixteen-performance run on November 18.

Of course, the play was still not written, but that didn't take long.

Charles wrote very quickly when he had a firm handle on the character that he would play. The star role, Gertrude Garnet, was partly inspired by a dress Charles had worn to an annual drag ball, the Night of a Thousand Gowns, that he had commissioned Bobby Locke to design and build. Charles was always a little sheepish about attending this event because he did not like to think of himself as a drag queen, but the ball was a guilty pleasure. The dress was a 1940s-style, long-sleeved, cream-colored, crepe evening gown with padded shoulders, a shimmering gold underskirt, and gold trim, influenced by the designs of Adrian for MGM stars. After the ball, Charles was frustrated that the dress was consigned to the closet, and he began imagining roles that would accommodate it. The muted, classic elegance of the line of the gown, accented by the flashy gold of the underskirt, suggested one of his favorite character types: an upwardly mobile, pretentiously sophisticated woman whose soignée exterior masked a tough-talking dame from the wrong side of the tracks. This duality was there in the dress, which could have been designed for Barbara Stanwyck in her prime. Very much in the tradition of Madeleine Astarté, Theodora, and Irish O'Flanagan, Gertrude Garnet (pronounced Gar-NAY), is a world-famous classical concert pianist who got her start playing honky-tonk piano in sleazy dives in Brooklyn.

The gown dictated the period (1940s) and the character of the protagonist, but the milieu of the play came from another source. Charles and I often improvised scenes to entertain ourselves at home and, perversely, one of our favorite subjects was over-the-top Nazis. I would usually play a cold-as-ice officer whose capricious cruelty went well beyond that of the bumbling villains of *Hogan's Heroes*, and Charles would often play a calculating Nazi *frau*, among other characters. I don't know why we found these tasteless improvisations endlessly amusing, but we did. And we were both fans of Hollywood anti-Nazi melodramas, which were both scary and campy at the same time, with their brave heroes and clear-cut villains. The plot for our new show was easy to develop because it was lifted from a number of these classics from the early 1940s (which we were addicted to renting from the World of Video), primarily the Norma Shearer/Robert Taylor vehicle *Escape* (1940). Details and plot twists were culled from *Idiot's Delight* (1939), *Reunion in France* (1942), *Above Suspicion* (1943), and Hitchcock's *Notorious* (1946), among others.

The plot was also determined by the personas of the members of our company who were available to do the show. As always, Charles tailored

Gertrude Garnet (Charles Busch) takes vengeance on the evil Nazi Baron von Elsner (Kenneth Elliott) in The Lady in Question *at the WPA Theatre. Photo by Carol Rosegg*

each role for a specific actor. Arnie Kolodner was Erik Maxwell, a leading man in the Robert Taylor mold; Julie Halston, who was finally ready to give up her Wall Street career and get back into the company full-time, was Gertrude's best friend, the Eve Arden–inspired Kitty, the Countess de Borgia; Bobby Carey would play Karel Freiser, a handsome Hitler youth who ultimately sees the error of his ways; Theresa Marlowe was Heidi Mittelhoffer, Karel's estranged girlfriend, a professor's emotionally charged daughter working with the resistance; Mark Hamilton, who had been a reliable understudy at *Vampire Lesbians* but had never originated a part with the company, played the dual roles of Heidi's father, the kindly Professor Mittelhoffer, and the Mengele-like Dr. Maximilian. Charles insisted that I perform in this play because he saw me as the cruel-but-bumbling Nazi aristocrat, the Baron Wilhelm von Elsner. Meghan would be Raina Aldric, a legendary (and stentorian) actress who escapes from a concentration camp.

Charles originally planned to have Andy play my mother, Augusta von Elsner. But one night after we watched a film about brainwashed youth in wartime Germany, *Hitler's Children* (1943), I suggested to Charles that Andy should play an evil little Nazi girl with blonde braids. He immediately added a plotline for the Baron's niece, Lotte, for which Andy was perfectly suited. With the role of Augusta freed up, we were able to give Meghan the opportunity to play two mothers, one good and one evil.

Knowing the budget was minuscule, I was prepared to do the show on an empty stage with our usual setup of legs, borders, and backdrop, but while Charles was in the midst of writing the first draft, Kyle invited us to take a walk-through of the set for *Just Say No*, in case there was anything we wanted to salvage. Larry Kramer's play was set in the living room of a contemporary Washington, D.C., townhouse, which was beautifully designed with great detail by Edward Gianfrancesco, better known to his friends as Hawk, the house designer of the WPA. Although it was a modern setting, the style and decor were traditional. A magnificent staircase with a landing dominated the scene and, because *Just Say No* was a farce, there were seven doors. There was a portrait over the fireplace that was hinged to conceal a safe with a combination lock.

Charles and I were in heaven as we walked through the set, opening and closing doors, making entrances, improvising grand theatrical moments. After a brief conference, we told Kyle not to strike the set, that we would take the whole thing and recycle it for our play. The Washington townhouse would become the Baron von Elsner's schloss. It didn't take long to figure out how to make use of all seven doors, and Charles was able to work both the staircase and the fireplace safe into key reversals for the heroine. He was always inspired when writing with fixed circumstances in mind, and here he not only had a dress and a cast of available actors with defined personas, but a massive, detailed, realistic set as well.

Charles had always imagined himself performing in a realistic setting, and Brian Whitehill and I had always denied him that fantasy. I called Brian to tell him about our plan and also to express some misgivings about it. The play took place mostly in the Baron's schloss, but there were a couple of exterior scenes as well. How could we accommodate those scenes within the fixed walls of a box set? More important was the question of style. The Theatre-in-Limbo design team had developed a distinctive, non-illusionistic visual aesthetic over four years and nine productions. Should that be completely jettisoned to play our show on a set designed for Larry Kramer's farce? Brian had recently seen *Just Say No*, and he thought that we could use the set but that we had to make it our own. His solution was to obscure the realistic detail by painting the entire thing battleship gray and then overlaying a misty range of mountaintops, trees, and a spray of snow on top of the gray base coat, as if the Alps were projected on the interior walls of the house. That effect added a surreal element that suggested the outside is the inside as well. The gray evoked coldness and hinted at the visual look of black and white movies—the source films were shot in black and white. We got rid of all the furniture except for a sofa at center. This was still (mostly) a "stand-up" play.

The obvious solution to the exterior scenes was to play them "in one," that is, in the furthest downstage area, usually in front of a drop or traveler curtain. But there was no fly system at the WPA to bring in a drop, and Hawk's set was so massive that there was very little room downstage. Brian solved the problem by creating a folding screen (also gray) that resembled a giant travel brochure painted in his signature ironic graphic style. It featured a happy-go-lucky red-headed girl skier waving cheerfully, and it was emblazoned with the slogan, "Tour Carefree Bavaria." We played the opening train station scene in front of this screen, which had the added benefit of delaying the reveal of the schloss interior. The final scene of escape in the Alps was painted on the reverse side of the folding screen, and to simulate a long shot of the leading characters fleeing the Nazis on skis, a pair of puppets appeared through slots and slid down the mountains—the perfect touch of Limbo cheap theatrics. Despite the many film references,

I also wanted our show to resemble a 1940s Theatre Guild production for the Lunts. Bobby Locke, whose costumes for *Gidget Goes Psychotic* had been a bit too realistic, designed and built a dazzling parade of period gowns (Jennifer Arnold designed the costumes for the men), and I was able to keep my promise to work with him on a future project after having fired him from *Psycho Beach Party*.

The working title of the show was *Fighting Girls Against the Blitzkrieg or Kraut on the Side Please!* It was a typical Theatre-in-Limbo title meant to get an immediate laugh, thought up for curtain speeches long before a word of the play had been written. But as the script developed, it became apparent that it was misleading. Not only did the plot have nothing to do with a blitzkrieg, but the overall tone of the play was more serious and suspenseful than the silly title suggested. Charles had created an elegant parody of the source material, and I argued that it demanded a dignified title. We settled on *The Lady in Question* (unrelated to the 1940 Rita Hayworth film of the same title), which had a double meaning, referring both to the main character, Gertrude Garnet, and to the actor/actress playing her (a questionable lady). The new title may not have been good for an instant laugh, but it was much more appropriate for the play.

The title aside, I worried that the play itself lacked humor. It hewed closely to the conventions of early 1940s suspense films, and the characters, while admittedly melodramatic types, were more subtly drawn than those in Charles's previous work. The plot concerned issues of life and death, and it was as well crafted as most of the original films. Gertrude Garnet, a celebrated but utterly self-centered American classical pianist, is on a concert tour in Germany in 1940, which she had refused to cancel, oblivious to the horrors of the Nazis all around her. She is traveling with her wisecracking friend, Kitty, the Countess de Borgia (an American married to an Italian aristocrat), who is less sanguine about the political climate. When they arrive in a small Bavarian town where Gertrude is to play in the local *festspielhaus*, they discover the hotel has lost their reservations and they are unable to find other accommodations due to Oktoberfest. The oily Baron von Elsner, who is immediately smitten with Gertrude, comes to their rescue and invites them to stay at his very large, magnificent schloss. Gertrude accepts the Nazi hospitality: "Baron, I simply can't wait to see your magnificent schlong. I mean, schloss!"[7] At a dinner hosted by the Baron that night, Gertrude meets Professor Erik Maxwell, an American who entreats her to help in the effort to rescue his mother, the great actress Raina Aldric, who has recently escaped from a concentration camp and is hiding in the catacombs beneath the schloss. Gertrude at first demurs, insisting that she is apolitical and only concerned with her own business; but when Kitty is murdered by the Baron's niece, Lotte, she changes her tune and assists Raina's escape, which involves the wheelchair-bound Raina dragging herself up the grand staircase while Gertrude distracts Lotte and the Baron. Gertrude falls in love with Erik in the process, and the final scene is Gertrude's own escape, fleeing her Nazi pursuers down the Alps on skis with Erik, who is shot in a hail of bullets. But he revives just as Gertrude realizes by the position of the brightest star overhead that they have indeed escaped across the border, and she rhapsodically envisions a world that will be free for all people and free of the Nazi menace. I scored the show with a mix of Richard Wagner and Max Steiner film scores that emphasized both the sentiment and the suspense.

The Lady in Question worked like a charm in the intimate, cozy WPA Theatre, which Kyle explained had once been a house owned by Clement Moore, author of "A Visit from St. Nicholas." The main publicity for this short, three-week run was our reliable Limbo mailing list and minimal print advertising. Critics were not invited; we wanted to be able to work on the show without being judged. I needn't have worried about the laughs; they were plentiful, and our loyal, mostly gay audiences were giddy. The response took me by surprise. Although it contained plenty of witty twists, the script so lovingly recreated the source material that it could, with only a few alterations, have been filmed by Warner Bros. in 1940. Aside from the schlong gag, there was only one word in the entire play that would not have made it past the Hays Code: when Gertrude refuses to help Erik rescue his mother, he calls her "a coward, a selfish, egocentric, opportunistic, vulgar, manipulating cunt!" (Her reply: "Vulgar! Now that did it!")[8] Charles's star turn as Gertrude Garnet was his most seamless performance to date, and the entire company was in peak form; but the tone and style of the production was much less outrageous than our previous work had been. As the first Theatre-in-Limbo show to premiere in an actual theatre rather than a club, Charles and I wanted it to ooze legitimacy, yet the audience was delirious with laughter.

Without critics, we could relax and enjoy the run. But the sellout crowds and enthusiastic response almost immediately generated talk of a commercial transfer. Kyle approached me about it one night after a performance, and with a peculiar combination of excitement and utter dread, but with a sense that we *had* to proceed, I agreed. He suggested that he and I co-produce, and Albert put together a $250,000 budget for the transfer, which was more in line with most commercial Off-Broadway productions than our bargain-basement Theatre-in-Limbo productions had been.

The lack of reviews made it hard to raise money, and it would take a full six months before Kyle and I could assemble the capitalization. With *Vampire Lesbians* still running at the Provincetown Playhouse, I was busy casting and putting in what seemed like constant replacements while meeting with potential *Lady* investors and being occasionally summoned to the Public Theater to meet with Mr. Papp to confer about *Up Against It*. In late January 1989, I traveled to Key West to put together a production of *Vampire Lesbians* for the Waterfront Playhouse with Charles, Julie, Andy, and Tom Aulino recreating their roles (the other parts were cast locally). The weather was spectacular, and we got to hobnob with local literary celebrities like the poet James Merrill (who became a *Lady in Question* investor), but we were housed together in a small "conch" house, and the close quarters exacerbated tensions within the company—especially between Andy and Charles.

When I got back to New York, I decided it was time for me move out of the railroad flat I shared with Charles and finally get my own apartment. In the nine years we lived together we almost never had an argument, and we had lots of fun improvising scenes and fantasizing about theatre projects. But a railroad flat offered no privacy; Charles had to walk through my bedroom to get to the bathroom, and I had to walk through his bedroom to get to the living room. With a long-running show and two soon-to-open productions, I thought my prospects looked pretty bright, so why not buy a condo? I found a spacious studio at 299 West Twelfth Street, just two blocks away.

Not long before I moved, at about the time the capitalization for *The Lady in Question* was finally coming together, Meghan called and asked to meet with Charles and me at our place. She arrived looking spectacular, wearing a simple summer shift punctuated by a pair of her trademark wacky earrings. She had come to tell us something we already knew: she had AIDS. She was very brave about it. She said her health was fine, that she was taking AZT, and that her condition had stabilized. She said she had no idea how she got it. Her Canadian husband, Maxim, had died of AIDS the previous year, but she insisted that they had never been intimate. She wanted us to know that she was more than well enough to recreate her roles for the transfer, but if we felt we needed to replace her she would understand. Both Charles and I immediately told her that we wouldn't think of replacing her, that we wouldn't even consider proceeding without her. She was pleased, but she had one request: she asked us to keep her HIV status a secret and to tell no one else in the company. We promised that we would.

With the substantial investment of Morton Swinsky, one of Kyle's WPA angels, we were finally able to capitalize *The Lady in Question* in May, and Albert booked us into the Orpheum Theatre on Second Avenue in the East Village, where another WPA transfer, *Little Shop of Horrors*, had been a huge hit a few years earlier. We launched our publicity campaign with an extravagantly campy float in the gay pride parade. Charles and a few of the cast members (along with some cute boys in lederhosen) waved to the crowds, while I and a cadre of volunteers walked alongside handing out flyers.

At about the same time I moved into my new condo. Charles seemed ambivalent about losing his longtime roommate, but I don't think he was pleased—he was used to me doing the shopping, cooking, and most of the cleaning, and he wasn't sure how he was going to get along by himself. He often referred to me as "Harriet Craig," the obsessive-compulsive housewife from George Kelly's play, portrayed on the screen by Joan Crawford. (To be fair, Charles always did the dishes.) I assured him that I would be just down the street if he needed me, but the move certainly changed our relationship. We were never quite as close after that.

We still saw a lot of each other, however, as we moved into tech and dress rehearsals. At 347 seats, including a balcony, the Orpheum was by far the largest house we had ever played. It had been a Yiddish theatre as early as 1904, but was converted to a movie house in the 1920s. Live theatre returned with the debut of *Little Mary Sunshine* in 1959, and it became one of the top commercial Off-Broadway theatres. Despite its storied history, it seemed like a bit of a barn to me, and I worried about how some members of our company would project to the last row of the balcony. All of the design elements were upgraded, and Brian and I had fun with a high concept idea for the lobby decor. While thumbing through some 1940s issues of *Life* magazine, I noticed advertisements with star endorsements of every type of consumer product imaginable. I suggested to Brian that he recreate some of these ads, inserting the image of Charles as Gertrude Garnet, to show that she had no scruples and would endorse anything from cigarettes to vacuum cleaners. We mounted them in the lobby instead of the usual production photos and press quotes.

We embarked on a breakneck schedule to save money. We had only two days of rehearsal before we moved into the theatre and two days of tech before an invited dress on Thursday, July 15. Our first preview was the following evening, and critics started coming just one week later. Fortunately, there were very few changes, and the cast was able to pick right up where we had left off in December at the WPA. My understudy, Richard Cuneo, went on for me a few times so I could watch from out front before the press nights. After his first performance, he told me that he had been amazed and slightly terrified by the overwhelming noise the audience made when they laughed. I told him to enjoy it. I certainly was, until Sam Rudy told me that the *Times* was sending Frank Rich to cover the show—that was when *I* felt terror, to the pit of my stomach. I kept this news to myself, and Sam promised not to tell me which preview he would be attending.

We opened on July 25, 1989. We must have been reasonably confident, because Kyle and I splurged on opening night gifts for the cast from Tiffany's (just as my former boss Michael Stewart always did): engraved crystal beer steins. The festive opening night party at Spaghetteria, a neighborhood restaurant up the street from the theatre, became a delirious celebration when the early edition of the *Times* arrived and Kyle did the honors of reading aloud Rich's glowing valentine to the show, the cast, and especially to Charles. In what appeared to be a complete reversal of his scathing pan of our entire company in what he had called "the lesser" *Psycho Beach Party*, he raved about every aspect of the show:

> As always, Mr. Busch knows his MGM schlock, but never previously has he or his director, Kenneth Elliott, dished it out with such sustained, well-paced discipline. Along with its double-entendre groaners, "The Lady in Question" actually offers some melodramatic chills and, thanks to the witty production design, the backlot shock effects allotted movies with B budgets.

He provided a thoughtful and perceptive analysis of the Busch versus Ludlam issue:

> While Mr. Busch's plays are often linked with Charles Ludlam's lighter efforts, such generalizing distorts the artistry of both. Mr. Ludlam, a theatrical classicist and a political iconoclast, usually had a second agenda, ideological or esthetic, percolating within his gender-flipped sendups. Mr. Busch's attitude is the simpler one of "Hooray for

Hollywood!" The man revels in trash. "The Lady in Question" mimics its source material so accurately and affectionately that it is as much homage as parody.

Curiously, Rich goes on to note that it wouldn't have made much difference if the role of Gertrude had been played by a woman, and he reiterates this point in his rhapsodic final paragraph: "That the lady in question is a man soon becomes beside the point. What matters here is that the performer in question is a star."[9]

Those were magic words to Charles, and well-deserved praise for his sublimely funny performance, but it was not exactly accurate to say that it was beside the point that the leading lady was a man in a dress. That *was* the point, and it was the reason why the audiences were convulsed with laughter. My original trepidation that the script was too serious, too genuinely faithful to the source material, did not take into account that the heroine of this melodrama was a man in a dress knowingly playing on gender stereotypes. Charles was skillfully having it both ways: conspiring with audience members who were "in the know," while "passing" for those who would ordinarily be turned off by drag performance, supported by the elegant costumes and majestic scenery. The show received lots of glowing notices, as well as a few pans, and almost all of them ignored the implications of the cross-gender casting. Clive Barnes, who had detested *Psycho Beach Party,* gushed in the *New York Post,* "I loved it. I couldn't have had a better time, unless someone had given me popcorn." Like Rich, he was taken in by the story and the accuracy of the playing style: "A parody I suppose it is, but this is a very serious, even loving parody, that almost but definitely not quite—it runs a fine line of humor here—demands to be taken on the very same terms of that which it is satirizing. A neat trick."[10] For Barnes, the cross-gender casting was more of a stumbling block to get past than a central element of the production. He averred, "I have an abnormal prejudice against drag, but when the performance is as mistressful as this, my prejudice simply fades into wonder." A neat trick, indeed.

Three days after our opening was a typically sweltering New York July day. I arrived at the theater early to check in with the box office, and I was delighted to find we were sold out to the last row of the balcony. While I was there, I decided to make a few adjustments to the lobby display. I was up on a ladder when Meghan walked in wearing a light summer dress, pressing two plastic cups of ice to her cheeks. She was the first actor to arrive.

I always treated her as if she were Lynn Fontanne: "My darling, you're here early! You were brilliant last night. How are you?" "Not well," she replied with a soft, raspy voice, "I have a 104-degree fever." I froze for a moment as her words sank in, and then scrambled down the ladder to try to deal with the situation. Clearly, she should have gone to the hospital rather than the theatre, and I told her so. "No," she firmly insisted with great theatrical emphasis, "I'm going on tonight." Her understudy, Judith A. Hansen, had just gone on contract the day before opening; she had seen two performances, but probably had not yet started memorizing lines, and she had had no rehearsal. I sputtered as I attempted to work through the situation. "I'll cancel the performance. Please, Meghan, your health is more important than one performance." She had already started into the theatre, ignoring my entreaties with the wave of her hand, and was heading to her dressing room, unwilling to even entertain the notion of going anywhere until she had given her performance that night. I followed and sat down next to her in front of the makeup mirror, unable to speak. She took my hand, looked me in the eye, and emphatically insisted that she would be fine. I soon realized that there was no way to change her mind, so I finally agreed—providing that she cut some of the strenuous business, such as when Raina drags herself up the staircase and somersaults to safety in an upstairs bedroom. Once again, she was adamant: "No, I'm not cutting anything." For some reason, I kept arguing that she must cut the somersault, at the very least, as if that would help matters. "All right, I'll cut the somersault if you think that's best, but otherwise I'm going to give my performance as directed. It's very important to me. And please, don't tell any of the other actors. After the show, I'd like you to take me to Lenox Hill Hospital. Now let me get ready." I promised that I wouldn't tell anyone, and told her I would have a taxi waiting.

I didn't quite keep my word; I waited for Charles in the lobby to tell him about Meghan's condition, and when Julie arrived, she figured it out pretty quickly. I called Judith Hansen and told her to start working on her lines—fast. Meghan's performance that night was only slightly subdued, and she managed to hold it together and even collect most of her laughs, but as I played scenes with her, I could see the struggle to simply get the words out. Offstage, she was falling apart. Gradually, the entire cast became aware that something was very wrong with her, and they stood in the wings with worried expressions on their faces while the audience out front, oblivious to the dire situation, continued to laugh uproariously. It surprised no one that at the climactic moment of Raina's exit, Meghan managed to pull herself up the grand staircase, getting huge laughs, and then deftly somersault offstage. After the performance, I rushed her into a taxi and we rode to Lenox Hill Hospital together, neither of us saying much. I just held her hand tightly. The next day I found out that she had pneumocystis pneumonia. Amazingly, she would be back in the show in less than two weeks.

I was only able to remain in the cast through Labor Day weekend as I got busier with auditions and production meetings for *Up Against It*; Peter Bartlett replaced me. During a callback at the Public in early September, Mr. Papp asked me how *The Lady in Question* was doing. "Not bad," I told him, "but it's always a little slow after Labor Day, and we've got the Jewish holidays coming up." He raised an eyebrow and said, "The Jewish holidays! Oy. You sound like the Shuberts." The truth was that the box office was declining precipitously, and with weekly running costs fixed at around $40,000 we couldn't afford many bad weeks. Hal Luftig and Alan Perry, who ran the theatre, loved the show and were very generous, but we had to do something dramatic to reignite sales. After several meetings with Albert and Kyle at Great Scot Advertising, we decided to shoot a television commercial.

Albert knew a brilliant young TV director, Paris Barclay (later a two-time Emmy winner and president of the Directors Guild), who had his own highly successful production company called Black and White Television. His background was in advertising, but he had made a name for himself directing music videos, and he was very busy—I remember meeting with him only once, briefly, in the back of a taxi en route to his next appointment. We decided on a high concept ad that would recreate a trailer from a 1940s suspense film, shot in black and white with noir lighting. Charles, who had fantasized about being a film star for decades, was in seventh heaven during the shoot, and the finished product looked great. Unfortunately, it didn't sell tickets. For one thing, by the time the commercial was edited we didn't have enough money in our reserve fund for a substantial TV buy. Even more problematically, the ad confused viewers; it was so faithful to the style of old movie trailers that it was unclear that it was promoting a current Off-Broadway attraction.

As audiences at the Orpheum dwindled, relations between some members of the cast deteriorated (a familiar scenario). Andy became more openly hostile to Charles because of many slights, perceived and real. He became convinced that a line in the script where Gertrude addresses

Lotte as "my precious little monkeyface" was a direct dig at his appearance. Charles soon began to hang out in the ladies dressing room, but the atmosphere there was far from harmonious. As Meghan's illness grew more debilitating, the side effects of AZT made her irritable, and she often took out her frustration on Theresa Marlowe, whom she believed was not up to her professional standards. Julie tried to make peace, but Meghan, unmoved, explained, "I don't have time for that. Don't you understand? I don't have time."[11] Bobby Carey, who was also feeling the effects of AIDS, gave notice to fulfill a long-held dream of moving to Los Angeles. The excellent stage manager, Bob Vandergriff, did his best to maintain the show, despite the lack of comity backstage.

Up Against It

It didn't help matters that I was absent for most of this, preoccupied at the Public Theater trying to make sense of *Up Against It*, which was headed into production. Joe Orton's screenplay, originally written for the Beatles, was an intriguing, occasionally witty, meandering mess. Tom Ross, who worked with Gail Merrifield Papp in the literary department of the Public, had adapted it for the stage and pitched the idea to Todd Rundgren, who agreed to write the score. Neither Tom nor Todd had ever written a musical, and there was very little, if any, collaboration between them. When Todd completed a song, he sent along a demo tape and lyric sheet and left it to us to figure out how to insert it into the script. Through the development process of three staged readings, I had worked with Tom to try to give the book a narrative thrust, and the story was beginning to make as much sense as it could. Although there were some terrific tunes, I had lots of suggestions to help integrate the score into the book; Todd was not receptive. As a major rock star, he was accustomed to having his way about everything in the studio, and he was unfamiliar with the collaborative process of the theatre. However, Mr. Papp agreed with me about the changes needed to make the book and the score cohere, and he decided that *he* would give the notes to Todd. At a particularly uncomfortable meeting, Todd told Mr. Papp "no" to every note, explaining patiently but firmly that I was free to stage the show any way I chose, but the score could not be changed or cut. Take it or leave it. It was very clear who had the muscle in this show. Mr. Papp was not used to being told no, but he backed down, and I had to figure out how to make it work—a difficult task considering that some of the songs had no relation to the story whatsoever. I was spoiled by my experience with Theatre-in-Limbo, working with a playwright who trusted me and who enjoyed the collaborative process. I was unused to having my notes completely disregarded, and it caught me off guard. But it was the first of many lessons in what it's like to direct a show when you don't have the power to make major decisions.

I had never directed a musical, but I felt like I had because of my work with Jeff Veazey, and I so wished that I could collaborate with him again. Jeff was gone, but his partner, Susan Stroman, had a similar sensibility, and I wanted her as choreographer for the project. Mr. Papp was equivocal about her because he hadn't seen her work (this was years before her breakout success with *Crazy for You*), and so he, Tom Ross, and I traveled to Millburn, NJ, to see a production of *Jesus Christ Superstar* that she had choreographed for Paper Mill Playhouse. It was a fine production, but I don't think the show itself appealed to Mr. Papp, and Susan was deemed too commercial; he preferred Jennifer Muller, a well-regarded modern dance choreographer who, incidentally, was at the time the girlfriend of Mark Linn-Baker, the departed director of *Zero Positive*. Although I liked and respected Jennifer, I didn't know her, and we came from different worlds. As artistic director of the eponymous dance company she had founded in 1974, Jennifer Muller/The Works, she (like Todd) was accustomed to being the primary creative artist, and most of her previous work was in an abstract idiom quite different from raucous musical comedy. I had to call Susan to tell her that Mr. Papp was giving the job to Jennifer.

Casting went smoothly for the most part, but even this process presented an unexpected challenge to my authority as director. I wanted Tom Aulino to play the supporting role of Bernard Coates, the richest man in the world. As a member of the original Theatre-in-Limbo company, I knew he would understand the off-center style I was trying to create. Rosemarie Tichler, the casting director, preferred another actor she had worked with; he was talented and had Broadway experience but was much older and a completely different type. I explained my reasoning to Rosemarie, but she was adamant that I was wrong. I found her intransigence baffling and maddening. Jordan Thaler, the casting associate at the time, helpfully suggested that I sleep on it and call Rosemarie in the morning. The next morning, I had not changed my opinion, and I called Rosemarie to let her know, assuming that would be the end of it. After a long pause she sighed and said, with a tone of weary sadness, "Then we'll just have to take it to Joe." I was stunned that she was still not giving up, and I felt my ability to make aesthetic choices was being further eroded. Both actors were summoned for a callback to read and sing, but the real tension in the room was between Rosemarie and me. There's nothing like a high-pressure audition for Joe Papp! Tom got the part, but it was a decidedly sour episode.

I was grateful that Mr. Papp allowed me to hire my entire Limbo design team: Brian Whitehill, John Glaser, Vivien Leone, and Kathie Carr. The psychedelic fantasy elements of *Up Against It* lent themselves to the kind of outrageous look we had used for *Vampire Lesbians* and *Coma*, and so we gave it the visual look of a Theatre-in-Limbo production, right down to the wigs.

We ended up with a terrific cast that included Alison Fraser, Roger Bart, Toni DiBuono, and Philip Casnoff. Once rehearsals began, Mr. Papp and the staff more or less left us alone to create the show, and it came together despite the incongruities of the book and score. The invited audience at the final dress rehearsal was deliriously responsive—it was one of those magical nights. Mr. Papp, who was seeing the show for the first time, was so impressed that he called me into his office the next day. He had a plan: at the end of the scheduled three-week run (critics had not been invited because it was a developmental production), he would put the show back into rehearsal for a week, then reopen for three weeks of previews, during which we would polish it during afternoon rehearsals for the eventual press opening. At a meeting in the Anspacher Theater he told a stunned cast that he intended to move *Up Against It* to Broadway, where his long-running hit, *A Chorus Line*, was starting to flag.

In the midst of all this, I got a phone call from Albert Poland on Wednesday, October 25, who explained that Bob Vandergriff had gone home after the previous night's performance of *The Lady in Question* and died of a massive heart attack. I immediately called T. L. Boston, who had stage-managed *Psycho Beach Party*, and he agreed to take over the show. I took the night off from *Up Against It* to sit next to T. L. in the booth to train him to call the show from Bob's promptbook. Naturally, everyone at the Orpheum was in shock; Bob was particularly beloved by the cast. He was one of those rare stage managers who was truly adept at maintaining a show; he could give notes to the actors without ruffling feathers, and they trusted him.

That night in the booth would be the last time I would see *The Lady in Question* until its closing, because once Mr. Papp decided *Up Against It* had commercial possibilities most of my days and nights were spent at the Public Theater. There were casting sessions, chorus calls, and meetings in Mr. Papp's office to discuss book, staging, and design changes. The score was the only thing that would not change. As promised, Mr. Papp closed the show for one week of intense, full-time rehearsal to put in new cast members and to implement the revisions that he insisted on. Most of the changes were made in an attempt to straighten out the unwieldy plot and to rework the outrageous musical numbers in order to make the show more palatable for a commercial Broadway audience. One such change involved a number set in an asylum featuring Toni DiBuono as a whip-wielding dominatrix madly pursuing the three leading boys as they desperately tried to escape in wheelchairs. The number had gotten big laughs, but Mr. Papp had an aversion to wheelchairs, so it had to be completely restaged. It never got laughs again.

Mr. Papp continued to carefully monitor the show after we reopened, and we made changes every day, rehearsing for four hours in the afternoon and putting in the changes for the evening performances. It was an exhausting process, and tempers naturally flared along the way. The ultimate effect of all this upheaval was to quash the wacky, downtown spirit of the piece. Unlike Theatre-in-Limbo, where we "ironed in the kinks," here we ironed them out. But *Up Against It* could never be a satisfying Broadway musical for a mainstream audience—even second-tier Joe Orton was too transgressive for that.

Two Closings

Throughout this intense preview period at the Public Theater, the box office at the Orpheum continued to plummet, and *The Lady in Question* finally closed on December 3, 1989, after 14 previews and 151 performances, losing its entire investment. I attended the closing night performance, and what I saw appalled me. All the actors, including Charles, had let their performances get sloppy, and they were mugging like crazy. The success of *The Lady in Question* relied on an ensemble playing style that balanced fidelity to the source material with occasional outrageousness that was nevertheless grounded in *belief*, complete immersion into the world of the play. But the inconsistent audience response that had afflicted *Vampire Lesbians of Sodom* and *Psycho Beach Party* had become a problem again for *Lady* as the initial rush of gay fans was supplanted by a more mainstream crowd. The natural response of actors to a quiet house is to push. T.L. was a superb stage manager, but he had not been part of the rehearsal process. Without Bob Vandergriff (or me) around to give notes, the performances had deteriorated and the actors stepped outside the world of the play to comment on it in what seemed like desperation to get laughs.

The very next night, *Up Against It* opened at the Public. Meghan was once again my date, and this time her health allowed her to show up for the performance. Mr. Papp decreed that there would be no reviews allowed at the party. This was ostensibly so that we could all enjoy ourselves without worrying about the press, but it was not a good sign—Mr. Papp obviously had a mole at the *Times*. After the party, I walked Meghan to her new apartment on Sixth Avenue in the Village, and we picked up a copy of the next morning's *Times* at a newsstand along the way. It contained a devastating pan by Mel Gussow. When we got back to her apartment, the heat wasn't working so she lit the oven in her tiny kitchen and we sat in front of it, rereading the notice, trying to find a bright side, but it was hard to find in a review that claimed we had "obliterated whatever charm existed in the screenplay."[12] Meghan held my hand and had many comforting words for me that night. Although she made no reference to her illness, she was battling for her life, and she knew that a bad review, even in the *New York Times*, was just not that important. Nevertheless, *Up Against It* closed the following week, and we all knew why.

The reasons for the failure of *The Lady in Question*, however, were not so clear-cut. Press agent Sam Rudy commented that "it was one of the more sensational or head-scratching failures on or off Broadway in 1989."[13] Many in the cast blamed bad marketing choices—too much was spent on television and radio advertising, not enough on print and posters. Or was it the high running cost and large seating capacity of the Orpheum? Perhaps the title just wasn't funny enough. Could the high expectations of the *Times* review have set audiences up for a transcendent experience that the show could not live up to? Certainly, as Kyle Renick pointed out, word of mouth was not moving tickets at the box office.

The Lady in Question was marketed as mainstream theater, and most of the critics who praised the show did so *despite* the drag performances that were central to its humor. Although Frank Rich asserted that it wouldn't have mattered if the leading lady were a biological woman and Clive Barnes overcame his "abnormal prejudice against drag" to enjoy the performance, not all of the critics overlooked the elephant in the room—and prejudice against drag was unfortunately not "abnormal." Writing in the *Daily News*, Doug Watt asked, "If I told you that 'The Lady in Question' is a tacky-looking melodrama spoofing, from a gay viewpoint, those innumerable anti-Nazi movies of the 1940s, would you rush over to the Orpheum to soak it up?"[14] In his radio broadcast review on WNEW, Richard Shepard called it "a special kind of farce, spattered with gay jokes, and I'm sure its special audience will have a good time."[15] John Simon devoted an entire paragraph to our "special audience":

> The spectators, mostly men with other men, have a ball. Some of them, I observed, were rocked by transports of foot-stomping ecstasy; others talked back at the stage, like the youth behind me who, upon Gertrude's line over the prostrate Baron, "And before him trembled all of Schaffhausen," gasped "*Tosca!*" It is certainly one happy audience, moved by that emotional unison Jules Romains called *unanimismei*. It makes one wonder: Is this kind of communal joy to be had nowadays only in minority theater? Homosexual audiences at drag shows, black audiences at plays by blacks, and so on?[16]

The critic Peter Bowen perceptively noted in *Outweek*, "while nothing *in* the play is particularly gay, everything *about* it is."[17] The mainstream trappings of the production did not conceal that the play's primary address was to a gay audience, despite the fact that it did not contain any gay characters or situations. The humor was camp, and the gender inversion was meant to be noticed, not ignored; there were moments in the play when Charles dropped his voice and became pointedly male. Even the storyline, based as it was on mainstream Hollywood films, spoke to a gay audience. It was a play about overcoming the oppression of the dominant culture in order to be "free." The specter of AIDS was present as well. Gertrude's conversion from selfishness to altruism upon the death of her friend, Kitty, mirrored the inclination of many gay men of the period reacting to death all around them, to come out, act up, and fight AIDS. It made for stirring theatre, but it did not speak to everyone. After the closing of two promising shows in two weeks, I was beginning to think I had made a mistake buying that condo after all.

Chapter 6 **Limbo Sunset**

Pat Pilford (Julie Halston) and Mary Dale (Charles Busch) share a laugh, but Marta Towers (Judith A. Hansen) isn't in on the joke in Red Scare on Sunset. *Photo by T. L. Boston.*

The year 1989 had seemed so promising. I thought *The Lady in Question* would be a high-profile, sure-fire hit, Joe Papp had been confident that he would move *Up Against It* to Broadway for a long run, and *Vampire Lesbians of Sodom* continued to chug along at the Provincetown Playhouse. By the end of the year, the first two shows had closed precipitously, and the third was barely holding on. Charles and I were both a bit shell-shocked, so I was relieved to get a call from producer Gordon Crowe, who proposed a Los Angeles production of *Vampire Lesbians of Sodom.* Gordon was a blunt, occasionally foul-mouthed, old-school impresario who had been one of the producers of the original Off-Broadway and Broadway versions of *Oh! Calcutta!* (Unlike Arthur Cantor, he did not specialize in prestige productions.) *Variety* reports that he "pioneered" national bus and truck tours of popular Broadway musicals, usually featuring "a headline star who came out of retirement and a cast of talented unknowns."[1] His tours included *Sugar Babies* starring Pinky Lee, Cab Calloway in *Bubbling Brown Sugar*, and *A Funny Thing Happened on the Way to the Forum* with Jack Carter. Perhaps Gordon's pugnacious personality was formed by his early days working as a boxer and a newspaper copy boy. He could be charming when he chose to be, but his specialty was cut-rate productions; cost overruns really got his dander up. He must have thought *Vampire Lesbians* would be a good bet, cheap and easy to produce, given its long run at the Provincetown Playhouse. He planned an open-ended run at the Coronet Theatre on La Cienega Boulevard in West Hollywood, a mid-sized theatre notable for having housed the American premiere of Bertolt Brecht's *Life of Galileo*, starring Charles Laughton, back in 1947.

Meghan immediately began lobbying to recreate her role as La Condesa. She wanted to get to the West Coast to see if she could gain any traction in television or film, and she was desperate to keep working. Working meant being alive and in the game. If she had been well, I would have been thrilled to have her recreate her role, but her bouts of hospitalization had become more frequent, she had lost a lot of weight, and her health was quite precarious. I knew she wasn't up to traveling across the country, let alone playing such a large and demanding role, and I was also worried that it would be dangerous for her to be so far away from her doctors. She dismissed all my concerns, insisted she was fine, and practically begged me for the part. Giving her the news that Charles and I had decided to cast Julie Halston was excruciating. I felt truly terrible, but she accepted the decision with such stoic grace that I nearly burst into tears.

Tom Aulino and Andy Halliday journeyed with Charles, Julie, and me to Los Angeles, where we all stayed at the Highland Gardens on Franklin Avenue, a slightly seedy motel that specialized in housing actors on tour. To save money, the rest of the show was cast in L.A.—Bobby Carey already lived there, as did Monica Horan (who had replaced Theresa Aceves in New York), and they were glad to recreate their roles. The production looked great in the theatre, which had a larger stage than the Provincetown Playhouse, but Gordon had fits about the budget. In one of many blowups, he screamed at me over the phone, "That goddamn lighting designer is out of control!" He repeated the same line about the set designer and the costume designer during the course of load-in and tech, but none of them were out of control; the show was just a good deal more expensive to produce than he had anticipated. Gordon easily solved the problem by not paying the bills.

Sylvie Drake, reviewing for the *Los Angeles Times*, was favorable, if patronizing, as she resuscitated the old Ludlam versus Busch comparison: "Try besting the late Charles Ludlam at his own Ridiculous Theatre game. Busch has. And then some." She described the show as "camp transvestism punctuated by blatantly, ostentatiously vulgar jokes." Without calling it a gay show for gay audiences, she coyly asserted that it was "not for all markets, but certainly for some markets." She wrapped up her thoughts by predicting we would have a long stay at the Coronet: "'Vampire Lesbians,' with its guaranteed cult status, might run on and on, ad infinitum."[2] Unfortunately, cult status is rarely guaranteed, and there was one thing that Gordon Crowe surprisingly did not take into account: there was no equivalent to the Off-Broadway scene in Los Angeles. In general, Los Angeles is not a theatre-going town; there are a few large theatres, such as the Ahmanson, the Mark Taper Forum, and the Pasadena Playhouse, and lots of small (under 99 seats) theatres that produce "waiver" productions (which essentially means the actors waive their salaries), but almost nothing in between. There is no theatre district, and the town is such a sprawl that driving to a theatre through the inevitable L.A. traffic jams requires true dedication. Then there was the practical problem that there was no convenient parking near the Coronet, a major audience deterrent in L.A. The show sputtered along for a few months, hampered by a parsimonious and ineffective advertising campaign. I remember sitting at breakfast with Tom Aulino at our kitchen table in the Highland Gardens one morning, thumbing through the *Los Angeles Times*, when I stumbled across a tiny quote ad for our show that featured Brian's *Vampire Lesbians* logo followed by the bold, all caps headline, "MIGHT RUN." *Vampire Lesbians* might run? I was apoplectic. Was Gordon promoting our shaky box office as revenge for cost overruns? After careful scrutiny, I found the rest of Sylvie Drake's quote (". . . on and on ad infinitum")—but the ad was so small that it was almost necessary to use a magnifying glass to read it. This was typical of the hapless advertising campaign.

End of an Era

Although it might have run, it didn't, closing on May 13, 1990, after playing just over two months. Back in New York two weeks later, I finally had to close the Off-Broadway production of *Vampire Lesbians* after a much more spectacular run of 17 previews and 2,024 performances, surpassing *Vanities* (1,784 performances) as the longest-running nonmusical in Off-Broadway history. The box office had been too frequently dipping below our break-even point that spring, and I didn't see it returning to profitability. I had paid back the investors, which made it a "hit" by *Variety*'s definition, but I had no reserve fund to get us through the lean weeks to come.

How did this little show survive nearly five years, long after the hysteria of our gay Limbo Lounge audiences was a distant memory, while *Psycho Beach Party* and *The Lady in Question*—much stronger shows—had abbreviated and unprofitable runs? A combination of factors contributed to its unique success, some of which are obvious. The venue was critical; the Provincetown Playhouse was located in an active and iconic area of Greenwich Village on MacDougal Street between Washington Square Park and a strip of coffeehouses, restaurants, and nightclubs. There was always lots of street traffic, which resulted in plenty of "walk-up" ticket buyers. It was also an intimate space, which preserved the close actor/audience relationship we had established at the Limbo Lounge. The small size of the theatre also meant that we could maintain low running costs; everything from the rent to the actors' salaries was less expensive than in most other Off-Broadway theatres, which enabled us to survive bad weeks without going too deeply into the red. The catchy title was invaluable; it was naughty and fun without being obscene, and it generated ticket sales.

Most important, word of mouth, which Kyle Renick believed was the problem for *The Lady in Question*, remained strong for *Vampire Lesbians*. I suspected that as our audience became predominantly made up of tourists, *Vampire Lesbians of Sodom* came to represent an adventurous, edgy evening in the Village to tell the folks back home about, with the added advantage that it was presented in the safe environs of a traditional Off-Broadway theatre. Once in the door, most audiences could accept the drag performance in this lighthearted series of vignettes, especially since the leading drag performer was playing the role of the clown. Mainstream audiences were much more reluctant to accept Charles as the glamorous leading lady of more traditionally structured narratives in which the characters he played had romantic love interests, as was the case in his other plays. In *Vampire Lesbians*, the guy in a dress was interested in *girls*. Our tourist audiences could enjoy being exposed to transgressive ideas without having to experience genuine discomfort. In this regard, *Vampire Lesbians* was an anomaly among Theatre-in-Limbo productions, although we didn't realize it at the time.

Meghan's health continued to worsen, and she eventually suffered from aphasia caused by lesions on her brain. As this condition progressed, her speech was gradually reduced to gibberish. She had always been such a commanding personality—proud, grand, talented, and articulate—that it was nothing short of devastating to visit her during her final stay at Lenox Hill Hospital. She became so caring at the end, and she was always happy to see her friends, but she could no longer find the words to express herself. Charles recalled that when he saw her for the last time she had no words left: "She would just say to me, 'You're perfect, you're perfect.' And I'd say, 'You're perfect.' It was interesting that it was that phrase that she was left with."[3]

She died on November 18, 1990, at the age of 35. The *New York Times* obituary quoted Sam Rudy on the cause of death, who said "she had been ill with AIDS-related cancer."[4] We held a memorial service for her at the Orpheum Theatre on December 3, almost one year to the day after the closing of *The Lady in Question*. It was a big production; I rented the best large screen video equipment available at the time so we could show clips, as Susan Stroman had done for Jeff Veazey. The theatre was packed, and the audience applauded and cried as they watched the tape of Meghan pulling herself up the stairs one last time on the Orpheum stage.

Godiva Takes a Ride

Charles and I worked on projects independently of each other for most of the year after *Vampire Lesbians* closed; he rewrote the book of the Harold Arlen/Truman Capote musical *House of Flowers* for a stock tour starring Patti LaBelle and directed by Geoffrey Holder, and I directed a new play, *Grotesque Lovesongs* by Don Nigro at the WPA. By the end of the year, Charles was anxious to get back on the New York stage, and he had the beginnings of an idea for a new play for Theatre-in-Limbo. An entry in my 1990 date book for 3:00 p.m., December 4 (the day after Meghan's memorial service) notes our first "Godiva meeting."

Charles was becoming nostalgic about our early East Village performances, and he wanted to play Lady Godiva in a good, old-fashioned Theatre-in-Limbo costume pageant like *Theodora* or *Pardon My Inquisition*, something sure to please our fans. Kyle Renick had already agreed to produce it, sight unseen, at the WPA; we were set to open in March 1991. This timing was unfortunate for me because my agent at the time, Jeff Melnick, had arranged for me to spend six months in Los Angeles "observing" the directors on a soap opera called *Santa Barbara* (in hopes that I would transition into a more lucrative career as a television director), and I had leased my beloved condo beginning February 1. But I couldn't pass up the fun of doing a new Limbo show, so I made arrangements to come back and stay with New York friends during rehearsals.

As usual, there was no script. Charles came to our first meeting with a preliminary scenario for discussion. The subject matter had a Ridiculous provenance in Ronald Tavel's *Life of Lady Godiva*, and, like Tavel, Charles proposed to handle the story to comic effect with multiple anachronisms. But Tavel created a dark, dangerous world that featured sadomasochism and rape, and his dramaturgical approach emphasized a disturbing discontinuity. Charles's treatment of the story was lighter, and the narrative was clearly laid out based on the eleventh-century legend in which Godiva rides naked through the streets of Coventry to convince her husband, Leofric, to rescind a tax on the peasants. In Charles's outline, Godiva is herself a peasant whom Leofric meets while in disguise, and after they marry, she becomes "very highfalutin and pretentious," much like earlier Limbo heroines such as Gertrude Garnet and Irish O'Flanagan. And like Irish, Godiva learns the error of her selfish ways after being shown a series of visions. These visions depict how she will suffer in her future, reincarnated lives because of her apathy toward the plight of the peasants. In one vision, Godiva comes back as the Mexican artist Frida Kahlo, who is brutalized by her male chauvinist husband, Diego Rivera. Moved by the visions, she pleads with Leofric to rescind the tax. Leofric merely laughs and taunts her by saying he'll stop the tax if she rides naked in the streets. And so she mounts her steed, with nothing but her long hair to cover her nakedness, to come to the aid of the peasants, who agree not to watch. But Peeping Tom cannot resist taking a gander, and he goes blind. The working title of the play was *Godiva Takes a Ride*.

What intrigued and excited me about the scenario was a framing device Charles had created set in Hollywood in the early 1950s during the height of the red scare. Godiva's ride is actually the dream of all-American film star Mary Dale. Mary is married to Frank Taggert, an alcoholic, left-leaning stage actor; her best friend is a wacky comedienne and rabid right-winger called Pat Pilford. I encouraged Charles to expand the 1950s scenes, and it just so happened that some excellent research on the subject was available at the Museum of the Moving Image, which at the time was screening some rarely seen anti-communist films that weren't available at the World of Video: *The Red Menace* (1949) and *The Woman on Pier 13* (1949—originally titled *I Married a Communist*). We attended this double feature before our next meeting on December 12, and by that time Charles had created a revised scenario for our new project.

That meeting was also the first attended by theatre historian Richard Niles, who was working on a doctoral dissertation on Theatre-in-Limbo. Charles and I agreed to allow him to be a "fly on the wall" at all our meetings and rehearsals as we developed the new show, and his dissertation provides a detailed account of the process. Niles reports that at the December 12 meeting Charles read the new scenario and the rest of the meeting was taken up with my response to it.

By this time, Charles had fleshed out the Mary Dale story, which was beginning to be more than a mere framing device for a historical pageant. While looking for snapshots of their recent trip to Bermuda, Mary finds Frank's passport in his sock drawer at their beach house and discovers that his real name is Moishe Nisowitz, born in Ukraine. She is suspicious of his sudden interest in method acting and of his friendship with one of its proponents, Marta Towers, an actress whom Pat Pilford has identified as a "notorious pinko." Meanwhile, Pat's former lover, the Pulitzer Prize–winning playwright turned screenwriter Mitchell Drake, a communist, blackmails Pat. He confronts her just before the live broadcast of her radio variety show, threatening to release pornographic pictures he took of her "unless she becomes a commie tool." Mary is a guest on Pat's show that day, and she is aghast when Pat greets her with a hearty, "Welcome, comrade." During a commercial break, Mary confides that she is worried about Frank and his method acting class. Pat, "scared of commie goon squads," warns her to "stay away."

Mary doesn't take that advice, and she follows Frank to his acting class at the Yetta Felson Studio, which is a communist front organization. "She sneaks in and sees Frank tormented by doubts and Marta seducing him." Mary is discovered and "Frank humiliates her by sending her home alone." In the next scene at the movie studio, Mary breaks down on the set while "lip-syncing a musical number in her new film, 'Lady Godiva.'" Her director,

R.G. (whom she grows to suspect is also a communist), gives her a bottle of sleeping pills and she takes an overdose. This is where the Godiva dream sequence begins.

When Mary wakes up from her dream in a hospital room, most of the plot points are resolved at her bedside in this preliminary outline:

> Frank is with her, very upset at almost losing her. Mary convinces him the communist way is wrong. Pat visits. Frank makes Pat confess she's being blackmailed. She breaks down and says it's true. Mary says they must get the photos. Frank tells her she mustn't. It's too dangerous. Malcolm [Mary and Frank's gay valet] visits her. He is being hounded by the communists. He can't take it anymore and so he jumps out the window. Mary is now convinced she must do something.[5]

Mary and Pat sneak back into the acting studio to find the negatives of Pat's porn shots, and a series of reversals occurs: Pat murders Mitchell; R.G. and Yetta Felson, the method acting instructor, reveal themselves to be FBI agents; Marta reveals that "she is really Commissar Olga Kosavetskinya, who murdered the real Marta Towers in Mexico years before. Marta goes mad . . . R.G. convinces Frank to turn himself in." The final scene of the play is described in one sentence: "Mary climbs the steps of Congress and before HUAC, she gives a rousing patriotic speech and names names including Frank's as the curtain falls."

Many of the plot points in this scenario were lifted directly from the films we had just seen at the Museum of the Moving Image, outrageous, noir melodramas in which the Communist Party operates like organized crime by using front organizations, stopping at nothing in its quest to destroy the American way of life and luring unsuspecting victims into its tentacles by issuing membership cards that can never be revoked and that will haunt them for the rest of their lives. Beautiful femmes fatales entice decent-but-weak men into the party's clutches. Both films featured characters who spectacularly hurl themselves to their deaths from tall buildings as the only viable escape from the dreaded party. In a climactic scene in *The Red Menace*, evil party stalwart Yvonne Kraus (played with relish by Betty Lou Gerson, later known as the voice of Cruella de Vil in *101 Dalmatians*) admits before immigration officials that she is actually "Commissar Greta Block," and brags that she had the real Yvonne Kraus murdered in Mexico and then assumed her identity. She promptly goes mad, hearing in her head the drums of an imaginary advancing proletariat ("You fools! Don't you hear them?"), and erupts into peals of demonic laughter as she is led off by an officer to the psychopathic ward. Even the name of the director of Mary Dale's film, R.G., is an homage to R. G. Springsteen, the director of *The Red Menace*.

Charles and I found these films both hilarious and astonishing. It was disturbing to imagine the paranoia of a society that could take such blatantly absurd propaganda seriously, but that was the United States at the height of the Cold War. We assumed we lived in a much more sophisticated age that wouldn't be taken in by such nonsense, but this was well before the outbreak of fake news on the internet and in social media. The films were campy and ripe for parody, and very few changes were needed to convert their plots into truly Ridiculous Theatre. Nevertheless, some problematic issues remained in the preliminary scenario that Charles and I hashed through at that December 12 meeting. The McCarthy era, with its notorious smear campaigns and blacklisting that ruined lives, was still a vivid memory and a touchy subject for many people. How would the audience react to the heroine of the play, Mary Dale, naming names before a congressional committee, an act that could only be viewed as abhorrent, no matter how well-meaning the character's motives? We were concerned that the irony might not be obvious, and that some in our audience could think we were endorsing McCarthyism. But we were more concerned with a major structural problem: the Lady Godiva sequence had no function in the story of Mary Dale. It was as if two completely different plays had been taped together.

Over the course of several script meetings, I continued to argue for bolstering the 1950s plot, which I found much more interesting than the Godiva story. After years of collaborating and living together, Charles and I trusted each other so completely that I could be frank with him as an editor and dramaturg to help him shape the narrative and strengthen character motivation. I had always been fascinated by a 1953 media event: Arthur Godfrey's on-air firing of singer Julius La Rosa. I felt that the tone of the play could be set by opening the show with Pat Pilford's radio broadcast, during which she would fire an actor on the air for being a communist, and I brought an old recording of the classic radio show *Fibber McGee and Molly* to one of our meetings to provide some inspiration. To give the narrative a push, I suggested that the communists should hatch a plot to take over the Hollywood studios to spread their evil propaganda. I proposed that we add a character to spearhead this plot: a cigar-chomping, thuggish party boss. After Mary is discovered at the acting studio, the boss, Barker, should blackmail Frank into murdering her, which, because he was in the grip of the communists, he would reluctantly agree to do. This provided the cliff-hanger for the act 1 curtain: how would Mary escape this death sentence? I made a stab at justifying Mary's Godiva dream by proposing that it should somehow be a catalyst for her to take a stand against the communists. Charles incorporated most (but not all) of my notes into the first draft of the play, which he completed by the end of January 1991. That was the way we worked. As a result of our script meetings, the focus of the play had shifted from Lady Godiva to Mary Dale, and by the end of January the title had been changed from *Godiva Takes a Ride* to *Red Scare on Sunset*.

Limbo Reunion

Before Charles even started writing the play, he and I contacted members of our company to make sure they were available—it had, after all, been over two years since we had created a show together. Meghan was gone, and Bobby was in California, but the cast included three members of the original company: the role of Pat Pilford was tailored for Julie Halston, Arnie Kolodner filled his usual leading man role as the troubled Frank Taggert, and Andy Halliday was to play Frank and Mary's gay butler, Malcom, and double as the method acting guru Yetta Felson. The rest of the company had all been in Limbo shows at some point: Ralph Buckley, who had been in *Times Square Angel*, *Pardon My Inquisition*, and *Psycho Beach Party*, was set to play Mitchell Drake; Mark Hamilton, the longtime *Vampire Lesbians* understudy who had created dual roles in *The Lady in Question*, agreed to play the director R. G. Benson and several other roles; Judith Hansen, who had appeared in *Psycho Beach Party* and valiantly understudied Meghan in *The Lady in Question*, would be the femme fatale method actress Marta Towers. Roy Cockrum, my college roommate at Northwestern who had played over one thousand performances as a replacement in *Vampire Lesbians*, was Bertram Barker, the party boss. The Limbo design team was also reassembled. Brian and Vivien were set to do the scenery and lighting. John Glaser was unavailable to design the costumes, so we turned to Debra Tennenbaum, who had designed *Times Square Angel* and the Limbo Lounge version of *Coma*. T. L. Boston was once again our stage manager. Starting the production process with a cast and artistic staff that is already familiar with the style of the play is an unusual luxury, and it meant that we could work together quickly. We would need to.

Before I left for Los Angeles for my abbreviated stint observing on *Santa Barbara*, we had a production meeting at the WPA Theatre that proved to be tempestuous, and the bone of contention was money. The bifurcated structure of the play meant that we had an enormous costume plot covering two distinct periods: there were to be eleven medieval and twenty-eight early 950s costumes. Many of these costumes could be rented, but Charles's gowns would have to be built. Our costume designer, Debra Tennenbaum, was a tough cookie who refused to sugarcoat reality for the producers. She knew what it would cost, and she wasn't going to start working without assurance from Kyle that she would have the funds she needed to do it right. Kyle and the WPA staff were equally adamant that the budget could not be changed, and Debra would somehow have to cut $3,100 from her projected expenses. I argued that the budget had been created for a generic, small-cast WPA production with contemporary realistic costumes and that it made no sense to apply it to this play, but Kyle would not back down. We were at an impasse until I suggested that we cut one week of our proposed three-week rehearsal period to pay for the costumes. Kyle agreed, at which point Charles tartly inquired, "What are we going to do the second week?"

We had two weeks to put the show together before the first preview, so after one table reading on Tuesday, March 5, I started blocking immediately. By Friday the actors were off book and ready for their first run-through. That was when it became apparent that the Godiva sequence wasn't working; it really interrupted the flow of the story and served no dramatic purpose. At the height of the rising action, just after Frank attempts to murder Mary with a poison necklace, the play ground to a halt for a seemingly unrelated historical pageant in an entirely different style. After the Saturday run-through, I dismissed the company, sat for a moment, and then turned to our stage manager, T. L. Boston, and said, "I think the whole thing should be cut." I went up to Charles's dressing room and told him the same thing; he reluctantly agreed. I found Debra Tennenbaum in the hall and gave her the news that we wouldn't need the medieval costumes after all and, needless to say, she was dismayed. Brian Whitehill, who had been touching up some details on the set, overheard our conversation and soon both he and Debra were passionately trying to convince Charles and me to save the dream. Brian had concocted a blow-up horse that was inflated with a vacuum cleaner for Godiva's ride and that was sure to be one of the best visual jokes of the show, and he didn't want to lose it. Soon, T. L. Boston wandered in and joined the discussion. Richard Niles was there, too, and according to his account, Charles then "announced that no one was leaving until he had a new dream sequence."[6]

The brainstorming session went on for an hour or so, until Brian finally came up with a solution that we all agreed on. Rather than beginning an entirely new narrative introducing a new set of characters, the dream should be a surreal nightmare that takes place in the set of Mary and Frank's beach house. Charles went home and on his day off he completely rewrote the Godiva sequence from scratch, in the process cutting it from twenty minutes to six. The original Godiva scenes, including the visions, were jettisoned. After Frank attempts to murder her, Mary overdoses on the pills R.G. gave her at the studio, she collapses, and the dream music and lighting effects are cued in. The other characters of the play enter in medieval costumes—but they are still recognizable characters from the main narrative: Frank, Pat Pilford, Mitchell Drake, Barker, Marta Towers, and Malcom. They all address Mary as Lady Godiva, but she remains Mary throughout, utterly confused and suffering from an identity crisis: "Frank, look at me. I'm not Lady Godiva. That's just a role I play. I'm Mary Dale Taggert. No, that's not me. I'm Mary Dale. No, that's my stage name. I'm Mary Louise Hofstetter." At the climax of the dream, Mary threatens to throw herself into the moat in despair. Then the period abruptly changes with the entrance of the ghost of Mary's grandmother, an Auntie Em–type farm woman (played by Mark Hamilton in a simple 1930s cotton dress) who gives Mary some heartfelt advice: "Save yourself and save your husband. He's not a bad man, just so very scared. Save him darlin'. One little person can make a difference, you know. But sometimes you gotta do something kind of crazy to make people stand up and take notice."[7] This inspires Mary and leads directly to Mary-as-Godiva riding Brian's inflatable horse through the town square in brilliant white light—a fabulous *tableau vivant* of cheap theatrics. When Mary wakes up in the hospital in the next scene, she is a changed person; she is no longer confused, and she knows what she needs to do. This new dream propelled the action of the play rather than stopping it in its tracks. It worked.

When we returned to rehearsal on Tuesday, we had one week to put in the new material and tech the show before the first preview. I soon regretted having blithely given up that third week of rehearsal, because the technical demands of *Red Scare* were intense, and our underpaid crew was inexperienced. But, with the usual magic of show business, the first preview went smoothly and the audience was loving the show—that is, until it became clear exactly what Mary had learned from the dream: that she was to root out and expose communists in Hollywood, including her own husband. In the penultimate scene, Frank admits his membership in the party to R.G. (who is revealed to be a double agent working for the FBI): "I may have just joined, but I've been pink for years. Mary and I have discussed this and I'd like to go public and admit I was wrong. [*brightly*] We also thought it would be helpful if I gave the names of others I know to be disloyal." I could feel the air go out of the room at this moment, and when the play ended with Mary naming names, it was one of the most uncomfortable curtains I had ever experienced. The response was exactly what Charles and I had feared at our first script meeting. Of course, the ending was meant to be satirical and to demonstrate that otherwise "nice" people can do horrific things in the name of an ideology. To emphasize the irony, Brian designed cartoon stick figures of the Capitol, the Statue of Liberty, and the Liberty Bell, which stagehands waved upstage while Mary read her list. Charles assured the audience in curtain speeches, "I'm up here in a dress, why would I be for blacklisting?" That didn't matter, because the lovable heroine of a hilarious comedy turned out to be a right-wing red-baiter seemingly happy to destroy lives. The audience was disoriented and confused.

After a few previews with the same muddled response, Charles and I set out to fix the problem through dialogue, sound, and lighting. Mary's original speech to Congress revealed her to be an angry demagogue expressing a very specific, conservative ideology that was reminiscent of Ronald Reagan's embrace of anti-intellectual "traditional values" from a mythological morning in America, as she self-righteously addressed a congressional committee:

> Only in America, could the right to free speech be distorted and exploited by a corrupt foreign influence. They have taken our delicious freedom and forgive my vulgarity, kicked us in the you know what. We in show business must set an example to the rest of the country. We must represent honest emotion, traditional values, gay laughter, singing and dancing. That's entertainment. Definitely not obscene, pseudo-intellectual hogwash designed to amuse a decadent elite.[8]

In a rewrite, Charles cut the conservative dogma and made it clear that Mary's point of view was reductive, simplistic, and wrong. She begins by invoking a more anodyne Reaganesque trope of rising from Midwest poverty to Hollywood stardom:

Senators, Gentlemen, I stand before this august body terribly humbled. Only in America could a young girl raised by struggling farmers in Indiana grow up to be a movie star and also be able to speak to a distinguished panel of senators and may I add, most handsome. The world is so complicated today. A girl doesn't know which way to turn. One wants to do the correct thing. But what is the correct thing? What's smart today could be dumb tomorrow. But I had a dream about Lady Godiva, which is my latest film and I cordially invite all of you to the premiere at the Pantages. And from that dream I learned to apply the simple answers of a bygone era to the complicated questions of today.[9]

The new speech softened the ending considerably and made it clear that, despite her revelatory dream, Mary had not really changed into an ideologue. She was simply a naïve, harmlessly flirtatious actress, unsure if what she was about to do was really the "correct thing," blindly accepting the prevailing view of the times. When it came time to name names, Charles gave it the comical feel of an Academy Awards ceremony. As Mary opens an envelope containing a list of communists, she looks up nervously and says, "My, this is very exciting." She then proceeds to read the names: "I name Marta Towers, Bertram Barker . . . (SHE pauses for a moment, hesitantly.) and because I love him, Frank Taggert."[10] She continues with a roster of students from the Yetta Felson Studio. At this point, I worked with sound designer Guy Sherman (a.k.a. Aural Fixation) to add a sound cue that gradually drowned out the litany of names, a section from the final movement of Charles Ives's Second Symphony that treated patriotic themes such as "Columbia, the Gem of the Ocean," with a harsh, dissonant quality. Vivien built the lights to a glaring brightness on the cartoon cutouts waving upstage before going to a blackout rather than a gentle fade on the final chord—a loud, abrasive, sour note. We felt certain that these changes would clarify the ending by emphasizing the satire. We were only partially successful.

The Lady in Question had been presented as part of the WPA "Silly Series," which meant a short run without critics, but *Red Scare on Sunset* was part of the regular WPA season, and critics were invited. We may have only had two weeks of rehearsal, but Kyle very generously gave us four full weeks of previews before the first press night. He and I both knew that we could count on our Limbo audiences to fill the WPA Theatre for at least that long and that we didn't need reviews to sell tickets in the short term. We continued to make minor tweaks, but overall, the audiences were ecstatic despite the uncertain ending. The show felt like a hit, and I was starting to get the urge to move it to a commercial venue, so I began the laborious process of inviting potential investors to the show.

My efforts to transfer *Red Scare* were tinged with desperation. Over the past six years I had moved four shows to commercial Off-Broadway runs, and all but the first had been financial flops. This felt like a last chance. It didn't help that I was nearly broke at the time; like most Off-Broadway nonprofits, the WPA did not pay well. Living out of a suitcase in someone else's apartment contributed to my sense of anxiety and unease as I began to look for angels. And underneath it all was the constant awareness of the toll that AIDS was taking.

One night in April, Bobby Carey came to a performance. He had moved back to New Jersey from California to live with his parents so that they could take care of him as various AIDS-related illnesses ravaged his body. We all tried not to look shocked or heartbroken when we saw him. He was emaciated, walked haltingly with a limp, and was partially paralyzed on one side. I had just seen him in Los Angeles a few months earlier, and I was really shaken by how quickly his health had deteriorated. A lot of us went out to dinner with him after the show, and we all laughed together and reminisced about the old days at the Limbo Lounge. When it was time to go home, we hugged him extra hard; it was obvious that he was not going to get better.

The critics finally started coming during the fifth week of our run, and we were ready for them. But I was acutely disappointed when I learned that the *Times* was sending second-stringer Mel Gussow, who had been so patronizing about *Up Against It*, rather than Frank Rich. Jeff Richards, the WPA's press agent, explained that Rich was covering another opening that night at Manhattan Theater Club and that, at any rate, the WPA was Gussow's usual beat. I wasn't comforted by that explanation, and with growing horror and outrage at the thought of a bland Mel Gussow review, I met with Kyle in his office and demanded to know why we hadn't changed the date of the opening night to accommodate Rich's schedule. He just shrugged and said there was nothing we could do about it, adding that even if we changed the opening night there was still no guarantee that the *Times* would send Frank Rich. All we could do was hope for the best. Of course, Kyle was right, but that did nothing to assuage my sense of doom.

The official press opening was Sunday, April 21, and after the reception, Charles and I took a taxi up to the *Times* Building on Forty-Third Street so we could get one of the first copies off the presses of Monday's paper. We stood on the street breathlessly thumbing through the arts section, but there was no review. Other notices, mostly positive, started trickling in on Monday and Tuesday, but still nothing from the *Times*. Finally, on Wednesday, it appeared, relegated to the new "Theater in Review" section that featured a roundup of short, capsule reviews of what seemed to be less-than-noteworthy productions that didn't merit a stand-alone review. Mel Gussow did not get it, labeling the play "political commentary of a most peculiar sort." While he was amused by the Godiva dream sequence, "unfortunately that story is only the subplot of a B movie melodrama about a projected Communist takeover of the film industry." Despite all our efforts to make it clear that we were critiquing, not advocating blacklisting, Gussow averred, "The play could be regarded as an attempt to justify the blacklist, which would be perverse in the extreme," and he declared, "Mr. Busch is over his head and fuzzy-minded as a political theorist." While he admitted that "the play's brambled path is strewn with quirky comedy" and that Julie Halston was "amusing as an imperious Hedda Hopper–like radio vixen," the overall tone of the review was condescending dismissal.[11]

My heart sank as I read those brief paragraphs, and my first reaction was to abandon any hope of moving the show for an extended run. But the slight from the *Times* had no effect on our box office; we continued to sell out, the audiences were laughing just as loudly, more favorable notices continued to come out, and Kyle extended our run at the WPA to May 5. One of the most perceptive reviews was from Michael Feingold in the *Village Voice*, who found that "what makes Mary Dale different than earlier Busch heroines is that, instead of confining itself to film-genre parody, her adorable triviality trespasses, in disturbing ways, on real life." Feingold had no trouble understanding the play's ending:

> For the first time in the series of playful pieces that began with *Vampire Lesbians of Sodom*, Busch has represented the difference between "normal" and "deviant" (gay, leftist, artist, whatever) as an unbridgeable gap. Where the earlier Busch heroines were either glamorous comic threats or equally glamorous gals-to-the-rescue, in the chilling last scene of *Red Scare on Sunset*, it's simple, good-hearted, well-meaning Mary Dale, with all her Middle American

virtues, who turns out to be the horror at the core of the piece . . . . Busch goes beyond the jesting with right and left to kick at something nightmarish in the American character itself: the desperate, brainless optimism that insists that good "little people" can prevail without ever thinking about what they're doing, that the unexamined life is the only one worth living.[12]

Jan Stuart in *Newsday* and Clive Barnes in the *Post* were also positive. Even John Simon in *New York Magazine* found the show "surprisingly enjoyable," with "much sassy wit."[13] I talked myself into the notion that a bad *Times* review didn't matter, and I decided to press on with the commercial transfer.

Kyle Renick declined to co-produce this time, and Hal Luftig at the Orpheum passed as well. But producer Manny Kladitis encouraged me; he let me use a desk in his suite of offices in the Sardi Building to work the phones, and he eventually signed on as a producer. We set the budget at $150,000—$100,000 less than *The Lady in Question*—in the hope we could recoup quickly. I felt like Amanda Wingfield selling magazine subscriptions in *The Glass Menagerie* as I trolled for investors, but after weeks of relentless phone calls and meetings and the addition of several co-producers, we were able to move *Red Scare on Sunset* to the Lucille Lortel Theatre, one of the premiere Off-Broadway theatres, owned by the self-described "queen of Off-Broadway," on June 21. Miss Lortel dutifully attended a performance, but it was pretty clear that it was not her cup of tea. She usually insisted on billing over the title, "by special arrangement with Lucille Lortel," for plays that opened in her theatre; in our case, she preferred no billing.

Whereas we did sellout business in the initial run at the WPA, the commercial transfer struggled to find an audience from the outset. Most of the mainstream critics had already seen the show two months earlier, and it was difficult to get press. Sam Rudy had warned us that the WPA run was getting too much coverage and that we should have saved it for the transfer. I kept hoping the *Times* would run a feature or send Frank Rich to do a "Critic's Notebook," but Gussow's four paragraphs were all that appeared in the paper during the run of *Red Scare*. As I had learned, attention from the *Times* is no guarantee of success, but without it you flail around trying to find an audience. Sam did his best to get us some coverage, and a few additional reviews appeared, including a rave in the *New Yorker* from Mimi Kramer, who called *Red Scare* Charles's "funniest play so far, and also his most cohesive and deeply felt," although Charles wasn't pleased that she singled out Julie Halston as "very much the show's star."[14] (His private response was "Never again!") Our low capitalization meant we didn't have the funds for a float in the gay pride parade as we had done for *The Lady in Question*, so I rented a convertible instead, and Charles waved to the crowds while other members of the cast and crew handed out the flyers.

The parade was festive, as usual, but it turned somber with the moment of silence at 2:00 p.m., when the entire, noisy procession came to a halt in remembrance of those who had been lost to AIDS. The moment was more than usually freighted for us because Bobby Carey had died three days earlier, on June 27. He was just thirty-two years old. Charles and I had gone out to his parents' house in New Jersey a few weeks earlier to visit him, and it was clear once we got there that we would be saying our final goodbyes. Bobby was pretty much bedridden. We each spent some time alone with him. I held his hand and awkwardly told him that I loved him. He said, "I know," and then gave me a watch I had often seen him wear that had a map of the world on its face.

After we had been running at the Lortel for only three weeks, Ben Sprecher, the general manager of the theatre, came to me with an offer: he would cut the rent drastically if we would agree to close the show by September 15. (He wanted to book another show into the theatre in the fall, *The Baby Dance* by Jane Anderson.) Ben really put me in a difficult position, and because Miss Lortel was not a fan of the show, there wasn't much I could do about it. We were falling short of our weekly operating expenses and needed the rent reduction, but taking it almost certainly meant closing the show at a loss. At first I refused the offer, but after another slow week at the box office Manny and I decided we needed the rent reduction even to make it through the summer. *Red Scare on Sunset* closed on schedule on September 15, after playing 100 performances at the Lortel. It was the last new show produced by Theatre-in-Limbo.

The evening after we closed, we had a memorial service for Bobby. Arthur Cantor allowed us to hold it at the Provincetown Playhouse. None of us had been there since *Vampire Lesbians* closed, and it was haunting to walk in to what we thought of as "our theatre" without the familiar marquee and lobby signs, stripped of scenery, with empty dressing rooms. We didn't see any rats that night, but I am sure they had probably reclaimed the place. As had become standard practice for our memorial services, I rented video equipment so that we could show clips of Bobby, both onstage and clowning in the wings, beautifully edited by Andy Halliday. Bobby's sister

Lee and I moderated the service, and several company members and friends gave moving eulogies. I held it together until after the service, when I took the narrow backstage steps down to the dressing rooms to be alone for a moment and sobbed uncontrollably for about five minutes. By the time I got back up to the lobby, the company was filtering out into the night. As I walked home, it occurred to me that our group could never be the same again. Charles and I both wanted to move in other directions, as did other members of the company. The memorial service was a farewell not just to Bobby but to Theatre-in-Limbo itself.

Chapter 7 **Beyond Limbo**

Charles Busch in a tuxedo for his first Off-Broadway role out of drag in You Should Be So Lucky, *with Stephen Pearlman. Photo by Andrew Leynse.*

Charles and I lifted our spirits in December 1991 by getting much of our company together for a revival of *Times Square Angel* at Theatre for the New City, a vibrant, chaotic cluster of performance spaces in the East Village run by the indomitable Crystal Field. Broadway dancer Jim Borstelmann took over Bobby Carey's role, and Jim Mahady, an old friend from Northwestern, replaced Andy Halliday, who was working on a production of his new play, *I Can't Stop Screaming*. Otherwise, it was the original 1984 cast, and more or less the original version of the script (without the extended prologue), so it felt like the good old days at the Limbo Lounge, complete with the wildly enthusiastic fans. Those days were gone, but we didn't realize it at the time.

In the new year, I was preparing a production of *Vampire Lesbians*, with Charles recreating his roles, for a three-week engagement in Tokyo in

February 1992 that was to be taped for broadcast on Japanese television. I sent the company off to Japan, but I was unable to go on the trip because I was directing *Julie Halston's Lifetime of Comedy* at the Actors' Playhouse, the Off-Broadway transfer of her acclaimed club act. The show was warmly received; reviewing in the *Times*, Mel Gussow described Julie as having "the deftness but not the malice of Joan Rivers and the show business sassiness of Bette Midler." He added, "one could easily envision her moving along into a sitcom."[1] Gussow's prediction was at least partially realized; CBS executive Christopher Gorman fell in love with Julie's performance, the network signed her, and a sitcom pilot, co-starring Harvey Fierstein and Eileen Heckart, was made. Like most pilots, it was not picked up as a series. Japanese audiences were somewhat puzzled by *Vampire Lesbians*, although the physical comedy got some laughs. Instead of gay men, Charles found that his fan base in Tokyo consisted mostly of teenaged girls, who adoringly tossed flowers to the stage at the curtain call and regularly converged on the stage door to catch sight of him after the performances.

Theatre-in-Limbo gave its final performance on December 20, 1992, with another revival of *Times Square Angel* at Theatre for the New City. No intentional decision was made to dissolve the company, it just happened. Charles and I were in our late thirties, and we were both still trying to figure out how to make a living in the theatre. Theatre-in-Limbo had produced eight new plays over a seven-year period, five of which had transferred to commercial runs, but only *Vampire Lesbians*, our first show, had been a financial success. Starting with *Psycho Beach Party*, each successive show had a shorter run, despite substantial critical praise and the initial enthusiasm of our Limbo fans. Once we ran through what we called "our audience," box office inevitably dwindled. Yet expenses at Off-Broadway venues such as the Orpheum and the Lortel grew higher and higher. It finally dawned on us that perhaps *Vampire Lesbians* was a genuine anomaly, and there truly was a limited audience for Ridiculous Theatre and drag performance. Perhaps it just wasn't worth it to mount expensive, full productions of these plays. "I don't think these kinds of plays are meant to be commercial," Charles observed in a 1991 interview with Richard Niles:

> Unfortunately, I also enjoy playing these nice theatres and having my own dressing room, hot water, in a real theatre, and it is nice to reach out to a wider audience. They may not come in droves, but there are all sorts of people who wouldn't come to Theatre for the New City

who have seen us only at the Provincetown or the Orpheum, and who are big fans of mine now. I don't really know what the answer is.

The answer was elusive, but Charles noted that the problem was clear: "Unfortunately, we have to make a living."[2] We started to rethink our strategy.

Charles caused a stir when he published a novel in 1993, a rather self-aggrandizing *roman à clef* with a preposterous caper plot about an East Village theatre company attempting to move their cult hit, *Whores of Lost Atlantis* (also the title of the novel), to a commercial Off-Broadway theatre. Julian Young, the central character Charles based on himself, is a wacky, lovable genius who assembles a group of misfits and losers devoted to helping him execute his unique artistic vision. In an early chapter, Julian's best friend, Joel Finley (based on me), rapturously declares to him, "You are the living embodiment of theatre. Think about it. You're flamboyant, outrageous, emotional, obsessed with artifice but also tough, gritty, totally self-absorbed, a survivor, and very seductive."[3] That's how Charles saw himself, but I don't think I would have said it quite that way. Theatre-in-Limbo may have only recently disbanded, but he had already turned it into a myth. Many of the characters are thinly veiled representations of members of our company, and not everyone was pleased to be depicted as an eccentric oddball.

Charles was both jealous of and impressed by Julie Halston's successful club act, and he decided that he should have a crack at cabaret—but he wanted something grander. Instead of a solo act, we worked with music director Dick Gallagher (another old friend from Northwestern)[4] to put together an old-fashioned, Carol Burnett–style variety show, with musical numbers, monologues, comedy sketches, dancing boys, and "special guests." We played in what Charles called "the big room" at the Ballroom, a popular restaurant and cabaret in Chelsea. *The Charles Busch Revue* was a hoot that Stephen Holden, reviewing for the *Times*, described as "ramshackle" but "consistently charming and ebullient."[5] Frank Rich chimed in on WQXR, saying, "This show is a delightful introduction to the Busch sensibility, which is warm and incisively satirical about pop culture without being mean-spirited. . . . If somehow you haven't met him before, his revue at the Ballroom, spiffily directed by Kenneth Elliott, is an ideal introduction."[6] The high cover charge along with food and drink minimums made it a very expensive evening, however, and were a deterrent to the box office. Cabaret was clearly not the answer to our show business dreams.

The owner of the Ballroom, Tim Johnson, had a bigger idea: a huge drag revue at the venerable Town Hall on Forty-Third Street to coordinate with the Gay Games to be held in New York in 1994. Charles Busch, in his star persona, would be the mistress of ceremonies, and I would direct (or rather assemble) the show, which would be called *Charles Busch's Dressing Up! The Ultimate Dragfest*. Tim wanted to sign up every significant drag performer alive for this extravaganza. He knew that he could book the great Charles Pierce, who had played the Ballroom many times, to revive two of his greatest impersonations: Gloria Swanson as Norma Desmond and Bette Davis. A Norma Desmond impersonation had helped to launch Charles Ludlam's career in an early Play-House of the Ridiculous production, but Charles Pierce was a very different type of drag artist. Although he preferred to be called a "male actress," he was really a stand-up comedian who mostly played in clubs. He was revered by his devoted fans, was edging toward retirement, and hoped that the Town Hall event would be a fitting farewell New York performance. But Tim was also talking to representatives of an even bigger headliner who might steal the spotlight: Milton Berle. Charles and I were dubious that Tim could convince Berle to appear at an event aimed squarely at a gay audience but, amazingly, he agreed to do it.

Uncle Miltie

Berle, who was eighty-five at the time, required a lot of attention. Tim and I picked him up in a limo at Penn Station on a sweltering day in June. Unfortunately, we were a few minutes late and in a panic ran all over the meandering, dungeon-like station looking for him. We found him outside at the taxi stand wearing a cashmere overcoat and a fedora, oblivious to the heat; he was always cold, and he seemed very old and tired. I met with him numerous times over the next weeks for fittings and rehearsals. He didn't have his own drag costume, but as we drove past NBC Studios at Rockefeller Center in the limo, he suggested that we call NBC to see if any of his old wardrobe from Texaco Star Theatre was available. I wondered if he really thought they saved all that for him. (Costume designer Suzy Benzinger found a dress and wig that recalled his television drag persona.) He was very fussy about how Charles would introduce him and demanded several rewrites to the script. I was summoned to the Friars Club, where he liked to have long lunches with Henny Youngman and other old comedians, to deliver the changes. I peered into the dining room where he was holding forth while the receptionist paged him: "Abbot Emeritus Milton Berle, you have a visitor." Rehearsals were really production meetings in which he would go over every detail of what he required, down to the brand name of the follow spot (it had to be a Super Trouper). I never saw him actually rehearse, and he never revealed any of the material that he was planning to perform, but I heard bits of it on a small cassette player he carried around on which he recorded all his jokes. All I knew was that he was going to do twenty minutes in drag.

The afternoon of the performance, we had a dress rehearsal at Town Hall. Milton humiliated Charles in front of the cast and crew by insisting that he was mispronouncing his name ("it's Mil-TIN, Mil-TIN") and demanding that he repeat the introduction over and over until he got it right. Still, Milton did not show us what he planned to do. After the rehearsal, Beatrice Arthur, who was making a cameo appearance to support her good friend Charles Pierce, approached and darkly warned me to "be prepared." I didn't know what she meant. "I've worked with Milton Berle," she said. "You'll never get him off the stage. You better have a plan." I thanked her for the advice, but I thought she was being overly dramatic and ominous, and I was too busy with last-minute details to give it much thought.

That night, Town Hall was packed with gay men. Charles Busch worked the crowd brilliantly in his opening monologue. Ira Siff, who is now best known as a commentator for the Metropolitan Opera broadcasts, leavened the proceedings with classical camp as the "traumatic soprano" Vera Galupe-Borszkh. Vera was a character he had developed with his own group, La Gran Scena Opera Company, an all-male troupe that skillfully parodied grand opera. Randy Allen, a popular young drag artist who died of AIDS less than a year later, appeared as Marilyn Monroe. The fun culminated triumphantly in the act 1 finale with "Mr. Charles Pierce" as Norma Desmond, who entered to a huge ovation saying, "I couldn't decide what to wear, so I wore everything!" I ran backstage at the intermission, and the dressing rooms were buzzing with excitement. Charles Pierce was particularly thrilled and gratified by the enormous affection that the audience had shown him. I checked in with Milton, who was in his dressing room listening to the cassette recording of himself, mouthing the words to his jokes. He looked so very old and frail that I wondered how he would get through his twenty-minute set—but he said he was ready to go on. I nervously took a seat in the back of the orchestra.

Milton was to be the penultimate segment of act 2. Charles introduced him flawlessly, and the Super Trouper spotlight picked him up as he entered in a sequined red dress, blonde wig, and full drag makeup. The audience roared and gave him a sustained ovation as he posed and primped; then he abruptly yanked off his wig, shouted "It's me, Milton!" and proceeded to dive into his act, a series of timeworn Borscht Belt one-liners that somehow were amazingly hilarious. His energy soared and the years seemed to melt away with each huge laugh he earned from the audience. He didn't look frail anymore; he was in command, as he had been on NBC decades earlier. I was laughing along with the audience, unaware that, in his vampire-like need to milk every joke he had ever told, he had gone well over the twenty minutes we had allotted. I suddenly felt a tap on my shoulder. It was Virginia Giordano, Tim's producing partner. "You've got to get him off the stage, or we'll be going into overtime with the stagehands," she whispered. I was jolted into reality—how could I get Milton Berle off the stage? I rushed backstage to find Charles Busch, Charles Pierce, Ira, Randy, and others huddled in the wings, all wondering if Milton Berle would ever run out of one-liners. It was a surreal scene because all of the performers were dressed as Bette Davis for the big finale. Bea Arthur turned to me with a raised eyebrow and said, "I told you." Finally, Charles Pierce bravely volunteered to give him the hook. He took a deep breath, strode onstage in his Margo Channing dress and shouted, "Milton, darling, it's Bette!" Milton initially looked utterly disoriented, but he soon realized that Bette Davis was going to stand there with her hands on her hips until he made his exit. He quickly wrapped up and, although Charles Pierce sadly had to cut much of his planned farewell Bette Davis routine, the big finale ended before overtime kicked in.

I was sure that Milton would be livid and that I was going to get an earful about giving him the hook, so I dreaded going to his dressing room after the show. But when I knocked on the door, he was hunched in front of his makeup mirror in a reverie. He was shirtless, and his clownish drag makeup was running down his face onto his sagging chest; he once again looked like a frail old man. He turned to me and said with wonderment, "They liked me. I didn't think this would be my crowd. But they liked Berle." He needed the affection of the audience; it was like a miraculous drug that temporarily restored him to vigorous middle age, and when it was over, he was depleted.

There was something incongruous about Milton Berle appearing onstage with Charles Busch and other gay drag artists at an event celebrating the Gay Games and gay pride. As a major television star of the 1940s and

'50s, he was the ultimate mainstream, establishment figure. Although he often appeared in drag on his show, it was always clear that underneath the makeup and wig, "It's me, Milton!" This type of heterosexual drag stands in nearly binary opposition to the gender ambiguity of Ridiculous Theatre. The old-fashioned groaners that he reveled in could not be further removed from Ronald Tavel's literate, ornate wordplay. The savvy showbiz pro who demanded a Super Trouper would have been baffled by John Vacarro's "orgiastic" staging. Ludlam said that camp is "motivated by rage," and so was much of his theatre. But Milton Berle wanted to be loved.

Theatre-in-Limbo came directly from the Ridiculous tradition of Smith, Tavel, Vaccaro, and Ludlam. Comparisons were made from the earliest Limbo Lounge performances, and the Ludlam versus Busch critique came to be expected in almost every review we received. The plays we produced were larded with postmodern quotations from pop culture and contained coded camp humor that was targeted to our gay audiences. Drag performance, especially that of our playwright and star, was a central, signature aspect of every show. Our approach to drag harked back to the gender ambiguity of early Ridiculous Theatre. Charles as the Virgin Sacrifice in *Vampire Lesbians of Sodom* looked like an extra from *Flaming Creatures*, and his costumes for all of our plays, while often glamorous, did not conceal his maleness. He never padded his chest or wore falsies in those days.

And yet, as a playwright and performer, Charles Busch had almost as much in common with Milton Berle as with his Ridiculous Theatre predecessors—and that determined the direction of our company as much as anything. Like Berle, Charles needed the love of the audience. The joy he took in being the star, center stage, was palpable and infectious. He had an old-fashioned sense of how to structure a joke and a skillful mastery of plot conventions gleaned from countless hours of watching old Hollywood films, and he genuinely loved the material we were parodying. Most important, he wanted to cross over, he wanted mainstream success. He once remarked that he couldn't understand anyone who didn't want to be famous. Celebrity was always part of his goal.

You Should Be So Lucky

Charles and I continued to work together (and separately) throughout the 1990s after Theatre-in-Limbo faded away, trying to find a new direction. In the quest for a mainstream hit, I urged him to write a male role for himself—which was a challenging stretch. It was not easy for Charles to figure out what kind of man he would be comfortable playing, but the result was a charming play, *You Should Be So Lucky*, which proved to be a nonprofit hit at Primary Stages Theatre. But early on in rehearsal we realized that the second act wasn't working. During a frenzied break, Charles and I identified the problems and hammered out a new scenario. I sent him home to write while I worked with the other actors. Two days later, he returned with an entirely new second act that I thought worked brilliantly.

Charles played Christopher, an agoraphobic, bashful, dizzy, gay electrologist, who rescues Mr. Rosenberg (Stephen Pearlman), a kindly, older, heterosexual, Jewish man who had collapsed on the street, and brings him to his cluttered Village apartment to recover. Rosenberg takes a platonic shine to Christopher and becomes an electrolysis client—and then dies of a heart attack during the hair removal process. Not only does he improbably leave Christopher $10 million, he returns as a ghost to serve as his fairy godfather. Julie Halston gave a hilarious star turn as Rosenberg's harpy daughter, and Nell Campbell played Christopher's wacky, self-dramatizing sister. With Mr. Rosenberg's support, Christopher gains confidence, gets a boyfriend, overcomes his shyness, and becomes a national sensation with an appearance on an Oprah-type television talk show—theatre as wish fulfillment. Unlike our Theatre-in-Limbo shows, *You Should Be So Lucky* was a topical, contemporary comedy without drag performance; but as Ben Brantley pointed out in his glowing *Times* review, "it's really a spiritual cousin to the Cinderella-theme movies of the 1930's and 40's like 'The Good Fairy' and 'Now Voyager,' in which downtrodden heroines are transformed into glamorous swans."[7] It was also a reflection of Charles's own story: the awkward boy who couldn't be cast in a university production becomes a sensation.

The show was picked up by producer Rhoda Herrick for a commercial run at the Westside Theatre, this time with a comfortable $400,000 budget. Unfortunately, the transfer didn't last long; the box office slipped below the "stop clause" during some inclement February weather, and the theatre owner, Peter Askin, wanted us out so that he could book a more prestigious (and heterosexual) David Mamet play, *The Cryptogram*, into the Westside Theatre. This turn of events was very upsetting to all of us, but especially to Rhoda, who was the sole investor, having supplied the entire $400,000 capitalization herself. She offered to pay six months of rental fees in advance, and when that offer was refused, she took out a full-page ad in the *New York Times* denouncing Peter Askin; he was not swayed.

Since no other appropriate theatre was available, *You Should Be So Lucky* abruptly closed. Although *The Cryptogram* won an Obie and was a finalist for the 1995 Pulitzer Prize, we couldn't help but enjoy a certain amount of schadenfreude when it proved to be a commercial flop, closing after only sixty-two performances.

I brought Charles in to rewrite the book of an Off-Broadway musical I was working on about an all-girl band entertaining the troops during World War II. It was a jukebox musical called *Swingtime Canteen* that attracted an older audience nostalgic for such 1940s hits as "I'll Be Seeing You" and "Apple Blossom Time." There were many World War II veterans in our audiences, and they often sang along with the girls. When our leading lady, Alison Fraser, announced that she would be leaving the show after six months, Charles floated the idea that he could be her replacement. The producer, William Repici, was initially cool to this prospect, but was ultimately convinced that it would be great press—and the show needed it to keep running. Charles is not really a singer, so the close Andrews Sisters harmonies posed a challenge, but he was very effective in the role of a glamorous movie star of the period. Because *Swingtime Canteen* was never intended to be a drag show, however, some of our elderly patrons experienced a disconnect when they discovered that the leading lady was a man.

A much better fit for Charles was our retooled version of his club act as a solo show—*Flipping My Wig*—for the WPA Theatre in fall 1996. Describing Charles as a "popular crossover cross-dresser," Ben Brantley raved in the *Times* that he "holds a special place in the world of drag. Walking a delicate line between adulation and ridicule, he avoids both the polemics and pathos of most men who play women."[8] In his review, Brantley noted a character Charles had developed called Miriam Passman, an intellectual but frustrated housewife who yearns for fame as a cabaret artist. While her aspirations were clearly delusional, Charles had such empathy for her intense desire for recognition that the character was both touching and ridiculous.

As wonderful as it is to receive adulatory reviews in the *New York Times*, Charles and I were continually reminded that you can't make a living doing limited runs at small nonprofit Off-Broadway theatres. We thought we were on a more sensible (and remunerative) track when we collaborated with Alison Fraser and her husband, composer/lyricist Rusty Magee, on a new musical based on the short story, "The Green Heart," by Jack Ritchie (also the source for Elaine May's 1971 film, *A New Leaf*, in which she starred with Walter Matthau). Alison had obtained the rights to the story (but not to the film) for Rusty to musicalize, and she wanted me to direct and to convince Charles to write the book. I was on board, but it was not easy to talk Charles into it; he had bad experiences with musicals, and he didn't relate to the story. But Alison was very determined, and he was ultimately persuaded.

The Green Heart is the story of a dissolute playboy, Henry Graham, who runs through all his money and marries a rich heiress whom he intends to murder for her fortune. Ultimately, he falls in love with her in spite of himself. Manhattan Theatre Club expressed interest in the show, and after a series of successful staged readings over a period of years (the "development" process), they optioned it for a major production. The show was too big for their City Center space, and this was before they had acquired a Broadway theatre, so they decided to rent one of the largest available Off-Broadway houses at the time, the Variety Arts, run by Ben Sprecher. We had high hopes that this would be our real chance to "cross over." In the years since Joseph Papp died in 1991, MTC had easily become the most prominent and successful of the nonprofit theatres in New York, the epitome of establishment, mainstream theatre.

The production was plagued with problems from the outset, beginning with casting. Charles had tailored the two major male roles in the book for actors who proved to be unavailable. At the urging of the casting director, Jay Binder, and the artistic director, Lynne Meadow, and over the objections of Rusty, we were pressured to cast a comic actor who could not sing in one of the roles; he had to be fired and replaced early on in rehearsal. In fairness, it was a difficult role to cast. It required a character actor with strong comedic skills who could also sing tight harmonies. We made numerous offers for the leading male role, Henry Graham, but we were repeatedly turned down, and because the show was slotted into the MTC season, we could not postpone for actor availability—we *had* to find someone who was available. We finally settled on an actor none of us knew; he gave his best performance at the audition. We did have three terrific ladies in the key female roles: Karen Trott as Henrietta, the heiress; Ruth Williamson as her corrupt housekeeper; and Alison Fraser as Henry's scheming lover. Unfortunately, they didn't get along with each other, which made for some tense, acrimonious rehearsals.

Manhattan Theatre Club was not accustomed to producing musicals, so in preproduction conversations with the production manager I stressed that, given the team's inexperience with this genre, it was particularly important for us to hire a stage manager who read music and had experience calling multiset musicals. The production manager instead insisted that I hire a stage manager who had worked at MTC many times, but only on small cast, single set, straight plays. I took my argument to various people on the artistic staff; they all listened sympathetically and then told me to please just go along with the production manager. I tried to ameliorate the situation by advising that we hire a deck assistant stage manager with musical experience, but this time I was strongly pressured to hire a young, non-Equity production assistant with almost no experience at all—they wanted to give him his Equity card. I could see trouble coming.

The day before the first rehearsal, the managing director, Barry Grove, called to tell me that he could not reach an agreement over a billing issue with the agent of the choreographer I had been working with throughout preproduction and that I would have to find someone else. I tried to convince him to reconsider, but he was adamant; he didn't want to set a precedent for future MTC productions. This was not an auspicious way to begin the rehearsal process; I frantically called every choreographer I knew. Naturally, most of them weren't available to start rehearsal the next day. I spoke to Susan Stroman, Rob Marshall, and several others who made wonderful suggestions, but not one of them could do it. Joey McKneely was a long shot; he was in the midst of preparing the new Cy Coleman musical, *The Life*, so I was immensely grateful that he was willing to step in to help out—but only part-time. His assistant ran many of the dance rehearsals.

Naturally enough, Lynne and the MTC artistic staff were nervous about their investment in this production (the budget was close to $1 million—high for nonprofit Off Broadway at the time), and so I received a constant barrage of notes on every aspect of the show. Tech rehearsal was a nightmare. The massive set, handsomely designed by James Noone, was crammed into the shallow wing space of the Variety Arts Theatre, creating a backstage obstacle course for the actors, who had to hopscotch over wagons and around furniture to make their entrances. As I had predicted to the production manager, organizing the many scene changes was much more laborious than it should have been because no one on the stage management team had ever done a musical. It wasn't their fault—they had to learn on the fly.

The first preview for the MTC subscription audience was disheartening. Musical numbers that had gone over like gangbusters in staged readings received what Alison referred to as "golf applause," and major comic lines received only mild titters. We had a lot of work to do as we began the grueling process of making changes during afternoon rehearsals to be put in during evening performances. Post-performance note sessions with Lynne and the artistic staff took place nearly every night, and it was usually difficult to come to a consensus about how to fix the show. It was theatre by committee. Like my experience with *Up Against It*, I was hired to direct the show but was not given the authority to do the job. I often thought of Larry Gelbart's famous quip, "If Hitler's still alive, I hope he's out of town with a musical"—but it was even worse being *in* town with a musical. It felt like trying to move a mountain. Yet, very gradually, the changes started to work, and audiences became more responsive. The cast was beginning to really gain confidence, and we were hopeful as we headed into critics' previews. Unfortunately, we didn't have enough time to properly play in all the revisions, because we had to open on schedule. Charles, Rusty, Alison, and I had been working on this show for years, from the first story meetings to the opening night, so it was truly devastating to all of us when the *Times* review was mixed and decidedly unenthusiastic. I was utterly exhausted and depleted by the whole experience. Bob Mackintosh, the costume designer, and I were invited to Peter Rogers's grand beach house in Fire Island Pines the day after the opening, where we moped around and indulged in a weekend of relentless self-pity. The hoped-for commercial transfer didn't happen, and *The Green Heart* closed on schedule.

A few weeks later, Charles called and asked if he could take me to lunch at Food Bar, a popular gay restaurant in Chelsea. I thought this was a little odd because I couldn't recall Charles ever having taken me to lunch. Over salads, he informed me that he wanted his career to move in a different direction and that he would not be working with me on his next project, a play for the WPA Theatre called *Queen Amarantha*, for which I had already begun preproduction work. He told me he preferred to direct it himself, because he did not want to play the role (loosely based on Greta Garbo's performance in the film *Queen Christina*) for laughs; he wanted to be taken seriously this time, and he was afraid I would push him toward comedy. He was right about that, but I was surprised and more than a little shaken to have our collaboration of over a dozen years end so abruptly.

I didn't have time to fully process the break with Charles. I was soon headed to London for my next project: a production of Mart Crowley's *Boys in the Band* at the King's Head, a pub theatre in Islington. I had directed the first New York revival of the play for Kyle Renick at the WPA in 1996, and it later transferred to the Lortel Theatre. It has long been a controversial play that many consider to be a politically incorrect relic of the pre-Stonewall days. I wanted to make it clear in my production that this was *not* a play about pitiful, self-hating homosexuals; rather, it was group of witty, sophisticated friends who had an understandable reaction to the homophobic world of the late 1960s in which they lived. I didn't ignore the pathos, but I emphasized the comedy—and the script is hilarious. Mart was enthusiastic about a London revival and was involved with casting and rehearsals. The stage of the King's Head Theatre is one of the smallest I have ever seen, but with the help of set designer Nigel Hook, it was able to accommodate the entire cast and a few pieces of furniture. The reviews were largely positive, and the show transferred to the Aldwych Theatre in the West End, which was a real thrill. But when I returned to New York, no jobs were on the horizon, and the condo I had bought when I was so optimistic about *The Lady in Question* was becoming an untenable financial burden. Encouraged by my agent, Bill Craver, I moved to Los Angeles in the spring of 1998 to see if I could break into television directing.

I was surprised to hear from Charles when he called me a year later. We hadn't spoken much since I left town. He had taken a critical shellacking for *Queen Amarantha*, which he ended up co-directing with Carl Andress. We had met Carl when he was working as the wardrobe and hair supervisor on *Swingtime Canteen*, and he and Charles had since developed a very close working relationship. In his *Times* review, Ben Brantley called the overall effect of *Queen Amarantha* "deflating, like a first-rate comedienne taking on a classic tragedy. Imagine Lucille Ball doing Lady Macbeth, and you'll get the idea."[9] Charles preferred to debut his new play, *Die! Mommy! Die!*, far from the *New York Times*. Don Fairbanks, a handsome, soft-spoken, and seemingly easygoing young man who managed the Coast Playhouse on Santa Monica Boulevard in West Hollywood, had agreed to produce it, and Charles asked me to direct. He insisted on only one condition, to which I reluctantly agreed: I had to cast Carl Andress as his son, Lance.

A Brief Reunion

As if it were the old days, we worked together on the script. I sent him pages of notes to clarify plot developments and character motivations, most of which he incorporated. He did, however, resist one note. I tried to talk him into changing a scene in which the leading lady murders her husband by pulling down his pants and inserting a giant poison suppository. I argued that it was too vulgar, but he insisted it would work—and he was right. It got some of the biggest laughs of the show. It was back to comedy, a Limbo-type mash-up of early 1960s gothic-horror star vehicles like *Whatever Happened to Baby Jane?* and *Hush, Hush, Sweet Charlotte* crossed with elements of the classical Greek trilogy, Aeschylus's *Oresteia*. Charles was to play the Clytemnestra character, transported to 1960s-era Los Angeles.

Soon after Charles arrived in Los Angeles with Carl in tow, Don Fairbanks calmly and quietly announced that he hadn't raised the money for the production. We were dumbfounded and frantic. The show had already been announced in the trade papers, and it would be humiliating for us to cancel. Charles pressed me to serve as producer to keep the show alive; I was disinclined, but I ultimately agreed to do it. Once again, I was calling potential investors, dealing with attorneys, and, to my horror, taking on the entire financial responsibility for the production.[10] It was especially stressful because I had no experience producing theatre in Los Angeles. Somehow, the money came together at the last possible minute, and the show opened on schedule. Charles had a field day playing Angela Arden, a malevolent, revenge-seeking virago. *Die! Mommy! Die!* had a wonderfully witty, highly stylized, mid-century modern set by Brian Whitehill, featuring absurdly uncomfortable, retro furniture in eye-popping colors and dominated by an obviously fake, trompe l'oeil grand staircase up center. Brian spent hours attaching carpeting to its tiny, notched steps. Charles got a huge laugh when he headed for the staircase, pondered going "upstairs," then changed his mind and exited into the wings.

While we were in the midst of production for *Die! Mommy! Die!* Charles was simultaneously shooting the film version of *Psycho Beach Party* for Strand Releasing. He was not reprising his stage performance (the role of Chicklet went to Lauren Ambrose), but he did receive sole credit for the screenplay, and he added a character for himself to play in drag: a policewoman called Captain Monica Stark. A Hollywood film version of a Theatre-in-Limbo production (albeit a low-budget one) featuring Charles in drag is something we could never have imagined when we were originally playing *Gidget Goes Psychotic* in a converted sanitation garage in the East Village in 1986. The Ridiculous aesthetic, inspired by Jack Smith's underground film in the early 1960s, had come full circle. Whereas prints of Smith's *Flaming Creatures* had been confiscated by the authorities, and screenings of the film had been banned, even prompting congressional inquiries, less than forty years later the film adaptation of *Psycho Beach*

Charles Busch as Angela Arden ponders going "upstairs" on the set of Die!
Mommy! Die! *at the Coast Playhouse in Los Angeles. Photo by B. T. Whitehill.*

Party would play at multiplexes across the country without incident. *Die! Mommy! Die!* (with two exclamation points removed from the title and the spelling of Mommy changed to Mommie) was also later optioned and made into a commercial film, thanks to the rave review our production at the Coast Playhouse received in *Daily Variety*, which called it "Charles Busch's funniest, most accomplished and, without question, raunchiest work."[11] This time Charles would recreate his stage role in the film, fulfilling a life-long dream of starring in a motion picture.

The shooting schedule of *Psycho Beach Party* occasionally ran long, and we had to cancel several performances at the Coast Playhouse when Charles was needed on the set. This was a real financial hardship for a production that was only playing five days a week for a one-month limited run, so I decided to extend it for an additional month to see if we could recoup the investment. Business slumped during the extension, probably due to an insufficient advertising budget as well as the vagaries of Los Angeles theatre, and *Die! Mommy! Die!* played to some painfully small audiences. I called a company meeting to give the actors a pep talk and explain that we were doing everything we could to could to boost attendance. Most of the cast was sympathetic, but Charles was furious about the small houses and glared at me throughout the meeting, occasionally making a pointed remark about the incompetence of the advertising and publicity. He later apologized. When the production closed at a loss, I was personally responsible to pay thousands of dollars to vendors, including theatre rent that Don Fairbanks refused to waive, and I ran up massive credit card bills to cover the debt; in contrast, Charles got a movie deal. Sadly, we never worked together again.

Charles achieved the kind of mainstream success he had long sought the following year as the author of a conventional comedy that was more realistic than Ridiculous, *The Tale of the Allergist's Wife* (2000), directed by Lynne Meadow, which Ben Brantley described as "a nimble sitcom of a play" in the mold of "Neil Simon's mid-career comedies, plays that present harried New Yorkers speaking naturally in competitive one-liners."[12] It was a big Broadway hit that picked up a Tony nomination for Best Play and generated a successful national tour. There were no drag performers or gay characters in it. The title role, Marjorie Taub, was a frustrated Upper West Side matron brilliantly played by Linda Lavin. Charles wasn't in the cast; however, a drag persona was lurking in the subtext: Marjorie was more or less based on Miriam Passman, the character he had played to great success in *Flipping My Wig*.

Charles's theater career has continued in three distinct arenas: commercial productions, nonprofit Off-Broadway productions presented by established companies, and Limbo-type productions produced Off-Off Broadway at Theatre for the New City.

Despite his aversion to working on musicals, his next Broadway outing was as book writer for *Taboo* (2003), a high-profile extravaganza produced by Rosie O'Donnell with a score by Boy George. After my experience with *Up Against It*, I could have warned him about the difficulties of collaborating with a pop star on a musical. Boy George was not only the lyricist and one of several composers, he was also in the cast. It didn't help that O'Donnell was a novice producer with a mercurial personality. The show was notable for its predictably rocky road to opening, which was thoroughly documented in the tabloid press. As Ben Brantley remarked in his *Times* review, "the newspapers bubbled with stories of starry ego clashes, missed performances, and last-minute consultations with outsiders."[13] The reviews were brutal, business was tepid, and *Taboo* closed less than three months after it opened.

A few years later, Charles called me in California to tell me that producer Daryl Roth was producing a commercial Off-Broadway production of *Die Mommie Die!* (with the new punctuation and spelling), and that he had asked Carl to direct. Naturally enough, I was very hurt, and I icily reminded him to ensure that none of the staging or design elements from my production would be used. The Off-Broadway production was, in fact, quite different. Unlike Brian's stylized, mid-century setting, it was played on a completely realistic and detailed living room box set that looked like it had been designed by a pretentious Hollywood decorator; the realism of the set was at odds with the style of the play. The acting was a mix of styles, some realistic, some over the top. And Charles softened the character of Angela, which made her more sympathetic, but less funny. I read it as an attempt to make an absurdly off-center play, his "raunchiest work" to date, more palatable to a mainstream audience. Like *Taboo*, it ran less than three months.

Charles is at his most inspired when writing plays that contain juicy roles for himself, but following the success of *Allergist's Wife*, he authored two more plays for New York nonprofits in which he did not appear. *Our Leading Lady* (2007), which reunited him with director Lynne Meadow and the Manhattan Theatre Club, is the backstage story of actor-manager Laura Keene and her company performing *Our American Cousin* at Ford's Theatre the night Lincoln was shot. *Olive and the Bitter Herbs* (2011), directed by Mark Brokaw for Primary Stages, is a contemporary comedy, closer in style to *Allergist's Wife*, centered on a venomous, aging actress played by Marcia Jean Kurtz; it featured Julie Halston in a supporting role. Both plays received mixed reviews and closed after their scheduled runs. There was great anticipation for the onstage fireworks that might ensue when Charles co-starred with Kathleen Turner in *The Third Story* (2009), presented by MCC Theater at the Lortel, but it was a curiously muddled production; as David Rooney, reviewing for *Variety,* noted, "the two stars barely collide, or even seem to be in the same play."[14] Charles starred in another realistic comedy for Primary Stages, also featuring Julie Halston, called *The Tribute Artist* (2014), in which he played a drag performer involved in a Manhattan real estate scheme. He and I chatted briefly after I attended a matinee performance, and he was in a decidedly sour mood. *The Tribute Artist* was clearly an unsatisfying experience for him. He complained about the grind of performing eight shows a week, the low pay, the cramped dressing room, and the dreary audiences. He told me he was thinking of retiring from the theatre.

But of course he didn't retire. He kept returning to his theatrical roots in the East Village, where he starred in a series of highly popular Limbo-type plays at Theatre for the New City: *Shanghai Moon* (1999), *The Divine Sister* (2010), *Judith of Bethulia* (2012), *Cleopatra* (2016), and *The Confession of Lily Dare* (2018). All were directed by Carl Andress, with sets and graphic design by Brian Whitehill that created a strong connection to Theatre-in-Limbo. Critics were not invited because reviews were not needed to sell the limited runs, and the audiences were populated by enthusiastic fans rather than subscription audiences. These shows were genuine triumphs, presented for the sheer joy of performing. Three of them, *Shanghai Moon,* *The Divine Sister,* and *The Confession of Lily Dare* ultimately transferred for extended Off-Broadway runs where they received many laudatory reviews that showed genuine affection and nostalgia for Charles in the kind of roles that had made him famous.

But he was no longer a scrappy upstart; he had become the well-established grande dame of New York drag theatre. The critics had begun to revere Charles as a New York theatre legend and, unlike the early days, they treated him with respect even when reviewing his less successful shows. The casts were peppered with top-tier Broadway performers, many with extensive film and television credits, such as Becky Ann Baker, Daniel Gerroll, B. D. Wong, Alison Fraser, Mary Testa, and Howard McGillin, who often gave skillful performances that contributed a professional polish to the productions; but that kind of professionalism can be an uncomfortable fit with Ridiculous Theatre. There was no regular company of actors familiar with the camp, over-the-top style of Charles's plays. As a result, the playing styles often lacked consistency, and while these shows evoked Theatre-in-Limbo, they could not recreate it.

While Charles continued his New York theatre career, my attempt to break into television directing fizzled after a year or two of countless meetings on studio lots and hours spent observing on sitcoms like *Suddenly Susan* and *Veronica's Closet*. I didn't have the patience required for endless Hollywood networking (or any offers), so at the age of forty-five I decided to enroll in graduate school at UCLA, where I earned my PhD in theater. Since then I have enjoyed university teaching and directing students in productions of classic plays by Shakespeare, Molière, and Ibsen as well as contemporary plays by Luis Alfaro, Tony Kushner, Bruce Norris, and others, while occasionally working professionally as well. I directed and co-authored (with Buddy Thomas) a play in the Ridiculous style, *Devil Boys from Beyond* (2009), starring Ridiculous Theatrical Company veteran Everett Quinton and featuring Andy Halliday. It won the "Best of Fringe" Award at the New York International Fringe Festival and transferred for a brief commercial Off-Broadway run at New World Stages. During a rehearsal for *Devil Boys*, Everett remarked to me, "This material is so old-fashioned." I was perplexed, because I thought that the central plot concerning gay marriage was very au courant. On reflection, I surmised that he was probably referring to the show's style, not its subject matter. He seemed to be saying that this type of Ridiculous Theatre had become passé.

Primary Stages transferred *The Confession of Lily Dare* in January 2020 to the Cherry Lane Theatre, a small, historic, revered Off-Broadway house tucked away on a picturesque block of Commerce Street in the West Village. I attended one of the final performances just days before New York theatres were shut down due to the coronavirus pandemic. Charles wrote a plum role for himself in the tradition of his best Theatre-in-Limbo turns, and he gave a polished performance as Lily that evoked a dizzying array of female stars, from the wide-eyed innocence of a young Audrey Hepburn to tough-as-nails Barbara Stanwyck, with here and there a bit of Mae West, Bette Davis, Marlene Dietrich, and Ona Munson as Belle Watling. The audience was responsive, and almost entirely over fifty. As Ben Brantley had presciently observed years earlier in his review of *Die Mommie Die!*

> Enjoy it while you can. Mr. Busch belongs to a venerable downtown-born comic tradition that will some day seem as distant as vaudeville does to us today. The relatively dressed-down naturalism of contemporary movie actresses seems unlikely to produce a new generation of Busches. Who, after all, could make baroque art out of channeling Julia Roberts?[15]

Gay culture has changed considerably since Theatre-in-Limbo started performing in 1984, as has the New York theatre scene.

For us, moving to an Off-Broadway theatre for an extended run where the actors were actually paid was like a dream come true. But the once-vibrant commercial Off-Broadway scene is greatly diminished; the critic Chris Jones has referred to its "demise."[16] Many of the theatres that supported it are long gone, such as the Promenade, the Actors' Playhouse, the John Houseman, and the Douglas Fairbanks. The Variety Arts was demolished to make way for a condo tower; the Provincetown Playhouse was mostly demolished and then rebuilt by New York University for student use; the Lucille Lortel now houses only nonprofit theatre for limited runs; the Orpheum and the Astor Place theatres have for decades been taken over by the spectacles *Stomp* and *Blue Man Group,* respectively.[17] In addition, the rising costs of doing business Off Broadway have made it even more of a dubious economic proposition than it used to be.

Camp, as practiced by Smith, Tavel, Ludlam, and Busch, is no longer the lingua franca of young gay men who, as Brantley implied, have no connection to the screen divas of the 1930s, '40s, and '50s. AIDS is now considered to be a manageable condition. Since the *Obergefell v. Hodges* Supreme Court decision and the recent passage of the Respect for Marriage Act, gay marriage is the law of the land (at least for now), and the *New York Times* regularly features gay wedding announcements that describe extravagant, if bourgeois, ceremonies and receptions. All of this is not to suggest that LGBTQ culture has been seamlessly homogenized into the mainstream, as the horrific shootings at gay clubs and the recent spate of violent threats to drag performances attest. As part of the current culture wars, at the time of this writing some state legislatures are passing laws restricting drag performance. Nevertheless, great progress has been made, but with it something has also been lost. The artist David Hockney, who visited the cast backstage at the Provincetown Playhouse after seeing an early performance of *Vampire Lesbians of Sodom*, complained in a 2015 interview that contemporary gay men "want to be ordinary—they want to fit in," and he lamented that "Bohemia is gone now."[18] It's certainly gone from the East Village, where urban blight and gritty clubs and galleries have been replaced by luxury housing and upscale restaurants. The Christodora, the graffiti-covered building down the block from the Limbo, was converted into high-end condos decades ago. And currently no regularly performing companies in New York follow in the tradition of Play-House of the Ridiculous, the Ridiculous Theatrical Company, or Theatre-in-Limbo.

Of course, there are contemporary artists, like the dazzlingly talented Taylor Mac, whose work echoes the Ridiculous style, as Sean Edgecomb argues in *Charles Ludlam Lives*. But Ridiculous Theatre was deeply connected to a particular time and place, a product of the gay subculture struggling to make itself heard. It was a critique of the heteronormative dominant culture of the time, and it began as an outraged response to the status quo in the pre-Stonewall era. Charles Ludlam continued the outrage, but "won converts" to the Ridiculous Theatrical Company, and his theatre in Sheridan Square became a kind of cultural center of New York's gay community in the 1970s and early 1980s. Theatre-in-Limbo took a less confrontational approach as it provided comfort, escape, and community at the height of the AIDS crisis. It is the sense of community with our audiences and among the members of our company that I remember most fondly.

The vast majority of American theatre productions, both commercial and nonprofit, are assembled on an ad hoc basis. Actors are jobbed in and have often never met each other before the first day of rehearsal. It can be difficult to establish a cohesive ensemble in the typical rehearsal period of three or four weeks, but that's all that the financial model of this country allows. It was an extraordinary gift, and all too rare, to have the opportunity to collaborate with Charles, our designers, and our ensemble of actors over a period of seven years. Theatre-in-Limbo was a family. We knew each other so well, we trusted each other, we listened to each other, and there was great joy on the stage. While the scripts of all of our shows have been published by Samuel French and videotapes in the collection of the New

York Public Library for the Performing Arts at Lincoln Center document our performances, these can't replicate the experience of a viewer at a live performance on a downtown stage in such a fraught period in New York City history. I hope this book can help to fill in some of the gaps and keep the memory alive. Despite the tragedy of AIDS unfolding around us and within our company, I remember it as a magical time in the theatre.

Appendix
Theatre-in-Limbo New York Production List, 1984–1991

ORIGINAL CASTS, INFORMATION ON RUNS

ENTRIES IN CHRONOLOGICAL ORDER

ALL PRODUCTIONS WRITTEN BY CHARLES BUSCH

   AND DIRECTED BY KENNETH ELLIOTT

Vampire Lesbians of Sodom: *Limbo Lounge*

(CAST)

Ali, a guard	Robert Carey
Hujar, a guard	Arnie Kolodner
A Virgin Sacrifice	Charles Busch
The Succubus, a monster	Lola Pashalinksi*
King Carlyle, a silent movie idol	Kenneth Elliott
Etienne, a butler	Andy Halliday
Renee Vain, a starlet	Theresa Aceves
La Condesa, a silent screen vamp	Lola Pashalinski*
Madeleine Astarté, a stage actress	Charles Busch
Oatsie Carewe, a gossip columnist	Tom Aulino
Zack, a chorus boy	Arnie Kolodner**
P. J., a chorus boy	Robert Carey**
Danny, a chorus boy	Andy Halliday**

Opened April 6, 1984, at the Limbo Lounge, 339 East Tenth Street; played one
performance at 8BC, 337 East Eighth Street, May 18, 1984; closed June 22, 1984,
at the Limbo Lounge. Total run: Five performances.

Re-opened October 4, 1984, at the new Limbo, 623 East Tenth Street; closed
December 1, 1984. Total run: Eleven performances.

Re-opened March 22–31, 1985. Total run: Five performances.

*Lola Pashalinski was replaced by Julie Halston on May 18, 1984; Julie Halston
was replaced by Meghan Robinson on March 22, 1985.

**These roles were added for the run beginning October 4, 1984.

Theodora, She-Bitch of Byzantium: *Limbo Lounge*
(CAST)

Rita, a handmaiden	Theresa Aceves
Toso, a temple dancer	Andy Halliday
The Emperor Justinian	Kenneth Elliott
Aunt Vulva, his royal aunt	Julie Halston*
Andreas	Arnie Kolodner
Marcus	Robert Carey
Fata Morgana, a Gypsy queen	Tom Aulino

Opened June 8, 1984, at the old Limbo Lounge; closed June 30, 1984.
   Total run: Four performances.
Opened at the new Limbo October 25, 1984; closed December 2, 1984.
   Total run: Fifteen performances.
*Julie Halston replaced by Randi Klein at the new Limbo.

Times Square Angel: *Limbo*
(CAST)

Albert, an angel	Arnie Kolodner
Voice of the Lord	James Cahill
Milton Keisler	Kenneth Elliott
Georgie	Robert Carey
Irish O'Flanagan	Charles Busch
Peona	Yvonne Singh
Eddie	Andy Halliday
Chick LaFountain	Ralph Buckley
Valerie Waverly	Theresa Aceves
Old Mag	Kenneth Elliott
Agnes	Theresa Aceves

Opened December 6, 1984; closed December 30, 1984. Total run: Sixteen
   performances.

Sleeping Beauty or Coma: *Limbo*
(CAST)

Miss Thicke	Andy Halliday
Enid Wetwhistle	Meghan Robinson
Sebastian Loré	Kenneth Elliott
Fauna Alexander	Charles Busch
Ian McKenzie	Tom Aulino
Anthea Arlo	Theresa Aceves

Barry Posner... .... Robert Carey
Craig Prince .... Arnie Kolodner
Opened May 4, 1985; closed May 19, 1985. Total run: Eight performances.

Sleeping Beauty or Coma: *Off Broadway*
(CAST)
Miss Thicke .... Andy Halliday
Enid Wetwhistle .... Meghan Robinson
Sebastian Loré .... Kenneth Elliott
Fauna Alexander .... Charles Busch
Ian McKenzie .... Tom Aulino
Anthea Arlo .... Theresa Aceves
Barry Posner .... Robert Carey
Craig Prince .... Arnie Kolodner
Presented by Theatre-in-Limbo, Kenneth Elliott, and Gerald A. Davis as a
    double bill with *Vampire Lesbians of Sodom* at the Provincetown Playhouse.
    Scenery by B. T. Whitehill, costumes by John Glaser, lighting by Vivien Leone.

Vampire Lesbians of Sodom: *Off Broadway*
(CAST)
Ali, a guard .... Robert Carey
Hujar, a guard .... Arnie Kolodner
A Virgin Sacrifice .... Charles Busch
The Succubus, a monster .... Meghan Robinson
King Carlyle, a silent movie idol .... Kenneth Elliott
Etienne, a butler .... Andy Halliday
Renee Vain, a starlet .... Theresa Aceves
La Condesa, a silent screen vamp .... Meghan Robinson
Madeleine Astarté, a stage actress .... Charles Busch
Oatsie Carewe, a gossip columnist .... Tom Aulino
Zack, a chorus boy .... Arnie Kolodner
P. J., a chorus boy .... Robert Carey
Danny, a chorus boy .... Andy Halliday
Opened June 19, 1985; closed May 27, 1990. Total run: 17 previews;
    2,024 performances.
Presented by Theatre-in-Limbo, Kenneth Elliott, and Gerald A. Davis as a
    double bill with *Sleeping Beauty or Coma* at the Provincetown Playhouse.
    Scenery by B. T. Whitehill, costumes by John Glaser, lighting by Vivien Leone.

Times Square Angel: *Off Broadway*

(CAST)

Eddie	Andy Halliday
Johnny the Noodle	Robert Carey
Reporter	Tom Aulino
Abe Kesselman	Arnie Kolodner
Serita	Yvonne Singh
Irish O'Flanagan	Charles Busch
Miss Ellerbee	Meghan Robinson
Duke O'Flanagan	Ralph Buckley
Mrs. Tooley	Julie Halston
Cookie Gibbs	Theresa Marlowe
Olive Sanborn	Meghan Robinson
Dexter Paine III	Michael Belanger
Mrs. Paine	Tom Aulino
Stella	Julie Halston
Albert, an angel	Arnie Kolodner
Voice of the Lord	James Cahill
Milton Keisler	Tom Aulino
Georgie	Robert Carey
Peona	Yvonne Singh
Chick LaFountain	Ralph Buckley
Valerie Waverly	Theresa Marlowe
Old Mag	Meghan Robinson
Agnes	Tom Aulino

Opened December 11, 1985; closed February 9, 1986. Total run: Eight previews; twenty-eight performances.

An expanded version of *Times Square Angel* was presented by Theatre-in-Limbo, Kenneth Elliott, and Gerald A. Davis at the Provincetown Playhouse in repertory with *Vampire Lesbians of Sodom* and *Sleeping Beauty or Coma*. Scenery by B. T. Whitehill, costumes by Debra Tennenbaum, lighting by Vivien Leone.

Pardon My Inquisition: *Limbo*

(CAST)

Bruno .... Ralph Buckley
Manuel .... Michael Belanger
Topo .... Michael Leitheed
Pepe .... Robert Carey
Estrelita .... Randi Klein
Zulima .... Yvonne Singh
Vincenzo .... Andy Halliday
Don Arturo .... Arnie Kolodner
Maria Garbonza .... Charles Busch
La Marquesa Del Drago .... Charles Busch
The Marquis .... Tom Aulino
Rosa .... Becky London
Aleandro .... Michael Belanger
Beggar Woman .... Becky London
Señora Gonzalez .... Andy Halliday
Opened May 16, 1986; closed June 7, 1986. Total run: Nine performances.

Gidget Goes Psychotic: *Limbo*

(CAST)

Stinky .... Robert Carey
Dee Dee .... Lanette Hohl
Nicky .... Michael Leitheed
Provoloney .... Andy Halliday
Moondoggie .... Arnie Kolodner
Gidget .... Charles Busch
Kahoona .... Ralph Buckley
Marvel Ann .... Michael Belanger
Larue .... Becky London
Mrs. Forrest .... Meghan Robinson
Bettina Barnes .... Theresa Marlowe (a.k.a. Theresa Aceves)
Opened October 10, 1986; closed October 26, 1986. Total run: Nine performances.

Psycho Beach Party: *Off Broadway*

(CAST)

Yo Yo .... Robert Carey
Dee Dee .... Judith Hansen
Nicky .... Michael Leitheed
Provoloney .... Andy Halliday
Star Cat .... Arnie Kolodner
Chicklet .... Charles Busch
Berdine .... Becky London
Marvel Ann .... Michael Belanger
Mrs. Forrest .... Meghan Robinson
Bettina Barnes .... Theresa Marlowe

Opened June 20, 1987; closed May 15, 1988. Total run: 16 previews;
    344 performances.

Presented at the Players Theatre by Theatre-in-Limbo, Kenneth Elliott,
    and Gerald A. Davis. Scenery by B. T. Whitehill, costumes by John Glaser,
    lighting by Vivien Leone.

The Lady in Question: *WPA Theatre and Off Broadway*

(CAST)

Voice of the Announcer .... James Cahill
Professor Mittelhoffer .... Mark Hamilton
Heidi Mittelhoffer .... Theresa Marlowe
Karel Freiser .... Robert Carey
Hugo Hoffman .... Andy Halliday
Baron Wilhelm Von Elsner .... Kenneth Elliott
Gertrude Garnet .... Charles Busch
Kitty, the Countess de Borgia .... Julie Halston
Augusta Von Elsner .... Meghan Robinson
Dr. Maximilian .... Mark Hamilton
Lotte Von Elsner .... Andy Halliday
Raina Aldric .... Meghan Robinson

WPA run: Opened November 18, 1988; closed December 11, 1988.
    Total run: Sixteen performances.

Orpheum run: Opened July 14, 1989; closed December 3, 1989.
    Total run: 14 previews; 151 performances.

Presented as part of the "Silly Series," at the WPA Theatre, Kyle Renick, artistic director. Scenery by B. T. Whitehill, costumes by Bobby Locke and Jennifer Arnold, lighting by Vivien Leone.

The production was later presented by Kyle Renick and Kenneth Elliott at the Orpheum Theatre.

Red Scare on Sunset: *WPA Theatre and Off Broadway*

(CAST)

Ralph Barnes .... Mark Hamilton
Jerry .... Roy Cockrum
Pat Pilford .... Julie Halston
Frank Taggert .... Arnie Kolodner
Mary Dale .... Charles Busch
Malcom .... Andy Halliday
Salesgirl .... Mark Hamilton
Mitchell Drake .... Ralph Buckley
Bertram Barker .... Roy Cockrum
R. G. Benson .... Mark Hamilton
Granny Lou .... Mark Hamilton
Old Lady .... Andy Halliday

WPA run: Opened March 19, 1991; closed May 5, 1991. Total run: Forty-nine performances.

Lortel run: Opened June 21, 1991; closed September 5, 1991. Total run: 100 performances.

Presented by the WPA Theatre, Kyle Renick, artistic director. Scenery by B. T. Whitehill, costumes by Debra Tennenbaum, lighting by Vivien Leone, sound by Guy Sherman/Aural Fixation.

The production was later presented by Manny Kladitis, Drew Dennett, and Shaun Huttar at the Lucille Lortel Theatre.

Times Square Angel: *Theatre for the New City revivals*

(CAST)

Angel 1	Guyah Clark
Albert, an angel	Arnie Kolodner
Angel 2	Brian Winkowski
Voice of the Lord	James Cahill
Milton Keisler	Kenneth Elliott
Georgie	Jim Borstelmann
Irish O'Flanagan	Charles Busch
Peona	Yvonne Singh*
Eddie	Jim Mahady
Chick LaFountain	Ralph Buckley
Valerie Waverly	Theresa Aceves
Mr. Ellerbee	Kenneth Elliott
Old Mag	Kenneth Elliott
Agnes	Theresa Aceves

The 1991 revival: Opened November 29, 1991; closed December 15, 1991.
    Total run: Fourteen performances.

The 1992 revival: Opened December 3, 1992; closed December 20, 1992.
    Total run: Fifteen performances.

*For the 1992 revival, Yvonne Singh was replaced by Cheryl Reeves;
    the role of Helen was added for Andy Halliday.

Notes

INTRODUCTION

1. Arnold Aronson, *"Vampire Lesbians of Sodom* at the Limbo Lounge," *Drama Review* 29, no. 1 (Spring 1985): 39–42.

2. Throughout this book, I use the term "gay" rather than "queer" or "LGBTQ+" (more inclusive identifiers that came into popular use later) because that is how we self-identified at the time.

3. David M. Halperin, "Normal as Folk," *New York Times*, June 22, 2012, A23.

4. See *Camp: Queer Aesthetics and the Performing Subject*, an anthology of essays edited by Fabio Cleto, for multiple theoretical perspectives on camp.

5. For an overview of Ridiculous Theatre, see Stefan Brecht's decidedly idiosyncratic *Queer Theatre*; David Kaufman's detailed biography of Ludlam, *Ridiculous!*; and *Theatre of the Ridiculous,* Bonnie Marranca and Gautam Dasgupta's useful compendium of plays and articles. More recent academic studies include Kelly I. Aliano's *Theatre of the Ridiculous* and Sean F. Edgecomb's *Charles Ludlam Lives! Charles Busch, Bradford Louryk, Taylor Mac, and the Queer Legacy of the Ridiculous Theatrical Company*. These sources provide a detailed history and analysis of this groundbreaking genre.

6. Stefan Brecht, *Queer Theatre* (New York: Methuen, 1986), 32.

7. Brecht, *Queer Theatre*, 28.

8. Richard Foreman, "During the Second Half of the Sixties," in *Flaming Creature: Jack Smith, His Amazing Life and Times,* ed. Edward Leffingwell, Carole Kismaric, and Marvin Heigerman (London: Serpent's Tail, 1997), 25.

9. Arnold Aronson, *American Avant-garde Theatre, A History* (London: Routledge, 2000), 116.

10. Dan Isaac, "I Come from Ohio: An Interview with John Vaccaro," *Drama Review* 13, no. 1 (1968): 142.

11. Charles Ludlam, *Ridiculous Theatre: Scourge of Human Folly*, ed. Steven Samuels (New York: Theatre Communications Group, 1992), 25.

CHAPTER ONE

1. Tom Lavell, "Degeneracy to Reign at Midnight Madness," *Daily Northwestern*, February 27, 1976, 1.

2. Ronald Sullivan, "In City, AIDS Affecting Drug Users More Often," *New York Times*, October 21, 1984, 42.

3. William L. Chaze, "Behind Swelling Ranks of America's Street People," *U.S. News and World Report*, January 30, 1984, 57–58.

4. Craig Unger, "The Lower East Side: There Goes the Neighborhood," *New York Magazine*, May 28, 1984, 32–41.

5. Uzi Parnes, "Pop Performance in East Village Clubs," *Drama Review* 29, no. 1 (Spring 1985): 5–16.

6. John Epperson, interview with the author, July 28, 2003.

7. Michael Small, "Art after Midnight," *People*, August 20, 1984, 98–107.

8. Margo Jefferson, "The Downtown State of Mind," *Vogue*, July 1985.

9. Charles Busch, "Vampire Lesbians of Sodom" (unpublished manuscript, 1984), typescript.

10. Sean F. Edgecomb, *Charles Ludlam Lives! Charles Busch, Bradford Louryk, Taylor Mac, and the Queer Legacy of the Ridiculous Theatrical Company* (Ann Arbor: University of Michigan Press, 2017), 65. Charles Busch related this story to me on several occasions, but I was reminded of the details when reading the account in Edgecomb's book.

11. Busch, "Vampire Lesbians," manuscript, 7.

12. Busch, "Vampire Lesbians," manuscript, 1.

13. Busch, "Vampire Lesbians," manuscript, 7–8.

14. Ronald Tavel, *The Life of Lady Godiva*, in *Theatre of the Ridiculous*, rev. ed., ed. Bonnie Marranca and Gautam Dasgupta (Baltimore, MD: Johns Hopkins University Press, 1998), 40.

15. Tavel, *Life of Lady Godiva*, 45.

16. Busch, "Vampire Lesbians," manuscript, 7–8.

17. Cornelia Otis Skinner, *Madame Sarah* (Boston: Houghton Mifflin, 1967), 162.

18. Busch, "Vampire Lesbians," manuscript, 8.

19. *A Tale of Two Cities*, directed by Jack Conway, performed by Ronald Coleman, Elizabeth Allen, Edna May Oliver, Basil Rathbone, and Blanche Yurka (Culver City, CA: MGM, 1935).

20. Skinner, *Madame Sarah*, 162.

21. Skinner, *Madame Sarah*, 162.

22. Julie Halston, email to author, June 2, 2012.

23. Charles Tarzian, "8BC—From Farmhouse to Cabaret," *Drama Review* 29, no. 1 (Spring 1985): 108–112.

24. Richard Niles, "Charles Busch and Theatre-in-Limbo" (PhD diss., City University of New York, 1993), 91.

25. Halston email.

26. Tarzian, "8BC—From Farmhouse to Cabaret," 110.

27. Tarzian, "8BC—From Farmhouse to Cabaret," 108.

28. Parnes, "Pop Performance in East Village Clubs," 5.

29. These figures were supplied by Deborah Humphreys, director of Pueblo Nuevo, a community housing organization, and were quoted in Unger, "Lower East Side."

30. Christopher Mele, "The Process of Gentrification in Alphabet City," in *From Urban Village to East Village: The Battle for New York's Lower East Side*, ed. Janet L. Abu-Lughod (Oxford: Blackwell, 1994), 174.

31. Unger, "Lower East Side," 36.

32. Unger, "Lower East Side," 35.

33. Unger, "Lower East Side," 41.

CHAPTER TWO

1. Charles Busch, "Theodora, She-Bitch of Byzantium" (unpublished manuscript), typescript, 5.

2. Calvin Tompkins, "Profiles: Ridiculous," *New Yorker*, November 15, 1976, 55–98.

3. Busch, "Theodora," 2.

4. Busch, "Vampire Lesbians," manuscript, 5.

5. Charles Busch, interview by Richard Niles, October 24, 1991, Collection 006, Box 10, Folder 47, Richard Niles-Charles Busch Papers, Thomas J. Shanahan Library, Marymount Manhattan College, New York.

6. Busch, "Theodora," 6.

7. Busch, "Theodora," 6.

8. Busch, "Theodora," 9.

9. Busch, "Theodora," 7.

10. Michael Small, "Art After Midnight," *People*, August 20, 1984, 98–108.

11. Small, 99.

12. Charles Busch, *Vampire Lesbians of Sodom* (New York: Samuel French, 1985), 70.

13. José Esteban Muñoz, *Disidentifications: Queers of Color and the Performance of Politics* (Minneapolis: University of Minnesota Press, 1999), 4.

14. Busch, *Vampire Lesbians*, 71.

15. Busch, *Vampire Lesbians*, 76.

16. "Legit Bits," *Variety*, October 3, 1984.

17. Michael Sommers, "Sodom and Adorable," *New York Native*, November 18, 1984.

18. Brandon Judell, "Lesbian Fangs on Bite and Other Mouthfuls from N.Y.," *Advocate*, November 27, 1984.

19. Michael Feingold, "When We Undead Awaken," *Village Voice*, October 16, 1984.

20. Charles Busch, letter to the author, August 26, 1984.

21. Arnold Aronson, "*Vampire Lesbians of Sodom* at the Limbo Lounge," *Drama Review* 29, no. 1 (Spring 1985): 41.

CHAPTER THREE

1. Paul Woerner died of AIDS in 1992.

2. Maxim Mazumdar died of AIDS in 1988.

3. Helen Deutsch and Stella Hanau, *The Provincetown: A Story of the Theatre* (New York: Farrar and Rinehart, 1931), 45.

4. Charles Busch, "Sleeping Beauty or Coma" (unpublished manuscript, 1985), typescript.

5. D. J. R. Bruckner, "Stage: 'Vampire Lesbians of Sodom,'" *New York Times*, June 20, 1985, C18.

6. Bruckner, "Stage: 'Vampire Lesbians.'"

7. Mary Campbell, "Vampire Play Is Light Summer Send-up," *Associated Press*, June 19, 1985.

8. Robert Feldberg, "Vampire Camping It Up for Summer," *Bergen Record*, June 20, 1985.

9. Madd, review of *Vampire Lesbians of Sodom and Sleeping Beauty or Coma*, *Variety*, July 17, 1985, 112.

10. Marilyn Stasio, "Vamping Vampires in Drag," *New York Post*, June 20, 1985.

11. John Simon, "Christmas Corral," *New York Magazine*, July 22, 1985, 57–58.

12. Stasio, "Vamping Vampires."

13. Don Nelson, "Vampire Lesbians: Theatre Summer Camp," *New York Daily News*, July 23, 1985.

14. Allan Wallach, "Theater Review: Taking a Bite Out of the Dracula Legend," *Newsday*, June 25, 1985.

15. William A. Raidy, "Vampire Drag-Races through Campy Hilarity," *Newark Star-Ledger*, June 28, 1985.

16. Simon, "Christmas Corral."

17. Richard Niles, "Charles Busch and Theatre-in-Limbo" (PhD diss., City University of New York, 1993), 136.

18. Charles Ludlam, *Ridiculous Theatre: Scourge of Human Folly*, ed. Steven Samuels (New York: Theatre Communications Group, 1992), 254.

19. Ludlam, *Ridiculous Theatre*, 158.

20. Charles Busch, "Introduction," in *The Tale of the Allergist's Wife and Other Plays* (New York: Grove Press, 2001), xi.

21. Charles Busch, interview by Richard Niles, March 9, 1991, Collection 006, Box 10, Folder 18, Richard Niles-Charles Busch Papers, Thomas J. Shanahan Library, Marymount Manhattan College, New York.

22. David Kaufman, *Ridiculous! The Theatrical Life and Times of Charles Ludlam* (New York: Applause Books, 2002), 361.

23. Richard Hummler, "Mainstream Visibility for Gay Legit," *Variety*, July 17, 1985, 111.

24. Hummler, "Mainstream Visibility."

25. Frank Rich, "The Gay Decades," *Esquire*, November 1987, 87–100.

26. Walter Goodman, review of *Times Square Angel* by Charles Busch, *New York Times*, December 17, 1985, C22.

27. Charles Busch, interview by Richard Niles, October 7, 1991, Collection 006, Box 10, Folder 47, Richard Niles-Charles Busch Papers, Thomas J. Shanahan Library, Marymount Manhattan College, New York.

28. Charles Busch, "Pardon My Inquisition" (unpublished Limbo manuscript, 1986), author's collection.

29. Michael Sommers, "Cuba Si, Heaven No," *New York Native*, June 9, 1986, 37.

30. Charles Busch, "Pardon My Inquisition."

31. "New York Notes," *Advocate*, August 19, 1986, 32.

CHAPTER FOUR

1. Charles Busch, interview by Richard Niles, November 7, 1991, Collection 006, Box 10, Folder 51, Richard Niles-Charles Busch Papers, Thomas J. Shanahan Library, Marymount Manhattan College, New York.

2. Charles Busch, "Gidget Goes Psychotic" (unpublished manuscript, 1986).

3. Busch, "Gidget."

4. Busch, "Gidget."

5. Busch, "Gidget."

6. Busch, "Gidget."

7. Brooks Atkinson, "The Theatre: A Lusty 'Macbeth,'" *New York Times*, October 20, 1955.

8. Charles Busch, *Psycho Beach Party* (New York: Samuel French, 1988), 12.

9. Robert Freedman died of AIDS a few years later.

10. Jeremy Gerard, "Charles Ludlam, Avant-Garde Artist of the Theater, Is Dead," *New York Times*, May 29, 1987, A1.

11. Leon Katz, "In Memory: Charles Ludlam (1943–1987)," *Drama Review* 31, no. 4 (1987): 9.

12. Susan Stroman, "Eulogy for Jeff Veazey" (speech, Provincetown Playhouse, New York City, May 16, 1988).

13. Howard Kissel, "Leftovers Again?," *New York Daily News*, July 21, 1987.

14. Clive Barnes, "Beach Party Washout," *New York Post*, July 21, 1987.

15. Stephen Holden, "The Stage: 'Psycho Beach Party,'" *New York Times*, July 21, 1987.

16. Mimi Kramer, "The Theatre: Where the Boys Are," *New Yorker*, August 10, 1987.

17. Laurie Stone, "Sand Blast," *Village Voice*, July 28, 1987.

18. Frank Rich, review of *Psycho Beach Party*, WQXR, New York City, August 14, 1987.

19. Frank Rich, "Critic's Notebook," *New York Times*, August 20, 1987, C22.

20. Busch, *Psycho Beach Party*, 76–77.

21. Rich, "Critics Notebook."

22. Kenneth Elliott, letter to Frank Rich, August 21, 1987.

23. Frank Rich, letter to author, September 1, 1987.

24. Charles Busch, "Tribute to the *Vampire Lesbians* Cast" (speech, McBell's Restaurant, New York, October 18, 1987).

25. Alex Witchel, "Inside Theater: Zero Up, Nunn Down," *Seven Days,* May 18, 1988, 41.

26. Reed Birney, telephone interview with author, November 17, 2011.

27. Harry Kondoleon, *Zero Positive* (New York: Dramatists Play Service, 1989), 24.

28. Sonia Taitz, "A Meditation on Death Gets a New Life," *New York Times*, May 15, 1988, Section 2, 5.

CHAPTER FIVE

1. Andy Halliday, telephone interview with author, March 10, 2012.

2. Kenneth Elliott, personal journal, July 21, 1988.

3. Elliott, personal journal, July 22, 1988.

4. Halliday, telephone interview.

5. Craig Rowland, "Brittle Queens and Sex Slaves: Two New Plays Spice Up New York's Stage Scene," *Advocate*, July 1988, 58.

6. Elliott, personal journal, July 26, 1988.

7. Charles Busch, *The Lady in Question* (New York: Samuel French, 1989), 33.

8. Busch, *Lady in Question*, 49.

9. Frank Rich, "Scene: Europe 1940. Subject: True Kitsch," *New York Times*, July 26, 1989, C17.

10. Clive Barnes, "No Question—the 'Lady' Is a Champ," *New York Post*, July 26, 1989, 22.

11. Richard Niles, "Charles Busch and Theatre-in-Limbo" (PhD diss., City University of New York, 1993), 218.

12. Mel Gussow, "Review/Theater: Joe Orton's 'Up Against It,' a Screenplay Staged," *New York Times*, December 5, 1989, C17.

13. Niles, "Charles Busch and Theatre-in-Limbo," 220.

14. Doug Watt, "Second Thoughts on First Nights: Is 'Lady' Out of the Question?," *New York Daily News*, August 4, 1989.

15. Richard Shepard, review of *The Lady in Question*, 1130 WNEW, July 26, 1989.

16. John Simon, "East Village, West Bank," *New York Magazine*, August 7, 1989, 44.

17. Peter Bowen, "Taking Camp Seriously: Busch, New Age, and AIDS," *Outweek*, August 7, 1989.

CHAPTER SIX

1. "Legit Impresario Gordon Crowe Dies," *Variety*, May 20, 2008.

2. Sylvie Drake, "Stage Review: 'Vampire Lesbians' Soars Beyond the Ridiculous," *Los Angeles Times*, March 8, 1990.

3. Charles Busch, interview by Richard Niles, October 7, 1991, Collection 006, Box 10, Folder 47, Richard Niles-Charles Busch Papers, Thomas J. Shanahan Library, Marymount Manhattan College, New York.

4. "Meghan Robinson, Actress, Dies at 35," *New York Times*, November 21, 1990, D23.

5. Charles Busch, Outline for *Red Scare on Sunset*, in Richard Niles, "Charles Busch and Theatre-in-Limbo" (PhD diss., City University of New York, 1993), 233.

6. Niles, "Charles Busch and Theatre-in-Limbo," 243.

7. Busch, "Red Scare on Sunset" (unpublished manuscript, 1991), 57.

8. Busch, "Red Scare on Sunset" manuscript, 82.

9. Busch, *Red Scare on Sunset* (New York: Samuel French, 1991), 96.

10. Busch, *Red Scare on Sunset*, 96.

11. Mel Gussow, "Theater in Review," *New York Times*, April 24, 1991, C10.

12. Michael Feingold, "Heartland of Darkness," *Village Voice*, April 30, 1991.

13. John Simon, "'Night, Mandy," *New York Magazine*, May 6, 1991, 110.

14. Mimi Kramer, "The Theatre: On the Edge," *New Yorker*, August 5, 1991.

CHAPTER SEVEN

1. Mel Gussow, "Theater in Review," *New York Times*, February 5, 1992.

2. Charles Busch, interview by Richard Niles, December 20, 1991, Collection 006, Box 10, Folder 56, Richard Niles-Charles Busch Papers, Thomas J. Shanahan Library, Marymount Manhattan College, New York.

3. Charles Busch, *Whores of Lost Atlantis* (New York: Hyperion, 1993), 22.

4. Dick Gallagher died of AIDS in 2005.

5. Stephen Holden, "Review/Cabaret; Charles Busch on Drag and 'Dragnet,'" *New York Times*, May 22, 1993, A13.

6. Frank Rich, radio review, WQXR, July 9, 1993.

7. Ben Brantley, "Theater Review; Charles Busch Takes on a Trouser Role," *New York Times*, November 3, 1994, C19.

8. Ben Brantley, "Between a Female Image and Fantasy," *New York Times*, December 20, 1996, C3.

9. Ben Brantley, "Theatre Review: Charles Busch Plays It Straight, So to Speak," *New York Times*, October 24, 1997, E5.

10. To keep legal costs down and speed the process, we did not produce the show with a limited partnership, which would have limited my liability.

11. Robert Hofler, review of *Die! Mommy! Die!* by Charles Busch, *Daily Variety*, July 22, 1999, 12.

12. Ben Brantley, "Theater Review: A Woman on the Verge of Another Breakdown," *New York Times*, March 1, 2000, E5.

13. Ben Brantley, "Theater Review: Flagrantly Stylish, Outrageously Sexy," *New York Times*, November 14, 2003, E1.

14. David Rooney, review of *The Third Story* by Charles Busch, *Variety*, February 2, 2009.

15. Ben Brantley, "When Time Dims a Star, Life Can Be a Real Drag," *New York Times*, October 22, 2007, E1.

16. Chris Jones, *Rise Up! Broadway and American Society from* Angels in America *to* Hamilton (London: Methuen Drama, 2019), 117.

17. *Stomp* closed on January 8, 2023, after 13 previews and 11,472 performances, having occupied the Orpheum Theatre for nearly twenty-nine years.

18. Robert Mendick, "David Hockney: Too Many Gay Men Just Want to Lead Ordinary, Boring Lives," *Telegraph*, May 9, 2015.

Bibliography

Aliano, Kelly I. *Theatre of the Ridiculous: A Critical History*. Jefferson, NC: McFarland, 2019.

Aronson, Arnold. *American Avant-garde Theatre, A History*. London: Routledge, 2000.

Aronson, Arnold. "*Vampire Lesbians of Sodom* at the Limbo Lounge." *Drama Review* 29, no. 1 (1985): 39–42.

Atkinson, Brooks. "The Theatre: A Lusty 'Macbeth.'" *New York Times*, October 20, 1955.

Barnes, Clive. "Beach Party Washout." *New York Post*, July 21, 1987.

Barnes, Clive. "No Question—the 'Lady' Is a Champ." *New York Post*, July 26, 1988.

Bowen, Peter. "Taking Camp Seriously: Busch, New Age, and AIDS." *Outweek*, August 7, 1989.

Brantley, Ben. "Between a Female Image and Fantasy." *New York Times*, December 20, 1996.

Brantley, Ben. "Theater Review: Charles Busch Plays It Straight, So to Speak." *New York Times*, October 24, 1997.

Brantley, Ben. "Theater Review: Charles Busch Takes on a Trouser Role." *New York Times*, November 3, 1994.

Brantley, Ben. "Theater Review: Flagrantly Stylish, Outrageously Sexy." *New York Times*, November 14, 2003.

Brantley, Ben. "Theater Review: A Woman on the Verge of Another Breakdown." *New York Times*, March 1, 2000.

Brantley, Ben. "When Time Dims a Star, Life Can Be a Real Drag." *New York Times*, October 22, 2007.

Brecht, Stefan. *Queer Theatre*. New York: Methuen, 1986.

Bruckner, D. J. R. Review of *Vampire Lesbians of Sodom,* by Charles Busch. *New York Times*, June 20, 1985.

Busch, Charles. "Gidget Goes Psychotic." Unpublished manuscript, 1986, n.p. Typescript.

Busch, Charles. Interview by Richard Niles, March 3, 1991. Richard Niles/Charles Busch Papers. Marymount Manhattan College, New York City.

Busch, Charles. Interview by Richard Niles, March 9, 1991. Richard Niles/Charles Busch Papers. Marymount Manhattan College, New York City.

Busch, Charles. Interview by Richard Niles, October 7, 1991. Richard Niles/
  Charles Busch Papers. Marymount Manhattan College, New York City.
Busch, Charles. Interview by Richard Niles, October 24, 1991. Richard Niles/
  Charles Busch Papers. Marymount Manhattan College, New York City.
Busch, Charles. Interview by Richard Niles, November 7, 1991. Richard Niles/
  Charles Busch Papers. Marymount Manhattan College, New York City.
Busch, Charles. Interview by Richard Niles, December 20, 1991. Richard Niles/
  Charles Busch Papers. Marymount Manhattan College, New York City.
Busch, Charles. *The Lady in Question*. New York: Samuel French, 1989.
Busch, Charles. "Pardon My Inquisition." Unpublished Limbo manuscript, 1986,
  n.p. Author's collection.
Busch, Charles. *Psycho Beach Party*. New York: Samuel French, 1987.
Busch, Charles. *Red Scare on Sunset*. New York: Samuel French, 1991.
Busch, Charles. "Red Scare on Sunset." Unpublished Manuscript, 1991. Typescript.
Busch, Charles. "Sleeping Beauty or Coma." Unpublished manuscript, 1985, n.p.
  Author's collection.
Busch, Charles. *The Tale of the Allergist's Wife and Other Plays*. New York: Grove
  Press, 2001.
Busch, Charles. "Theodora, She-Bitch of Byzantium." Unpublished manuscript,
  1984. Author's collection.
Busch, Charles. *Vampire Lesbians of Sodom*. New York: Samuel French, 1985.
Busch, Charles. "Vampire Lesbians of Sodom." Unpublished manuscript, 1984.
  Author's collection.
Busch, Charles. *Whores of Lost Atlantis, A Novel*. New York: Hyperion, 1993.
Campbell, Mary. "Vampire Play Is Light Summer Send-up." *Associated Press*,
  June 19, 1985.
Canby, Vincent. "Don They Now Their Drag Apparel." *New York Times*, August 15,
  1996.
Carter, David. *Stonewall: The Riots That Sparked the Gay Revolution*. New York:
  St. Martin's Griffin, 2004.
Chauncey, George. *Gay New York: Gender, Urban Culture, and the Making of the Gay
  Male World, 1890–1940*. New York: Basic Books, 1994.
Chaze, William L. "Behind Swelling Ranks of America's Street People." *U.S. News
  and World Report*, January 30, 1984.
Cleto, Fabio, ed. *Camp: Queer Aesthetics and the Performing Subject*. Ann Arbor:
  University of Michigan Press, 1999.
Conway, Jack, dir. *A Tale of Two Cities*. Performed by Ronald Coleman, Elizabeth
  Allen, Edna May Oliver, Basil Rathbone, and Blanche Yurka. Culver City, CA:
  MGM, 1935.
Crowley, Mart. *The Boys in the Band*. New York: Samuel French, 1968.

Deutsch, Helen, and Stella Hanau. *The Provincetown: A Story of the Theatre*. New York: Farrar and Rinehart, 1931.

Drake, Sylvie. "Stage Review: 'Vampire Lesbians' Soars Beyond the Ridiculous." *Los Angeles Times*, March 8, 1990.

Edgecomb, Sean F. *Charles Ludlam Lives! Charles Busch, Bradford Louryk, Taylor Mac, and the Queer Legacy of the Ridiculous Theatrical Company*. Ann Arbor: University of Michigan Press, 2017.

Feingold, Michael. "Heartland of Darkness." *Village Voice*, April 30, 1991.

Feingold, Michael. "When We Undead Awaken." *Village Voice*, October 16, 1984.

Feldberg, Robert. "Vampire Camping It Up for Summer." *Bergen Record*, June 20, 1985.

Foreman, Richard. "During the Second Half of the Sixties." In *Flaming Creature: Jack Smith, His Amazing Life and Times*, edited by Edward Leffingwell, Carole Kismaric, and Marvin Heigerman. London: Serpent's Tail, 1997.

Gerard, Jeremy. "Charles Ludlam, Avant-Garde Artist of the Theater, Is Dead." *New York Times*, May 29, 1987.

Gussow, Mel. "Review/Theater: Joe Orton's 'Up Against It,' a Screenplay Staged." *New York Times*, December 5, 1989.

Gussow, Mel. "Theater in Review." *New York Times*, April 24, 1991.

Gussow, Mel. "Theater in Review." *New York Times*, February 5, 1992.

Halperin, David M. "Normal as Folk." *New York Times*, June 22, 2012.

Hofler, Robert. Review of *Die! Mommy! Die!*, by Charles Busch. *Daily Variety*, July 22, 1999.

Holden, Stephen. "Review/Cabaret: Charles Busch on Drag and 'Dragnet.'" *New York Times*, May 22, 1993.

Holden, Stephen. "The Stage: 'Psycho Beach Party.'" *New York Times*, July 21, 1987.

Hummler, Richard. "Mainstream Visibility for Gay Legit." *Variety*, July 17, 1985.

Isaac, Dan. "I Come from Ohio: An Interview with John Vaccaro." *Drama Review* 13, no. 1 (1968): 142.

Isaac, Dan. "Ronald Tavel: Ridiculous Playwright." *Drama Review* 13, no. 1 (1968): 106–15.

Jefferson, Margo. "The Downtown State of Mind." *Vogue*, July 1985.

Jones, Chris. *Rise Up! Broadway and American Society from* Angels in America *to* Hamilton. London: Methuen Drama, 2019.

Judell, Brandon. "Lesbian Fangs Bite and Other Mouthfuls from N.Y." *Advocate*, November 27, 1984.

Katz, Leon. "In Memory: Charles Ludlam (1943–1987)." *Drama Review* 31, no. 4 (1987): 8–9.

Kaufman, David. *Ridiculous! The Theatrical Life and Times of Charles Ludlam*. New York: Applause Theatre and Cinema Books, 2002.

Kissel, Howard. "Leftovers Again?" *New York Daily News*, July 21, 1987.

Kondoleon, Harry. *Zero Positive*. New York: Dramatists Play Service, 1989.

Kramer, Mimi. "The Theatre: On the Edge." *New Yorker,* August 5, 1991.

Kramer, Mimi. "The Theatre: Where the Boys Are." *New Yorker* August 10, 1987.

Lavell, Tom. "Degeneracy to Reign at Midnight Madness." *Daily Northwestern*, February 27, 1976.

"Legit Bits." *Variety*, October 3, 1984.

"Legit Impresario Gordon Crowe Dies." *Variety*, May 20, 2008.

Ludlam, Charles. *The Complete Plays of Charles Ludlam*. New York: Harper and Row, 1989.

Ludlam, Charles. *Ridiculous Theatre: Scourge of Human Folly*. Edited by Steven Samuels. New York: Theatre Communications Group, 1992.

Madd. Review of *Vampire Lesbians of Sodom and Sleeping Beauty or Coma,* by Charles Busch. *Variety,* July 17, 1985.

Marranca, Bonnie, and Gautam Dasgupta, eds. *Theatre of the Ridiculous*, rev. ed. Baltimore, MD: Johns Hopkins University Press, 1998.

"Meghan Robinson, Actress, Dies at 35." *New York Times*, November 21, 1990.

Mele, Christopher. "The Process of Gentrification in Alphabet City." In *From Urban Village to East Village: The Battle for New York's Lower East Side*, edited by Janet L. Abu-Lughod. Oxford: Blackwell, 1994.

Mendick, Robert. "David Hockney: Too Many Gay Men Just Want to Lead Ordinary, Boring Lives." *Telegraph*, May 9, 2015.

Muñoz, José Esteban. *Disidentifications: Queers of Color and the Performance of Politics*. Minneapolis: University of Minnesota Press, 1999.

Nelson, Don. "Vampire Lesbians: Theatre Summer Camp." *New York Daily News*, July 23, 1985.

"New York Notes." *Advocate*, August 19, 1986.

Niles, Richard. "Charles Busch and Theatre-in-Limbo." PhD diss., City University of New York, 1993.

Parnes, Uzi. "Pop Performance in East Village Clubs." *Drama Review* 29, no. 1 (1985): 5–16.

Raidy, William A. "Vampire Drag-Races through Campy Hilarity." *Newark Star-Ledger*, June 28, 1985.

Rich, Frank. "Critic's Notebook." *New York Times*, August 20, 1987.

Rich, Frank. "The Gay Decades." *Esquire*, November 1987.

Rich, Frank. Review of *Psycho Beach Party,* by Charles Busch. WQXR, New York, August 14, 1987.

Rich, Frank. Review of *The Charles Busch Revue.* WQXR, New York, July 9, 1993.

Rich, Frank. "Scene: Europe 1940. Subject: True Kitsch." *New York Times*, July 26, 1989.

Román, David. *Acts of Intervention: Performance, Gay Culture and AIDS*. Bloomington: Indiana University Press, 1998.

Rooney, David. Review of *The Third Story*, by Charles Busch. *Variety*, February 2, 2009.

Rowland, Craig. "Brittle Queens and Sex Slaves: Two New Plays Spice Up New York's Stage Scene." *Advocate*, July 1988.

Shepard, Richard. Review of *The Lady in Question*. WNEW, New York, July 26, 1989.

Simon, John. "Christmas Corral." *New York Magazine*, July 22, 1985.

Simon, John. "East Village, West Bank." *New York Magazine*, August 7, 1989.

Simon, John. "'Night, Mandy." *New York Magazine*, May 6, 1991.

Skinner, Cornelia Otis. *Madame Sarah*. Boston: Houghton Mifflin, 1967.

Small, Michael. "Art After Midnight." *People*, August 20, 1984.

Smith, Jack, dir. *Flaming Creatures*. 1963.

Smith, Jack. "The Perfect Filmic Appositeness of Maria Montez." *Film Culture* 27 (Fall–Winter 1962).

Sommers, Michael. "Cuba Si, Heaven No." *New York Native*, June 9, 1986.

Sommers, Michael. "Sodom and Adorable." *New York Native*, November 18, 1984.

Sontag, Susan. "Notes on Camp." In *Against Interpretation and Other Essays*, 275–92. New York: Farrar, Straus and Giroux, 1966.

Stasio, Marilyn. "Vamping Vampires in Drag." *New York Post*, June 20, 1985.

Stone, Laurie. "Sand Blast." *Village Voice*, July 28, 1987.

Sullivan, Ronald. "In City, AIDS Affecting Drug Users More Often." *New York Times*, October 21, 1984.

Taitz, Sonia. "A Meditation on Death Gets New Life." *New York Times*, May 15, 1988.

Tarzian, Charles. "8BC—From Farmhouse to Cabaret." *Drama Review* 29, no. 1 (1985): 108–12.

Tavel, Ronald. *The Life of Lady Godiva*. In *Theatre of the Ridiculous*, rev. ed., edited by Bonnie Marranca and Gautam Dasgupta, 37–75. Baltimore, MD: Johns Hopkins University Press, 1998.

Tompkins, Calvin. "Profiles: Ridiculous." *New Yorker*, November 15, 1976.

Unger, Craig. "The Lower East Side: There Goes the Neighborhood." *New York Magazine*, May 28, 1984.

Wallach, Allan. "Theater Review: Taking a Bite Out of the Dracula Legend." *Newsday*, July 25, 1985.

Watt, Doug. "Second Thoughts on First Nights: Is 'Lady' Out of the Question?" *New York Daily News*, August 4, 1989.

Witchel, Alex. "Inside Theater: Zero Up, Nunn Down." *Seven Days*, May 18, 1988.

Index

Note: Page numbers in *italics* refer to images.

STUDIES IN THEATRE HISTORY AND CULTURE